Customizing and Extending SharePoint Online

Design tailor-made solutions with modern SharePoint features
to meet your organization's unique needs

Matti Paukkonen

Customizing and Extending SharePoint Online

Group Product Manager: Aaron Tanna

Publishing Product Manager: Kushal Dave

Senior Editor: Ruvika Rao

Technical Editor: Rajdeep Chakraborty

Copy Editor: Safis Editing

Book Project Manager: Prajakta Naik

Indexer: Hemangini Bari

Production Designer: Prashant Ghare

Developer Relations Marketing Executives: Deepak Kumar and Mayank Singh

Business Development Executive: Thilakh Rajavel

First published: March 2024

Production reference: 1290224

Published by Packt Publishing Ltd.

Grosvenor House

11 St Paul's Square

Birmingham

B3 1RB.

ISBN 978-1-80324-489-1

www.packtpub.com

To my true love, Soile, and to my family who have been supporting and believing in me through this journey.

- Matti Paukkonen

Contributors

About the author

Matti Paukkonen is a modern work professional who has been working in the IT industry and Microsoft ecosystem for over 15 years and with Microsoft cloud solutions for over 10 years. He has been awarded the Microsoft Most Valuable Professional (MVP) in the Microsoft 365 app and services award category.

He is based in Kuopio, south central Finland and he holds a Bachelor of Engineering degree in telecommunications technology from Savonia University of Applied Sciences.

About the reviewers

Aaron Rendell is a Microsoft MVP and Professional Services Director at Encodian, leading a team of experts in delivering business solutions for customers using Microsoft 365 and Azure technologies. Aaron specializes in information, document, and records management, as well as low-code and pro-code development platforms such as Power Automate, Power Apps, and SharePoint.

He has more than 15 years of experience in the Microsoft cloud ecosystem, and has a proven track record of successfully orchestrating digital transformations for a diverse range of organizations, from small and medium enterprises to large enterprises, across all sectors and industries.

Randolph Perkins-Smart is a motivated, successful senior leader with an entrepreneurial mindset, specializing in Microsoft technologies. BCS Chartered IT Professional and AgilePM Practitioner adept in Microsoft 365, SharePoint, and web-based information systems. He leverages acute business and commercial acumen to introduce initiatives using a proactive, results-focused style. A seasoned leader with proven success across cross-functional team management, operations, problem-solving, stakeholder management, market analysis, marketing, and branding strategy.

He is experienced across multiple industries including IT, Finance & Insurance, Health, Construction, Education, Public Sector, Transport and the Arts, and different organizations leading their field such as Tate, Sky, British Heart Foundation, IBM, and Anglia Ruskin University. Randolph is exposed to global markets and has worked in Belgium, Dubai, Jersey, and the USA.

Table of Contents

Part 1: Exploring SharePoint Online

1

2

3

Access Controls in SharePoint   31

4

Lists and Libraries   45

5

Describing Content with Site Columns and Content Types   69

6

Creating Informative and Stunning Content with Modern SharePoint Pages   89

Part 2: Enhancing the SharePoint Content

7

Search in SharePoint   109

Part 3: Automate and Extend SharePoint Experiences

12

Part 4: Create Your Own Customization using SharePoint Framework and Microsoft Graph

Preface

SharePoint Online is a powerful and versatile platform and one of Microsoft 365's core services. It supplies experiences to other applications, such as OneDrive, Microsoft Teams, or Viva Connections. Since the modern SharePoint experience, launched in 2016, it has been evolving rapidly bringing new features at a monthly pace.

SharePoint offers various methods for building solutions to support daily work life, communications, and collaboration. Besides the out-of-the-box features, SharePoint Online can be extended in various ways from simple view customizations made by browser to extensive customizations including custom code, APIs, and backend systems.

This book will first introduce the fundamental concepts and structural elements, such as sites, lists and libraries, and supporting services, such as search and managed metadata of SharePoint Online. It will present various ways to extend SharePoint Online using just a browser, such as editing list views or column styles. SharePoint Online supports low-code tools that help you create solutions without coding. You can use Power Automate to create workflows that automate processes, and Power Apps to create simple apps that customize your SharePoint Online experience.

SharePoint Framework is an application development platform for creating applications to SharePoint Online, but also different Microsoft 365 services and applications, such as Microsoft Teams, Outlook, and Viva Connections. This book will introduce various customization models SharePoint Framework provides.

Who this book is for

Power users, developers, and administrators who are looking into extending SharePoint Online in a modern way. This book is also a good reference for people in an owner role of communication and collaboration solutions built using SharePoint Online.

To make complete use of this book, the reader should have experience in managing SharePoint sites and services, basic knowledge of Power Platform capabilities, and basic software development skills using TypeScript.

What this book covers

Chapter 1, SharePoint Online in a Nutshell, provides an introduction to SharePoint Online.

Chapter 2, Organize Content with SharePoint Sites, provides an overview of sites and site types in SharePoint Online. It shows how to use sites and hub sites to organize content within SharePoint. This chapter also explains basic site managements tasks.

Chapter 3, Access Controls in SharePoint, provides a detailed overview of access permission management in SharePoint. It shares best practices for managing permissions and how to use groups in permissions management.

Chapter 4, Lists and Libraries, explains the concepts of lists and libraries in SharePoint, and what is the difference between them. It also introduces available settings and basic features like different views and list columns.

Chapter 5, Describe Content with Site Columns and Content Types, provides an overview of content types and site columns, and how they can be used within SharePoint's lists and libraries. It also explains who to centrally manage content types and site columns using Content Type Gallery feature.

Chapter 6, Create Informative and Stunning Content with Modern SharePoint Pages, provides how to use modern SharePoint pages to create informative and stunning content. It explains targeting content to different audiences and how to use page templates. It also shared how to use SharePoint content within Microsoft Teams.

Chapter 7, Search in SharePoint, provides an overview of SharePoint's search capabilities and how it can be extended using crawled and managed properties and query rules. It also explains the role of Microsoft 365 search.

Chapter 8, Managed Metadata, provides an overview of SharePoint's managed metadata term store and how it can be used to create structured metadata. It also explains how managed metadata can be used to describe SharePoint content.

Chapter 9, Understand Information with Microsoft Syntex, provides an overview of intelligent document processing capabilities. It also explains premium taxonomy features of Syntex, and upcoming features such as e-signature, Microsoft 365 Archive and Microsoft 365 Backup.

Chapter 10, Bring SharePoint Content to Teams with Viva Connections, provides an overview of Microsoft Viva Connections service and how it can be used to bring SharePoint content within Microsoft Teams. It also explains how to setup and manage Viva Connections features.

Chapter 11, App Catalog and SharePoint Store, provides an overview of managing customized application in SharePoint and how third party applications can be deployed from the SharePoint Store.

Chapter 12, Automate SharePoint with Power Automate, provides an overview and examples how to build automations on top of SharePoint using Power Automate.

Chapter 13, Extend SharePoint with Power Apps, provides an overview how Power Apps can be used to customized SharePoint list forms and access SharePoint content. It also explains how to embed Power Apps applications in SharePoint pages.

Chapter 14, Site, List, and Document Templates, provides an overview of how to create and manage reusable site and list templates. It also explains how to publish Office document templates from centralized location to Office desktop applications.

Chapter 15, Improving List Experiences with View Formatting, provides an overview customizing list views advanced column formatting, and with custom JSON-based column and list formattings.

Chapter 16, Introduction to SharePoint Framework, provides an overview of SharePoint Framework application development model. It also explains how to install needed tools, and create and deploy an example project to SharePoint.

Chapter 17, Access SharePoint Data using Microsoft Graph, provides an overview of the Microsoft Graph API. It also explains how to use Microsoft Graph to access SharePoint content and how Microsoft Graph can be used within custom SharePoint Framework project.

Chapter 18, Web Parts and App Part Pages, provides an overview of SharePoint Framework Web Parts and App Part Pages. It explains how web parts can be used within Microsoft Teams as a tabs or personal applications.

Chapter 19, Extending User Experiences with SharePoint Framework Extensions, provides an overview of different ways to extend SharePoint. It explains Application Customizers, Field Extensions, Form Customizers and List View Command Sets developed using SharePoint Framework. It also explains extending Viva Connections, which is also done using SharePoint Framework's Adaptive Card Extensions.

Chapter 20, Community Solutions for Extending SharePoint Online, provides an overview to available, open-source community solutions which can be used to extend SharePoint. It also introduces three valuable community-driven solutions and tools.

To get the most out of this book

You will need to have an understanding of Microsoft 365 services and SharePoint Online.

Software/hardware covered in the book	Operating system requirements
SharePoint Framework v1.18	Windows, macOS, or Linux
TypeScript 4.7	Windows, macOS, or Linux
NodeJS v18	Windows, macOS, or Linux

Download the example code files

You can download the example code files for this book from GitHub at `https://github.com/PacktPublishing/Customizing-and-Extending-SharePoint-Online`. If there's an update to the code, it will be updated in the GitHub repository.

We also have other code bundles from our rich catalog of books and videos available at `https://github.com/PacktPublishing/`. Check them out!

Conventions used

There are a number of text conventions used throughout this book.

`Code in text`: Indicates code words in text, database table names, folder names, filenames, file extensions, pathnames, dummy URLs, user input, and Twitter handles. Here is an example: "Let's first open the web part class, which, in this example, is the `OnboardingTasksWebPart.ts` file, and go through the basic elements."

A block of code is set as follows:

```
GET https://graph.microsoft.com/v1.0/sites/ tenant.sharepoint.
com,28e328a9-00f4-4b6e-b850-abf67531ec21,f3d3bc0d-216a-4b27-a2bd-278bb
a0c9e1a/lists?$select=displayName,webUrl
```

When we wish to draw your attention to a particular part of a code block, the relevant lines or items are set in bold:

```
this.context.msGraphClientFactory.getClient("3").
then((client:MSGraphClientV3): void=>{client.api("/me").get((error,
response:any, rawResponse?:any)=>{
        this.userProf.displayName = response.displayName;
        this.userProf.mail = response.mail;
        this.userProf.jobtitle = response.jobTitle;
    });
});
```

Any command-line input or output is written as follows:

```
export interface IOnboardingTasksState {
    items: IOnboardingTask[];
}
```

Bold: Indicates a new term, an important word, or words that you see onscreen. For instance, words in menus or dialog boxes appear in **bold**. Here is an example: "Creating a new model starts in the content center by selecting **New** on the content center homepage "

> **Tips or important notes**
> Appear like this.

Get in touch

Feedback from our readers is always welcome.

General feedback: If you have questions about any aspect of this book, email us at customercare@packtpub.com and mention the book title in the subject of your message.

Errata: Although we have taken every care to ensure the accuracy of our content, mistakes do happen. If you have found a mistake in this book, we would be grateful if you would report this to us. Please visit www.packtpub.com/support/errata and fill in the form.

Piracy: If you come across any illegal copies of our works in any form on the internet, we would be grateful if you would provide us with the location address or website name. Please contact us at copyright@packtpub.com with a link to the material.

If you are interested in becoming an author: If there is a topic that you have expertise in and you are interested in either writing or contributing to a book, please visit authors.packtpub.com.

Share Your Thoughts

Once you've read *Customizing and Extending SharePoint Online*, we'd love to hear your thoughts! Scan the QR code below to go straight to the Amazon review page for this book and share your feedback.

https://packt.link/r/1-803-24489-5

Your review is important to us and the tech community and will help us make sure we're delivering excellent quality content.

Download a free PDF copy of this book

Thanks for purchasing this book!

Do you like to read on the go but are unable to carry your print books everywhere?

Is your eBook purchase not compatible with the device of your choice?

Don't worry, now with every Packt book you get a DRM-free PDF version of that book at no cost.

Read anywhere, any place, on any device. Search, copy, and paste code from your favorite technical books directly into your application.

The perks don't stop there, you can get exclusive access to discounts, newsletters, and great free content in your inbox daily

Follow these simple steps to get the benefits:

1. Scan the QR code or visit the link below

https://packt.link/free-ebook/978-1-80324-489-1

2. Submit your proof of purchase
3. That's it! We'll send your free PDF and other benefits to your email directly

Part 1:
Exploring SharePoint Online

In this part, you will get an overview of SharePoint Online's fundamental concepts and structures, such as sites, lists, and libraries. In addition to this, you will also learn about access permission management, usage of site columns and content types, and how to use modern SharePoint pages for creating engaging and stunning content.

This part has the following chapters:

- *Chapter 1: SharePoint Online in a Nutshell*
- *Chapter 2: Organize Content with SharePoint Sites*
- *Chapter 3: Access Controls in SharePoint*
- *Chapter 4: Lists and Libraries*
- *Chapter 5: Describe Content with Site Columns and Content Types*
- *Chapter 6: Create Informative and Stunning Content with Modern SharePoint Pages*

SharePoint Online in a Nutshell

Microsoft SharePoint Online is a content and collaboration platform for intranets, document management repositories, teamwork, and collaboration across organizations. It's one of the core technologies in Microsoft 365, supplying rich experiences to other services; nowadays, examples are file management capabilities on the Microsoft Teams **Files** tab and storage for content, such as news articles and videos, to different Microsoft Viva Suite services. Versatile security, access management capabilities, and integration to **Microsoft Entra ID (ME-ID)** ensure the data is available for the correct audiences and kept inside of managed borders. Governance policies at different levels ensure that compliance requirements can be met, data is retained for the required period of time, and outdated content is automatically cleaned up.

SharePoint Online is also an application platform enabling the management and publishing of apps extending SharePoint, Teams, Viva, and Office applications. The novel application development model, **SharePoint Framework (SPFx)**, enables developers to create solutions with modern development tools, also using open source tooling and frameworks. Power Automate workflows can be used to automate and create processes on top of SharePoint content, and Power Apps can be used to extend SharePoint lists or create simple apps to access and modify data on SharePoint lists and libraries.

In this chapter, we're going to cover the following main topics:

- A brief history of Microsoft SharePoint
- SharePoint Online as a platform for portals and teamwork
- SharePoint Online as an app platform
- How SharePoint supplies experiences to other Microsoft 365 services

Over 20 years of SharePoint

Microsoft SharePoint is already an over-20-year-old product. SharePoint started at the end of the 1990s as codename Tahoe, and the first versions under the SharePoint brand were released in 2001, called **SharePoint Portal Server 2001** and **SharePoint Team Services**. The next releases followed the update cadence of Microsoft Office:

- Microsoft Office SharePoint Portal Server 2003 in 2003
- **Microsoft Office SharePoint Server (MOSS)** 2007 in 2007
- Microsoft SharePoint Server 2010 in 2010
- Microsoft SharePoint Server 2013 in 2013
- Microsoft SharePoint Server 2016 in 2016
- Microsoft SharePoint Server 2019 in 2019
- Microsoft SharePoint Server Subscription Edition in 2021

These SharePoint Server versions were and are hosted in the customer's data center and are quite often referred to as **on-premises SharePoint** in discussions.

The cloud journey of SharePoint started in 2008 when SharePoint Online was released as a part of the **Business Productivity Online Suite (BPOS) Software-as-a-Service (SaaS)** offering, which also included Exchange Online email services and Live Meeting capabilities. In 2011, BPOS was rebranded as Office 365, and SharePoint Server 2010 became the core of SharePoint Online. One of the biggest milestones was in the May 2016 announcement of new, modern user experience SharePoint team sites, integrations with Microsoft Flow (rebranded later as Microsoft Power Automate) and Power Apps, and the SPFx client-side software development model:

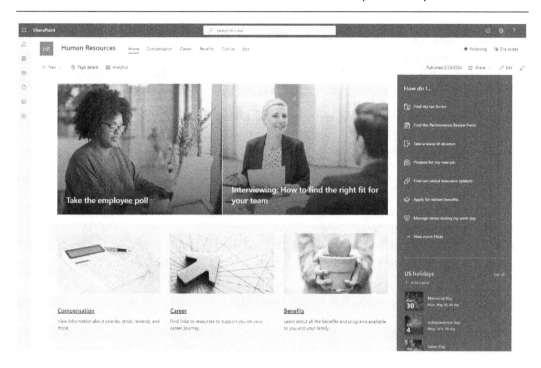

Figure 1.1 – Modern SharePoint site

Nowadays, when talking about SharePoint Online, it's common to hear the terms *classic* and *modern*:

- **Classic** refers to the experience used in SharePoint 2013. The classic experience in SharePoint Online is still needed for some mostly administrative or configuration tasks, but end users are using SharePoint Online's features with modern user experience.

- **Modern** refers to the new SharePoint user experience, which is also included in SharePoint Server 2016 and later versions. The modern experience is natively responsive and supports mobile devices, tablets, and computers, supporting all common, modern internet browsers.

SharePoint Online as a platform for portals and teamwork

SharePoint is a platform for an organization's news, guidance, policies, videos, and important links – commonly the intranet. SharePoint's rich content pages are used for bringing text, images, documents, and videos together in an easily accessible format using any device. Rich document views and a native video player reduce the need for the user to jump back and forth between content. Native web parts enable adding questionnaires or surveys using Microsoft Forms or creating small apps with Power Apps to rich content pages, again improving the user experience.

Lists and libraries are core building blocks of storing data in SharePoint and can be used in various solutions. A SharePoint list itself can be a small application, extended with views and workflows.

A document library is a place for documents, but when adding an approval workflow, it already transforms into a document management solution. Transforming a list from Excel to a list in SharePoint can make it more usable with prepopulated choices, users and groups, and views, enabling even more functionality with Power Apps and Power Automate workflows.

Users can access and process content hosted in SharePoint using different channels. Document libraries, folders, and files integrate natively into Office applications, such as Word, Excel, and PowerPoint. With mobile, users can use the SharePoint mobile app or just a browser to access content and files. Portals can be brought to Microsoft Teams with Viva Connections or adding tabs to Teams' channels. In some cases, users aren't even aware that they are using SharePoint.

Even though teamwork has largely moved to Microsoft Teams, SharePoint is still a key technology enabling the co-authoring of files, controlling access to content, and sharing content internally and across organizations. Users can access files via Teams' **Files** tab, using Office Online or Desktop applications, and can synchronize files and folders to Windows File Explorer or Mac Finder.

SharePoint Online as an app platform

Extending and customizing SharePoint has also evolved. With on-premises SharePoint versions, customizations were commonly made by modifying master pages and page layouts with SharePoint Designer or another HTML editor, running server-side C# code hooked into different events or loaded as a control during page load, or even creating customized APIs for accessing data. Development environments were heavy, consumed a lot of RAM, and required a local installation of SharePoint Server, which also required other services such as a Microsoft SQL database engine. The client-side implementation was quite commonly made by loading JavaScript using Script Editor web parts or injecting code directly to master pages or page layouts.

Since SharePoint Online is a SaaS offering, and actual servers are managed by Microsoft, there aren't possibilities to run custom server-side code as in SharePoint Server environments hosted in customers' data centers. With SharePoint Server 2013, Microsoft introduced the SharePoint Add-in model, which enabled developers to run client-side code and host it either in SharePoint (SharePoint-hosted) or outside of SharePoint (Provider-hosted). The main difference between these was that SharePoint-hosted add-ins could only run client-side code. The SharePoint Add-in model is still available today, but it is no longer preferred as the model for novel solutions, and new solutions should be rather developed using SPFx, Power Automate, Power Apps, SharePoint's REST APIs, and the Microsoft Graph API.

SharePoint is not just an app platform for hosting SharePoint-related customizations. SPFx can also be used to develop solutions for Microsoft Teams and Office. The same solution can be used on all platforms. Of course, when developing solutions to support SharePoint, Teams, Outlook, and Office, it is essential to consider all specialties of each platform, such as layout, user interface elements, and theming. SPFx is also the development platform for extending Microsoft Viva Connections, in which experiences are hosted in SharePoint.

When solutions are developed using SPFx, code can be hosted completely inside of the SharePoint environment without the need for a separate hosting environment. Solutions can be deployed just by uploading to the app catalog. The deployment process can also be automated using SharePoint REST APIs or PowerShell. Third-party solution offerings are available on the SharePoint Store, which also allows simple deployment and installation.

How SharePoint Online supplies experiences to other Microsoft 365 services

As mentioned earlier, SharePoint supplies rich experiences, content management capabilities, and a platform for other Microsoft 365 services. We'll look at how that works here with the different services.

Microsoft Teams

The **Files** tab on Microsoft Teams channels is a view of files and folders stored in the SharePoint document library connected to the Teams team. The **Files** tab is actually hosted on an application page on the SharePoint side:

Figure 1.2 – The Files tab in Teams

Also, the **Lists**, **SharePoint**, and **Document Library** tabs and content are hosted on SharePoint.

Sharing files and folders

The sharing dialog, which allows granting permissions for files and folders stored on SharePoint document libraries, can be used from different Microsoft 365 services, such as the new Microsoft 365 home app, OneDrive, and Teams:

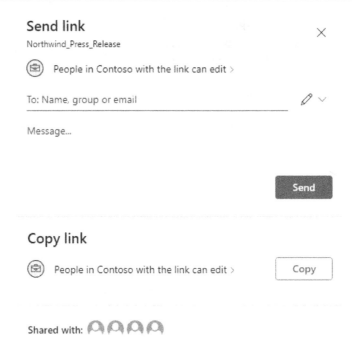

Figure 1.3 – Sharing dialog

OneDrive

OneDrive for Business, which is a personal storage location for users, is run on top of SharePoint. SharePoint enables co-authoring, version history, and permissions management capabilities for OneDrive.

Viva Connections

Microsoft Viva Connections, which is an employee experience communications solution for Microsoft Teams, uses news articles and videos stored on SharePoint. **Viva Connections Dashboard** is a page hosted on the SharePoint Home Site, and the dashboard's content is managed on a separate Dashboard page in SharePoint. Extensions and customizations for Viva Connections are developed using SPFx.

Videos

The new Stream video service uses SharePoint document libraries and OneDrive storage for videos. The same permissions and governance features as for other documents in libraries apply to videos. Stream's video player experiences are nowadays run on SharePoint or OneDrive.

Data, automation, and apps

SharePoint lists are quite a common data source for small-scale applications and automations. A SharePoint list can be used as a data source for Power Apps and Power BI reports. SharePoint can be a channel for publishing Power Apps or Power BI reports since it natively supports adding them to the content pages. Power Automate automations and workflows can use SharePoint lists as a data source or modify data stored in lists.

SharePoint can also be as a data source for custom applications extending Microsoft 365 via SharePoint's RESTful APIs or using the Microsoft Graph API.

Summary

With this chapter, we learned how SharePoint is a versatile communication and collaboration platform for organizations to manage their content, information, and business processes. SharePoint is one of the core technologies in the Microsoft 365 cloud service, integrating and providing experiences for other services. As a content platform, SharePoint hosts rich content pages, which can combine content with other Microsoft 365 services, such as Forms questionnaires or videos, and include Power Apps and Power BI reports without users needing to navigate away from the page.

SharePoint Online is also an application platform that enables extending and customizing SharePoint using modern web development technologies. The SPFx development model supplies capabilities for creating apps for other Teams, Outlook, and Viva Connections services, and these applications do not require a separate hosting environment. Developers can choose their development tools; open source tooling is 100% supported. Deploying SharePoint to a local development environment is no longer required. There is also a large developer community around SharePoint, bringing guidance, examples, and support to other developers.

In the next chapter, we will learn the concept of a site, what different site types there are, and how sites can be used to organize and share content.

2
Organize Content with SharePoint Sites

Sites are the foundation of organizing, structuring, securing, and bringing context to content in **SharePoint Online**. As this book focuses on the modern experiences of SharePoint Online, the term **site** is used to describe what was earlier called a **site collection**.

For on-premises SharePoint and classic experiences, site collections and sub-sites were used for widespread practice in terms of structuring and organizing content. In the modern SharePoint experience, sub-site hierarchies are no longer recommended for organizing content. Modern sites can be connected using navigation, linking, or connecting sites in the same context using hub sites.

A site holds lists for list items and libraries for files, folders, documents, and pages, depending on the purpose of the site; for example, human resources can have a site for their published guidance using pages and documents and a human resources team in Microsoft Teams for their documents, task lists, and conversations. A site also acts as a security boundary. Access to a specific site does not automatically give access to other sites. External sharing is also managed at the site level if enabled at the tenant level.

In this chapter, we're going to cover the following main topics:

- Different site types and special sites
- Organizing and categorizing sites with hub sites
- Creating multilingual content with SharePoint
- Managing sites in the SharePoint Admin Center

Different site types and special sites

In the modern SharePoint experience, there are three main site types:

- Communication site
- Team site
- Content center

> **Important note**
> Classic site types still exist and can be created, but these are not covered in this book.

Users can create both communication and team sites (if enabled) at the tenant level. New sites are always created underneath predefined managed paths. The managed path is either `/sites/` or `/teams/`, depending on the site creation setting in the SharePoint Admin Center.

Communication site

Commonly, these sites are used for communicating intranet-like content, guidance, document centers, archiving, and some extranet-like cases. The focus of communication sites is to make content, documents, business processes, reports, and apps easily accessible via rich content pages. Content is organized according to pages, news articles, lists, and document libraries. Communication sites can be used for collaboration and teamwork purposes as well, but since Microsoft Teams launched in 2018, the role of SharePoint as an actual surface for collaboration has decreased. A communication site cannot be connected to a Microsoft Teams team, and it's not linked to a Microsoft 365 group with linked resources such as a shared mailbox or calendar. Permissions regarding the communication sites are managed using SharePoint groups and at the site level. The following is an image of the communication site:

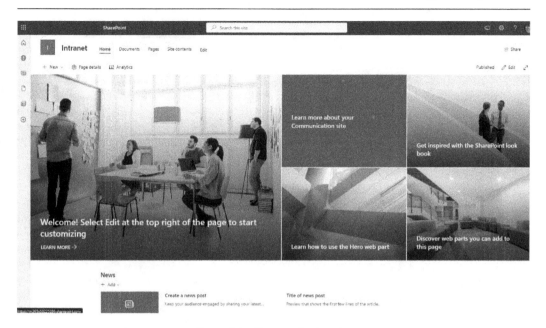

Figure 2.1 – Communication site

Team sites

A team site is a site type for collaboration and teamwork. By default, a team site is connected to a Microsoft 365 Group; this is the option for user-created team sites. A Microsoft 365 Group is an entity in **Microsoft Entra ID**, which connects group members and related services together (such as a SharePoint team site, a shared group mailbox and calendar, Planner, and OneNote notebook).

A group's services can be extended with a Teams team or a Yammer community, as well as with a Microsoft Project workspace. Group members have access to connected services based on group membership. Group owners will also act as owners for a SharePoint site, Teams team, and a Yammer community. Groups can be used to give access to other resources and applications from Microsoft or a third party as well. When a Microsoft 365 Group is created, a SharePoint site is also automatically created for that group.

Administrators can create team sites without a group connection from the SharePoint Admin Center. Permissions for these types of sites are managed using SharePoint default membership groups or creating custom permissions. The following is an image of the team site:

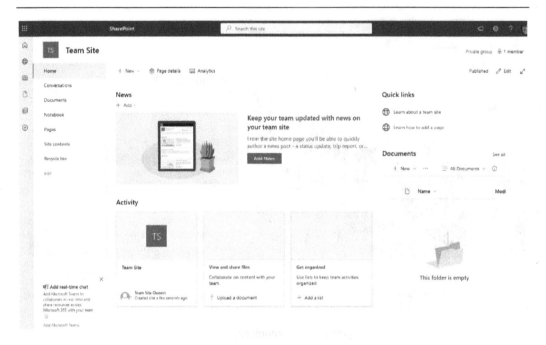

Figure 2.2 – Team Site

Channel sites

Channel sites are special sites related to Microsoft Teams' private and shared channels. A channel site is automatically created when a new private or shared channel is created for a team in Teams. These sites host files and other SharePoint experiences for related channels. Channel site permissions are managed only with channel permission management in Teams, and managing permissions in SharePoint is disabled. Separate sites for private and shared channels are for ensuring content security with a site-level boundary.

Channel sites are named following this pattern "**Team name–Channel name**", for example, "**HR Team–HR Managers**". The URL follows this pattern "Team URL–Channel URL", for example, "HRTeam–HRManagers". When a channel is renamed, the site name also changes, but the URL stays the same.

A small difference between private and shared channels on the SharePoint side is that a private channel's **Files** tab in Teams is linked to a subfolder named as the channel, whereas a shared channel's **Files** tab in Teams is linked to the site's default document library.

Channel sites are mainly used via Teams, and, for example, new lists are created using Teams's functionality. In some rare cases, such as restoring files and folders from the recycle bin, users may end up using a channel site via SharePoint.

The root site

Every Microsoft 365 tenant also has a root site, which is found at the tenant's root address, for example, https://your-tenant.sharepoint.com. Depending on when the root site is created, it might be a modern experience or a classic experience. If the root site needs to be upgraded or renewed, it can be replaced with an existing site. The root site cannot be deleted since it leads to all sites in the tenant being inaccessible. Replacing the root site can be done from the SharePoint Admin Center or with PowerShell using SharePoint Online Management Shell:

Replace root site

Specify a different site to use as the root (top-level) site for your organization. The site you select must be a team site or communication site. It can't be a hub site or connected to a Microsoft 365 group. Learn more about modernizing your root site

URL of the site you want to use *

Example: https://contoso.sharepoint.com/sites/home or /sites/home

Note

The current root site will be moved to https://mattip.sharepoint.com/sites/archive-2023-01-01T100649Z

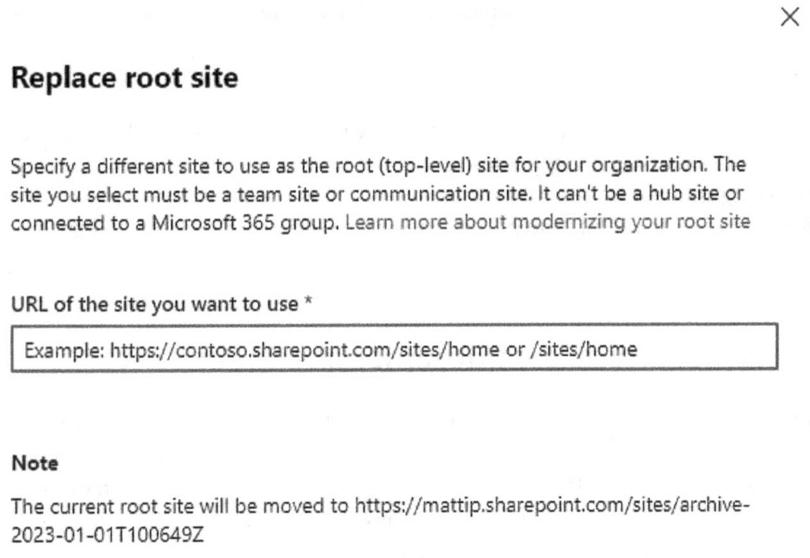

Figure 2.3 – Replace site in SharePoint Admin Center

With PowerShell, replacing the root site is done by using the Invoke-SPOSiteSwap cmdlet, which is found in SharePoint Online Management Shell. For the script SourceUrl, the parameter is the URL of the site, which should be set as the new tenant root site; TargetUrl is the tenant root address, and ArchiveUrl is the URL where the existing root site is moved:

```
Invoke-SPOSiteSwap -SourceUrl https://contoso.sharepoint.com/sites/
new-root-site -TargetUrl https://contoso.sharepoint.com -ArchiveUrl
https://contoso.sharepoint.com/sites/archive
```

Before replacing the root site, make sure that it's not promoted as a hub site, which can be used to connect sites together, and that it's not configured as a SharePoint home site. The site that will replace the root site needs to be a communication site or a modern team site (which is not connected to a Microsoft 365 Group and cannot be promoted as a hub site or associated with a hub site). If the target site is registered as a hub site, then do the following:

- Unregister it.

- Do a root site replacement operation.

- Register the site as a hub site after replacing it. All associated sites will be re-associated.

> **Important note**
>
> Note that the featured links are not copied to the new root site and need to be re-created. Site policies and permissions are not copied from the old root site to the new root site. It is good practice to configure these to the new root site before the replacement operation. The new root site needs to be indexed for search, so the search results are incomplete before the search index is up to date.

SharePoint home site and an organization's news sites

The SharePoint home site is the organization's landing site, which is quite commonly the front page of an organization's intranet portal and is linked to the root site of the tenant. Currently, only a single site can be registered as the home site. The home site brings global, left-side navigation to the SharePoint app bar and enables integration with Microsoft Teams and Viva Connections. Global navigation is either a home site's site navigation or, if the home site is registered as a hub site, then a hub site navigation. Global navigation is available on every modern SharePoint site and can be accessed from Viva Connections in Teams. The following is an image of the global navigation:

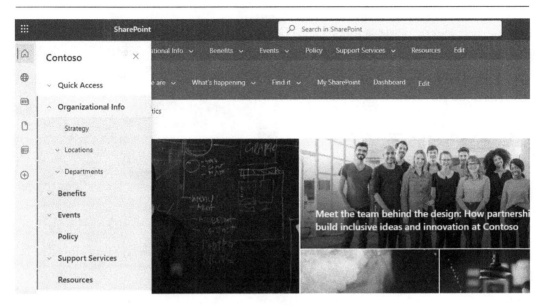

Figure 2.4 - Global navigation in the SharePoint app bar

The home site can be set up from SharePoint Admin Center's **Settings** section:

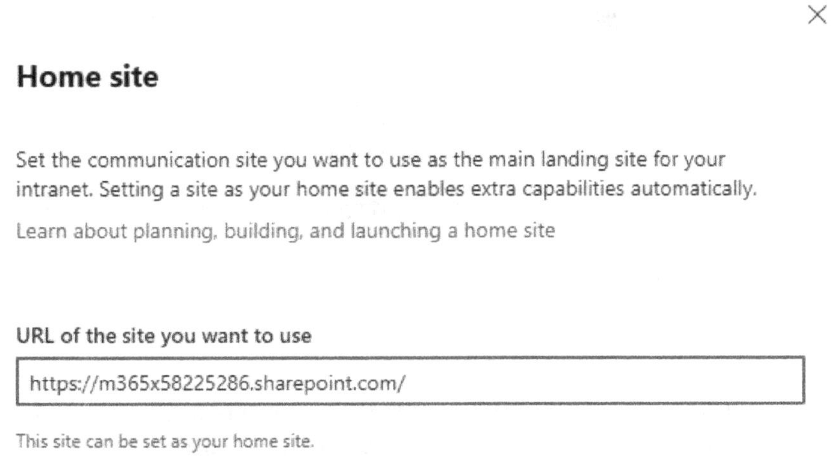

Home site

Set the communication site you want to use as the main landing site for your
intranet. Setting a site as your home site enables extra capabilities automatically.

Learn about planning, building, and launching a home site

URL of the site you want to use

https://m365x58225286.sharepoint.com/

This site can be set as your home site.

Figure 2.5 – Setting a SharePoint home site

The home site can be set using SharePoint Online Management Shell:

```
Set-SPOHomeSite -HomeSiteUrl https://contose.sharepoint.com/
```

The home site is also the official site for an organization's news. News articles from an organization's news sites get a visual color block indicator around the site name on the news feeds:

Figure 2.6 – An organization's news articles on the news feed

In addition to the home site, it is possible to set another important site as the organization's news source. Other news sites are managed using SharePoint Online Management Shell:

```
Set-SPOOrgNewsSite -OrgNewsSiteUrl https://contoso.sharepoint.com/
sites/news
```

To remove a site from an organization's news sites, do the following:

```
Remove-SPOOrgNewsSite -OrgNewsSiteUrl https://contoso.sharepoint.com/
sites/news
```

Microsoft Teams and SharePoint sites

Every team in Microsoft Teams has a SharePoint team site connected to it. The **Files** tab in the channels has a corresponding folder in the document library on the connected site. As an exception, private and shared channels have separate channel sites. When a channel is renamed on Teams, the connected folder name is also renamed accordingly. The **Files** tab is hosted as an application page on SharePoint, and it supports the same features as the document library view in SharePoint. Changes made either in the **Files** tab or in the document library view are reflected in each other.

Other SharePoint resources can be added to Teams channels as well. These resources can live on the site behind the team or on any other site.

> **Important note**
>
> Keep in mind that since permissions are respected, users will also need to have access to the resource to view it inside Teams.

The **Document Library** tab could be used to make the organization's central repository of guidance documents available to the **General** channel. With the **SharePoint** tab, it's possible to bring pages and news to the tab, for example, creating a feed of important news articles. With the **Lists** tab, it's possible to bring any list to the Teams channel, for example, an HR employee onboarding list to an HR team's **General** channel.

From a permission perspective, the privacy setting in Teams gives different permissions to the linked SharePoint site. In a private team, only those team members and owners have access to the site. In a public team, everyone in the organization has access. This access is given by the **Everyone except external users** permission.

> **Important note**
>
> A good practice with SharePoint sites linked to a team is to manage permission in Teams. There are always exceptions to permissions, but consider solving these with private or shared channels before making permission exceptions on SharePoint.

Organize and categorize sites with hub sites

A hub site serves as a central point for connecting related sites together, providing common context for news, content pages, and search, and providing consistent navigation and themes across sites. A hub site can be registered for a specific function, such as human resources or for a department or region, as well as, for example, creating a hub for all project sites. The most important thing is that the hub site and connected sites share a common context and that it's clear to the users. Nowadays, it's quite common to register an intranet landing site as a hub and other sites with it.

> **Important note**
>
> The maximum number of hub sites is 100 per Microsoft 365 tenant. In the hub site settings, hub owners can pick a logo for the hub and change the hub name and then the name will be visible on the navigation. Owners can select a site template, which is applied to a site associated with the hub. More about site templates can be found in *Chapter 14*. Hub association can also start an approval workflow when a site is associated.

The following is an image of the hub site settings:

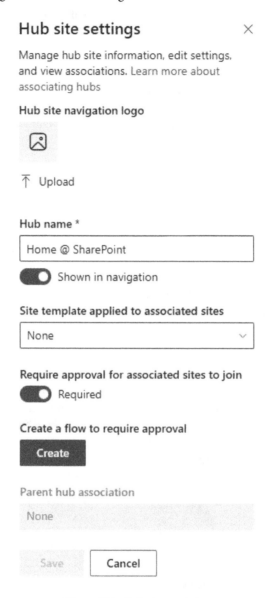

Figure 2.7 – Hub site settings

In SharePoint pages, **Events**, **Highlighted Content**, **News**, and **Sites Web Parts** support aggregating content using **All sites** in the hub as context. **Web Parts** also shows a list of associated sites when specific sites are selected as the source.

Depending on the search settings of the site, the search box in the navigation bar can search from the site, across the hub, or across the whole tenant. When the search box is set to search from the hub, it offers search results across all sites from the hub, and the search results page is set to hub context:

Figure 2.8 – Hub site in the search results

By default, the hub site's context searches across the hub, and the associated site's context is from the specific site. More on managing search settings in *Chapter 7*.

Permissions from the hub site are not copied to associated sites, so each site has separate owners, members, and visitors. Visitor access to the hub site and associated sites can be granted from the hub site permission settings:

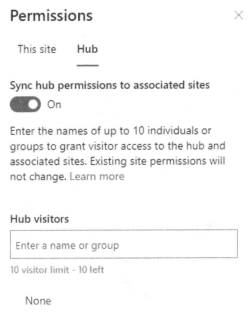

Figure 2.9 – Hub site permission sync

Synchronized permissions can have 10 individuals or groups. Synchronization can be disabled on each of the associated sites. It's good to have just a few named owners for sites. When the same members need to be distributed across all sites in the hub, it's a good practice to use security, mail-enabled security, or Microsoft 365 Groups to centralize membership management. A Microsoft 365 Group is a practical choice when membership management needs to be in the hands of the site owners, for example, creating a team for intranet content authors to manage permissions and collaborate and have discussions around the content.

Connecting hub sites

Hub sites can be associated with a parent hub site to create a wider search context across multiple hub sites. This could be used to create, for example, a regional hub for regionally named hub sites or create a hub for certain functions to gather content from a regional function's hub sites. Hub site associations also support multi-layered hub site structures.

Search and content roll-up web parts support three-level hub associations, so it's not reasonable when creating deeper hub associations. Information architecture planning is crucial with associated hubs. In the search results, each association level is displayed in the breadcrumb.

Links to the parent hub and associated child hubs can be added to the navigation with **Associated hubs** and **Associated child hubs** options in the navigation settings:

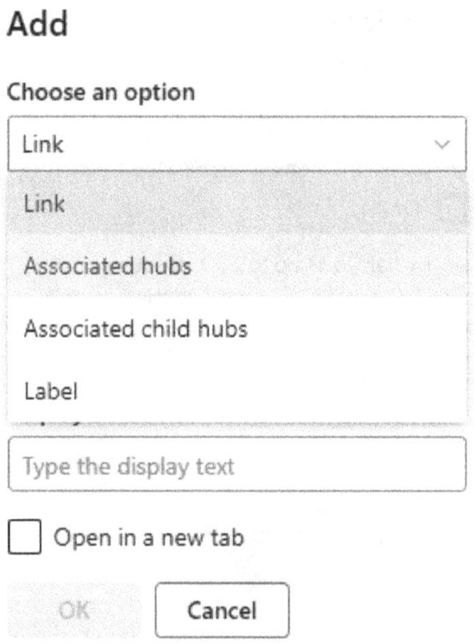

Add

Choose an option

Link	⌄

Link

Associated hubs

Associated child hubs

Label

Type the display text

☐ Open in a new tab

OK   Cancel

Figure 2.10 – Connected hub site navigation links

Navigation links are not automatically updated when hub associations are changed.

Navigation in sites

Each site has its own separate site navigation. In communication site navigation, the header area of the site can be found and is called global navigation. On team sites, navigation is placed on the left and is called a quick launch navigation. Navigation in team sites can also be changed to the header area if needed:

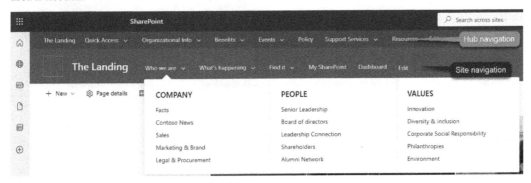

Figure 2.11 – Navigations in the SharePoint site

The site navigation is consistently visible on all pages, as well as in the list and library views on the site. The navigation links and structure are managed by site owners by using **Edit link** after the navigation headers.

The hub navigation is placed on top of the page on the hub and all associated sites. Owners of the hub site can manage the navigation content on the hub site.

Both navigation elements support a three-level deep hierarchy and can be styled as a fly-out menu or a megamenu. The fly-out menu displays the second-level navigation links or headers when the first-level links are selected. If there are third-level navigation links, they are displayed by clicking the second-level navigation link or header. The megamenu (in *Figure 2.11*) displays second- and third-level navigation links and a header when the first-level link or header is selected.

Navigation headers can be used on the first level and the second level to group navigation links into logical entities, which is useful for large navigations. For example, grouping all traveling and accommodation-related pages as third-level navigation links underneath a "Traveling and Accommodation" second-level navigation header.

Creating multilingual content with SharePoint

Modern SharePoint supports multilingual content and user experience. By default, user interface functionality, such as menus, library names, and command buttons, is translated into either being based on the user's preferred language on the user's profile, and if these are not set, then it is based on the user's browser language. Site owners can choose the available languages on the site's advanced language settings. Note that a site's primary language is chosen when a site is created, and it cannot be changed afterward.

Owners can enable the translation of content into multiple languages and assign translators, either persons or groups, for each language, who will be notified when the default language content is updated:

Figure 2.12 – Language and translation settings

Enabling translation into multiple languages allows for the translation of the site name, navigation, footer, pages, and news. It will also provide the users with a language menu, where they can change the language manually:

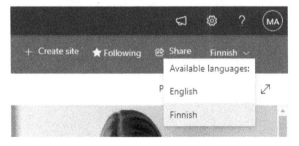

Figure 2.13 – Language menu in SharePoint

Translation for each content page and news article needs to be created separately from the translation pane:

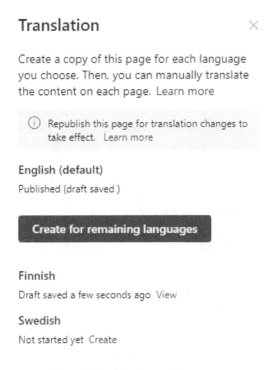

When a translation is created, editors can access it using the language menu on the page. All translated pages are placed in the site pages' library underneath a language-specific folder.

Managing sites in the SharePoint Admin Center

Users with a **SharePoint Administrator Azure Active Directory** role or higher can manage sites in the **SharePoint Admin Center**. The Admin Center can be found using the direct URL https://your-tenant-admin.sharepoint.com or navigation using the Office app launcher in the top left corner.

Active and deleted sites

On the active sites list, administrators can manage all sites in the tenant and see basic information, including the site's name, URL, when the site was created (and by whom), site template, last activity, and statistics (such as file views, page views and visits, and the number of files). Users with a SharePoint Administrator role can see all the sites but, by default, cannot access the content of the site:

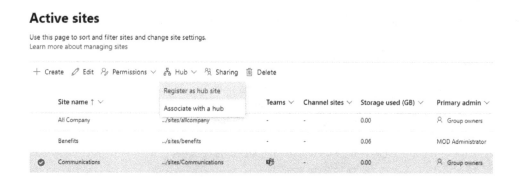

Figure 2.15 – Active sites list on SharePoint Admin Center

On the management pane, which opens on the right when a site is selected, administrators can see the basic permissions, add owners and additional administrators, and see and change a site's external sharing policy and sensitivity label. Hub site settings and hub associations are also managed in the active sites view:

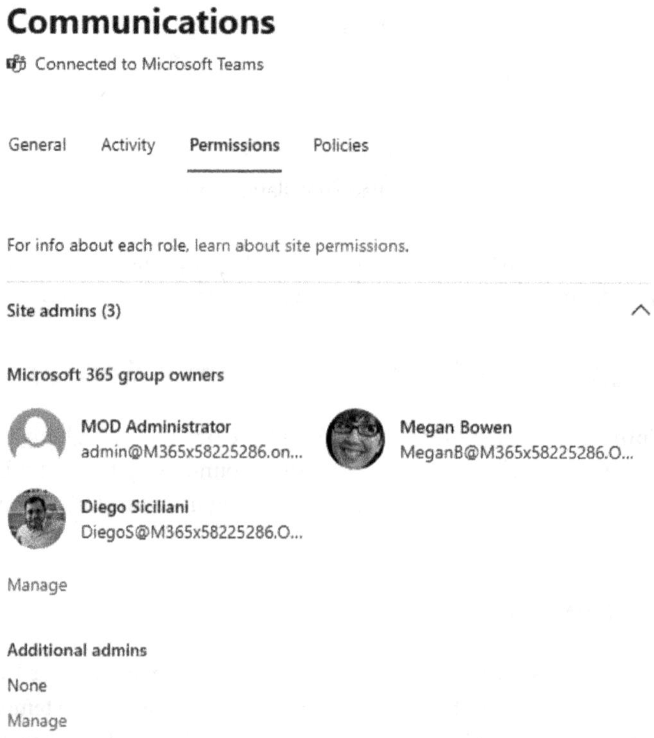

Communications

📧 Connected to Microsoft Teams

General   Activity   **Permissions**   Policies

For info about each role, learn about site permissions.

Site admins (3)   ⌃

Microsoft 365 group owners

MOD Administrator   **Megan Bowen**
admin@M365x58225286.on...   MeganB@M365x58225286.O...

Diego Siciliani
DiegoS@M365x58225286.O...

Manage

Additional admins

None

Manage

Figure 2.16 – Site management pane in SharePoint Admin Center

On the deleted site list, administrators can see all deleted sites (which are kept for 93 days, about 3 months) and restore deleted sites.

Registering a hub site

A hub site can be registered from the SharePoint Admin Center or by using SharePoint Online Management Shell. In the Admin Center, hub registration is done by selecting a site from the active sites list and selecting **Register as hub site** from the toolbar:

Figure 2.17 – Registering a site as a hub site

In the dialog, an administrator can give a name to the hub and define who can associate a site with the specific hub.

With SharePoint Online Management Shell, a hub site is registered with the following command:

```
Register-SPOHubSite –Site <site url or id> -Principals <user or group
ids>
```

The users and groups who can associate sites with the hub can be set by using the **Principals** parameter. A principal can be the email address of a user or a group, a user's account name, or the unique ID (GUID) of the user or the group.

Changing the site URL

Sometimes, it might be reasonable to change a site's URL, for example, when a site is renamed. The site's relative part of the URL, which is the part after the managed path (`/sites/` or `/teams/`), can be changed from the SharePoint Admin Center or with SharePoint Online Management Shell:

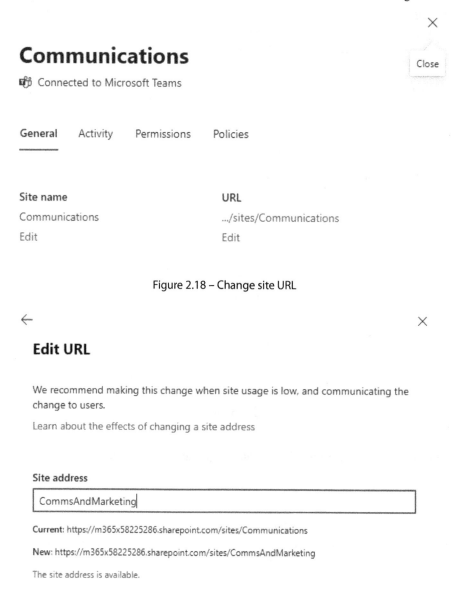

Figure 2.18 – Change site URL

Figure 2.19 – Renaming the site URL

Changing the URL with SharePoint Online Management Shell:

```
Start-SPOSiteRename -Identity https://contoso.sharepoint.com/sites/
Communications -NewSiteUrl https://contoso.sharepoint.com/sites/
CommsAndMarketing
```

By adding a `-ValidationOnly` parameter, it is possible to verify if the change is possible.

When a URL is changed, SharePoint automatically creates a redirect, so links pointing to the site's content, files, or folders are not broken. Redirects can be managed with SharePoint Online Management Shell.

To list all redirects, you can use the following:

```
Get-SPOSite -Template REDIRECTSITE#0
```

To remove a redirect, you can use the following:

```
Remove-SPOSite -Identity https://contoso.sharepoint.com/sites/
Communications
```

Summary

We learned how sites are a key part of SharePoint's information architecture. When implementing intranet portals, it's important to design how many sites and hub sites are needed, how site associations are configured, and whether there is a need to group hub sites together (always keeping clarity in mind). We later saw why the role of the SharePoint home site and other organizations' news sources need to be defined. Each site needs an owner; responsibility can be centralized for specific people or distributed, but it's important that owners understand their responsibilities.

In the last part, we observed how the sites and channel sites that are connected to Microsoft Teams channels are commonly accessed from the **Files** tab in Teams, and users might not use SharePoint's user experience at all when using Teams' teams. Permissions for these sites are managed using team owners, members, and guests.

Administrators have a key role in managing sites, setting up hub sites and associations, managing permissions, restoring deleted sites, and managing policies. Administrators need to familiarize themselves with the SharePoint Admin Center and with SharePoint Online Management Shell capabilities.

In the following chapter, we delve into how permissions work in SharePoint, how they are managed, and what good practices exist for effective permission management.

3
Access Controls in SharePoint

SharePoint Online provides granular options for controlling access to sites and content. There are 33 individual permissions, such as **Add Items** and **Manage permissions**, in total. In modern experiences, a list of different permission sets is mapped to five default permission roles – **Full Control**, **Design**, **Edit**, **Contribute**, and **Read**. These permission levels are then mapped to three default site permission groups.

Access to this content can be granted at different hierarchical tiers, including the site level, list or library level, folder level, and item or document level. Permission can be given through a group membership or directly to the user. By default, permissions are inherited from the site level to all lists and libraries, folders, items, and documents in that specific site. When permissions are changed, such as on a specific folder, permission inheritance continues to folders and items underneath that specific folder. Permission inheritance can be broken at all levels, which means that permissions are managed separately past where entity inheritance is broken.

Access for users outside the organization is managed at the Microsoft 365 tenant level with external sharing policies and **Azure Active Directory** (**AAD**) guest settings. External sharing policies can be set at the site level as well, but they can't override tenant-wide settings.

In this chapter, we're going to cover the following main topics:

- Managing access to content
- Controlling access with groups
- Permission levels
- External sharing
- Good practices to govern permissions

Managing access to content

In the modern SharePoint experience, there are three different roles by default:

- **Site owners**: Site owners have full control over the site and can manage content, settings, permissions, and applications

- **Site members**: Site members have edit permissions, allowing them to manage lists and libraries, list items, and documents

- **Site visitors**: Site visitors only have read access to the site

These roles are mapped to SharePoint groups, which are named after the site's title and respective access level – for example, "HR Team Owners," "HR Team Members," and "HR Team Visitors."

Site permissions

Regarding communication sites and team sites, which are not connected to Microsoft 365 groups, permissions are granted using the sharing dialogue. This dialogue can be opened using the **Share** button at the top right-hand corner of the page or from the site's **Permissions** panel, which can be opened from the settings menu:

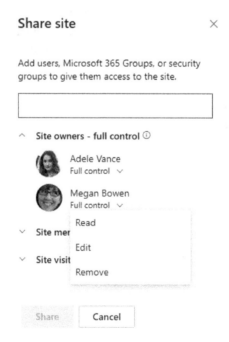

Figure 3.1 - The sharing dialogue on a non-group-connected site

On a Microsoft 365 group-connected site or a site connected to Microsoft Teams, the sharing experience is different. Microsoft 365 group owners and members can be managed from the group membership panel, which can be opened from the top-right corner of the page:

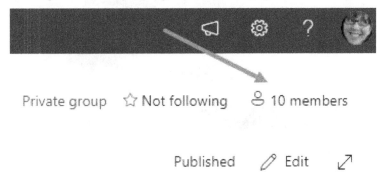

Figure 3.2 - Group membership management

It is also possible to manage permissions to a SharePoint site using the site's **Permissions** panel. This panel shows the underlying group's owners and members as separate objects. Here, a member's permission to the site can be changed to **Full control** or **Read**:

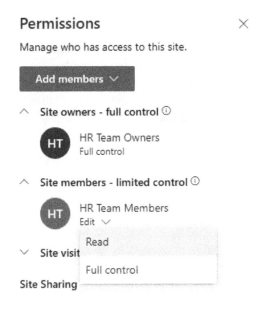

Figure 3.3 - Managing permissions

Permissions to the site can be given through the underlying Microsoft 365 group by adding members to it. This choice grants access to other linked resources too, so when access is granted to the group in SharePoint, the user also has access to the Teams team. Using the **Share site only** option gives permissions directly to the site, not to linked resources:

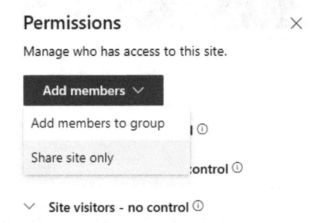

Figure 3.4 - The Permissions panel on group-connected sites

Advanced permissions

From the advanced permissions view, site owners and site collection administrators can create new groups, edit detailed group permissions, manage permission levels, and check permissions. The experience for the advanced permission settings is still in SharePoint's classic mode. The advanced permissions settings should only be used for specific requirements, such as adding approval permissions to the site members group or managing permission inheritance settings when permissions are limited within the site.

The **Check Permissions** view is sometimes a handy tool to confirm which permissions certain users have to the content:

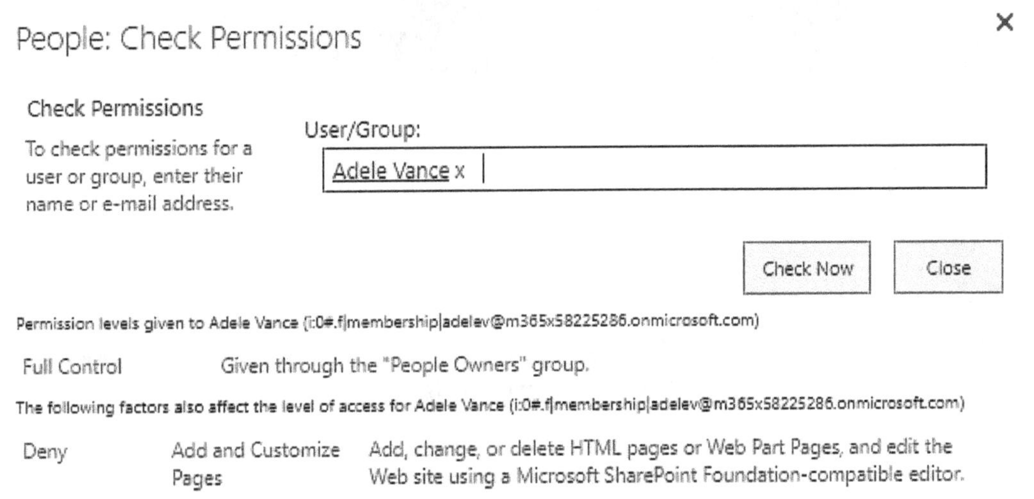

People: Check Permissions   ✕

Check Permissions

To check permissions for a
user or group, enter their
name or e-mail address.

User/Group:

Adele Vance ✕

Check Now   Close

Permission levels given to Adele Vance (i:0#.f|membership|adelev@m365x58225286.onmicrosoft.com)

Full Control   Given through the "People Owners" group.

The following factors also affect the level of access for Adele Vance (i:0#.f|membership|adelev@m365x58225286.onmicrosoft.com)

Deny   Add and Customize   Add, change, or delete HTML pages or Web Part Pages, and edit the
               Pages   Web site using a Microsoft SharePoint Foundation-compatible editor.

Figure 3.5 - Check Permissions

Permission inheritance

Permission inheritance in SharePoint means that permissions are automatically assigned from a parent object to all objects underneath it. For example, by default, permissions are inherited at the site level to all lists and libraries, folders, list items, and documents.

Permission inheritance can be broken by site owners and site collection administrators if unique permissions need to be granted to a specific object, such as a library containing sensitive information. When permission inheritance is broken, permissions that change from the parent object, such as a site or a parent library, are not automatically replicated. It is possible to remove all permissions that have been assigned from the parent when permission inheritance is broken. This can be useful in situations where certain users need to have different levels of access to a specific object, such as a confidential document library:

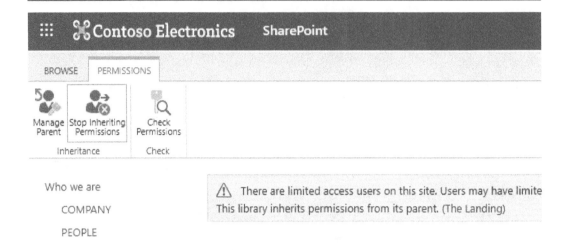

Figure 3.6 - Stop permission inheritance

Permission inheritance is a powerful and sometimes risky tool as it allows site owners and administrators to manage permission in a more granular way for sensitive content. For example, on a site for managing contracts, there might be a need for a library for more sensitive or personal contracts that should be visible to a limited group of people. It's not feasible to break permission inheritance at many levels, such as at the library level and several sub-folder levels, because it's difficult to figure out who has access and where afterward.

Custom permissions for lists and libraries

Custom permissions for a list or library are managed via the list or library settings. These settings can be accessed from the site menu (the gear icon in the top-right corner) and then selecting **List settings** or **Library settings**. These settings still use the SharePoint classic experience. **Permissions for this document library** and **Permissions for this list** can be found in the **Permission and Management** section. By default, permissions are inherited from the site:

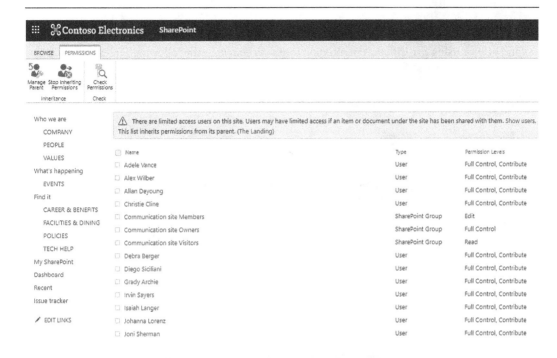

Figure 3.7 - List and library default permissions

After permission inheritance for the list or library is broken, permissions can be managed via the permission management toolbar. From here, you can do the following:

- **Delete unique permissions**: This restores permission inheritance and permission from the parent object – in this case, the site

- **Grant permissions**: Grant permissions for users and groups

- **Edit permissions**: Edit permissions for selected users or groups

- **Delete permissions**: Remove permissions from selected users or groups

- **Check permissions**: Check the permissions of a specific user:

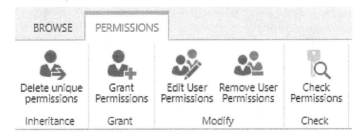

Figure 3.8 - The permission management toolbar

New permissions can be granted using the classic sharing dialogue. Permissions can be granted to users and groups using five different permission levels, as shown in the following screenshot:

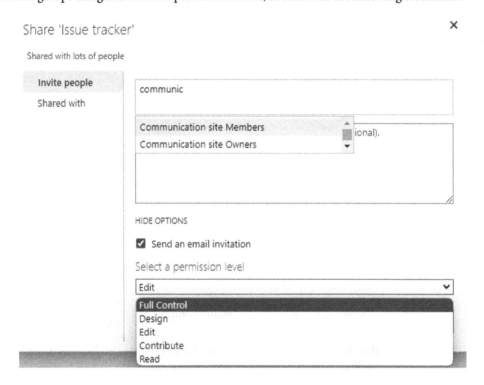

Figure 3.9 - Granting permissions to the list

Custom permissions for folders, list items, and files

Setting custom permissions for a folder, list item, or file involves using the same mechanisms that are used for lists and libraries. Advanced permission settings can be accessed by opening the information panel (the small info-icon at the top right of the list or library view) and selecting **Manage access**:

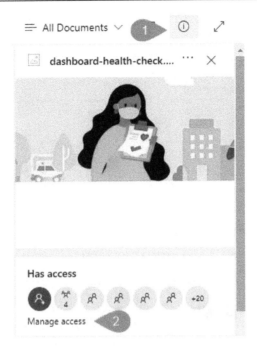

Figure 3.10 - Item-level permissions

The **Advanced** link can be found at the bottom of the **Manage access** dialogue box.

Sharing folders, items, and documents

Each folder, item, and document can be shared individually using the sharing dialogue. Sharing should be done carefully since sharing an item changes the permission inheritance setting to the item and to the list or library it's shared from. When sharing links with people who already have access to the site, it's recommended to use the **Copy link** feature or share using the **People with existing access can use the link** setting:

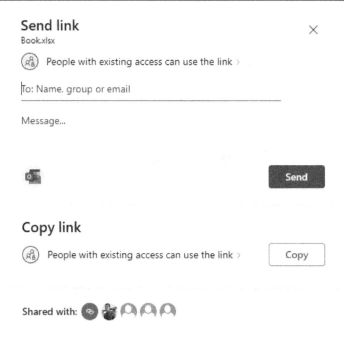

Figure 3.11 - Sharing with people with existing access

Controlling access with groups

SharePoint Online enables permission management via SharePoint groups and security-enabled groups on AAD. SharePoint groups are created at the site level, so each site has individual groups. By default, three groups are created automatically for each site.

SharePoint Online enables permission management using SharePoint and AAD groups. SharePoint groups are created at the site level, so each site has dedicated SharePoint groups. By default, three groups are created automatically for each site:

- **Site owners**: They have full control over the site, settings, content, and navigation

- **Site members**: They have editing capabilities for lists and libraries, pages, list items, and documents

- **Site visitors**: They have read-only access to content

In the modern experience, these groups are automatically mapped to the sharing experience permission levels on communication sites. On group-connected team sites, Microsoft 365 group members and owners are automatically mapped to site owners and site members.

A SharePoint group can contain individual users and AAD-hosted groups. SharePoint groups cannot be nested and used across sites but are useful in cases where the same custom permission level needs to be shared across multiple individuals and/or groups on the site.

SharePoint groups can be created and managed via the advanced permissions view:

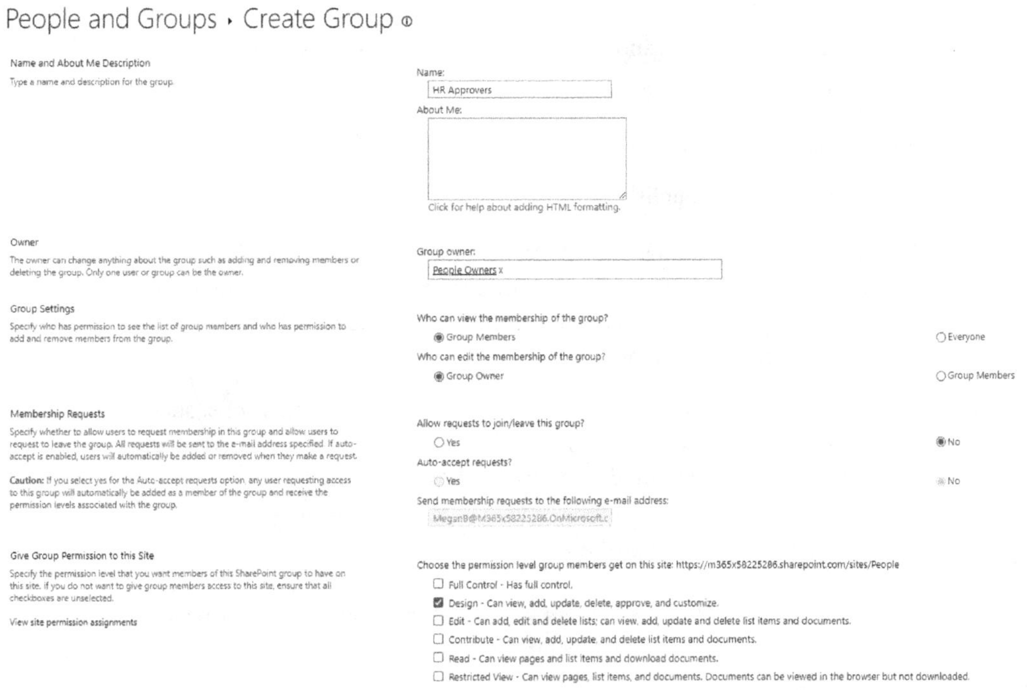

People and Groups › Create Group ⓪

Name and About Me Description
Type a name and description for the group.

Name:
HR Approvers

About Me:

Click for help about adding HTML formatting.

Owner
The owner can change anything about the group such as adding and removing members or deleting the group. Only one user or group can be the owner.

Group owner:
People Owners ×

Group Settings
Specify who has permission to see the list of group members and who has permission to add and remove members from the group.

Who can view the membership of the group?
⦿ Group Members   ○ Everyone
Who can edit the membership of the group?
⦿ Group Owner   ○ Group Members

Membership Requests
Specify whether to allow users to request membership in this group and allow users to request to leave the group. All requests will be sent to the e-mail address specified. If auto-accept is enabled, users will automatically be added or removed when they make a request.

Caution: If you select yes for the Auto-accept requests option, any user requesting access to this group will automatically be added as a member of the group and receive the permission levels associated with the group.

Allow requests to join/leave this group?
○ Yes   ⦿ No
Auto-accept requests?
○ Yes   ○ No
Send membership requests to the following e-mail address:
MeganB@M365x58225286.OnMicrosoft.c

Give Group Permission to this Site
Specify the permission level that you want members of this SharePoint group to have on this site. If you do not want to give group members access to this site, ensure that all checkboxes are unselected.

View site permission assignments

Choose the permission level group members get on this site: https://m365x58225286.sharepoint.com/sites/People
☐ Full Control - Has full control.
☑ Design - Can view, add, update, delete, approve, and customize.
☐ Edit - Can add, edit and delete lists; can view, add, update and delete list items and documents.
☐ Contribute - Can view, add, update, and delete list items and documents.
☐ Read - Can view pages and list items and download documents.
☐ Restricted View - Can view pages, list items, and documents. Documents can be viewed in the browser but not downloaded.

Figure 3.12 - Creating a new SharePoint group

When using **Group Settings**, consider the group owner who has permission to change the group settings. The group owner can be also a group, and it's quite common to set the site owner's group as an owner. Consider other settings based on the requirements. During group creation, permissions can be set based on five default permissions levels, but permissions can be specified more precisely after the group is created if required.

From AAD groups, Microsoft 365, security, and mail-enabled security group types are supported for controlling access in SharePoint. When using Microsoft 365 groups, access can be granted to group members. This includes owners and isn't limited to just the Microsoft 365 group's owners. Nowadays, it's quite common to control SharePoint permissions with Microsoft 365 groups since groups can be managed by group owners and do not require IT to be involved in all membership changes.

Permission levels

By default, there are five permission levels on SharePoint sites:

- **Full Control**: Full control over site content, lists and libraries, permissions, and settings. Site owners have this permission.

- **Design**: Manage lists, libraries, and content, as well as approve content.

- **Edit**: Manage lists, libraries, and content.

- **Contribute**: Manage content.

- **Read**: View and download published content.

By default, the owner has the **Full Control** permission and members have the **Edit** permission. Custom permission levels can be created, but these should only be used for specific requirements. Sometimes, you might need to add an approve permission to site members, which can be achieved by adding the design permission level to the site members group.

The individual permission level comprises a collection of specific permissions, such as **Manage Lists** and **Approve Items**, which are selected from a total of 33 available permissions. Some of these permissions are no longer effective in modern SharePoint experiences.

Controlling external sharing

You can manage how you externally share content via several access controls. Sharing files and folders is managed with sharing policies via the SharePoint admin center. There are four levels when it comes to sharing files and folders:

- **Anyone**: Files and folders can be shared anonymously and are accessed using a link. Anyone with the link can access the shared content.

- **New and existing guests**: People are invited via email to share content. They can sign in with their Microsoft account or use a one-time passcode with other email providers. Only people with invited email addresses can access the shared content. Users can invite new guest users to AAD.

- **Existing guests**: Content can only be shared with external users who have already been invited via AAD.

- **Only people in your organization**: External sharing is disabled for the whole tenant and cannot be overridden:

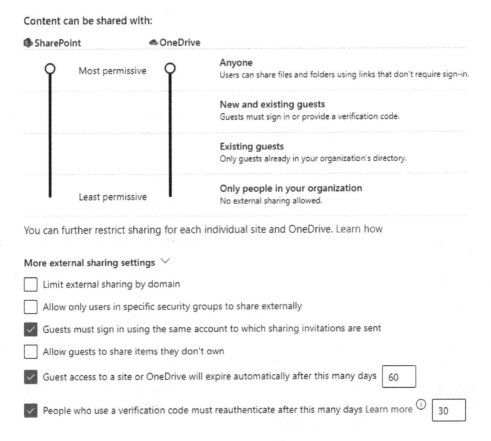

Figure 3.13 - External sharing policy

When it comes to the sharing policy, sharing can be restricted to specified domains. Sharing policies can be set at the site level but do not override the tenant-level policy. There are other controls on the AAD for inviting guest users and who can send invites.

External sharing is controlled at several levels in Microsoft 365. Regarding AAD, there are controls that users can use to invite external users from other organizations. This affects sharing content from SharePoint to guest users.

Good practices for permissions management

As we have discovered, SharePoint supplies flexible and granular ways to manage permissions, which can lead to uncontrolled situations and uncertainty about who has access to which areas. Here are a couple of helpful tips to keep in mind with SharePoint permissions:

- When sites are connected to teams, manage permissions using Teams' permission management. Solve restricted content areas using private or shared channels, depending on the case.

- Use AAD groups for permission management whenever possible. If possible, use Teams-connected Microsoft 365 groups and externalize permissions management to team owners.

- Use default permission levels whenever possible (**Full Control**, **Edit**, **Read**, and so on) by default. Create a new SharePoint group whenever custom permissions are required.

- Avoid breaking permission inheritance. Try to solve permission requirements at the site level. If that is not possible, do so at the document library or list level.

- It's important to remember to document any exceptions to the standard permission settings.

Summary

In this chapter, we learned how access to content in SharePoint is managed. SharePoint provides several different methods for permissions management and granular options, as well as individual document-level permissions. We saw how permissions are managed at the site level, how permissions can be customized, and how permission inheritance affects those permissions.

Later, we observed how permissions can be managed using SharePoint and AAD groups, and how individual permission levels are managed. Finally, we covered external sharing controls and good practices for permission management in SharePoint.

In the next chapter, we'll investigate lists and libraries, as well as control settings and how they can be modified using out-of-the-box tooling.

4

Lists and Libraries

As we learned in *Chapter 2*, sites are key elements for organizing and structuring content. SharePoint lists and libraries are also important since the content is stored in either a list or a library.

A list can be as simple as storing a list of items with just a title to a comprehensive database of dozens of site columns, attachments, and workflows. Likewise, a library can be a list of documents or a large document repository with dozens of site columns, content types, folder structures, and versioning policies.

The main difference between lists and a library is that, in a library, an item is always a document at the same time. Lists can also have files as an attachment – in fact, multiple if needed – but these are not required for list items. Attachments can be added and removed on the edit form of the item. Both lists and libraries are versatile and simple to extend using simple browser tools and advanced view and column formats.

In this chapter, we're going to learn the following main topics:

- Creating new lists and libraries
- Managing list and library settings
- Enabling the power of lists and libraries
- Microsoft Lists

Everything is a list or a library

When exploring how content is stored in SharePoint, it's quite clear that content on SharePoint sites is stored either in a list or a library. The main difference between these two is that a library always stores a document or a file as a list item and a list stores just list items. However, lists can also have files attached to list items. Both types can have metadata fields, which are used as properties to describe a list item or a document. Metadata can be, for example, the person who added a list item, description, choice, or number. In SharePoint, term lists or site columns are used. The difference between these column types is that list columns are only available and managed on the list or library specified, and site columns are available for all lists and libraries on a SharePoint site. Content from both can be surfaced using list views or different aggregation components and can be rendered as an HTML page or via APIs in **line-of-business (LOB)** applications.

Lists and libraries offer versatile storage possibilities. A list can have 30 million list items, and a document library can hold the same number of files and folders. Each list and library can have a maximum of 5,000 site columns for storing metadata. It might sound like a clever idea to use SharePoint lists as a database, but it should be kept in mind that list and library views only support retrieving just 5,000 items at a time. Also, having hundreds of site columns in a list or library starts affecting performance. There isn't any real relation between list or library items, which might lead to duplication of data. A SharePoint list can work as a database for lightweight applications; for example, a Power App used to support new employee onboarding or using list views itself as a user interface. Large lists are quite commonly used for archiving a substantial number of rows or files.

Creating new lists and libraries

Lists and libraries can be created from various locations. Each site can have 2,000 lists and libraries in total. Since this book focuses on the modern SharePoint experience, let's focus on modern ways of creating new lists and libraries. Using the new menu appearing on modern sites, it is possible to create both lists and libraries for the current site:

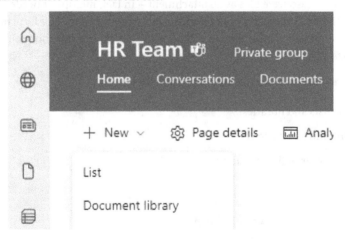

Figure 4.1 - Creating a new list or library

Creating a document library

Document library creation is simple; it just requires the name of the library and an optional description. It can also be defined if it is visible on the site navigation. A library URL is automatically generated based on the name:

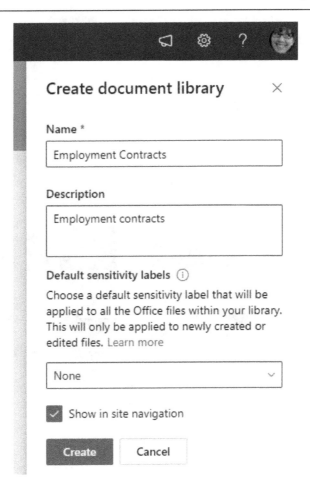

Figure 4.2 - Creating a new document library

Creating a new list

When a new list is created, the user is directed to a dialog with several options:

- **Blank list**: Blank list with just default site columns.

- **From existing list**: The user can choose a list from sites they have access to as a template. All list settings are copied with list content.

- **From Excel**: The user can upload or use existing Excel files from the site with a defined table. Table columns are mapped as list columns, and all rows from the Excel files are automatically added as list items.

- **From CSV**: Same as using Excel, but with CSV files.

- **Templates:** Microsoft provides several list templates with predefined site columns and settings. Organization can also publish their customized list templates:

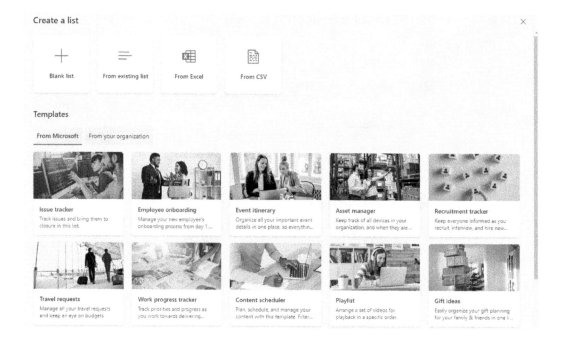

Figure 4.3 - Picking a template for a new list

> **Note**
>
> When lists are created from Excel or CSV files, the internal names of list columns are `field_0`, `field_1`, and so on. This needs to be taken care of when accessing list data from custom applications such as Power Apps.

Creating a list from an Excel spreadsheet

When creating a new list based on an Excel spreadsheet, data needs to be defined as a table. Each table of the spreadsheet is available to be selected:

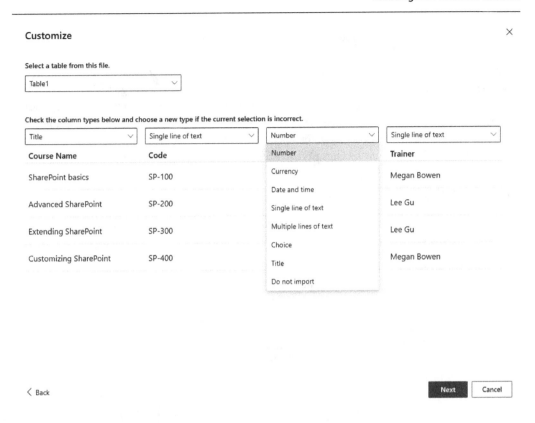

Figure 4.4 - Creating a list from an Excel spreadsheet

One of the imported columns needs to be mapped to the **Title** column of the list. The available data types are the following:

- **Number**
- **Currency**
- **Date and time**
- **Single line of text**
- **Multiple lines of text**
- **Choice**

Data types are available based on the data in the Excel spreadsheet. Not all the SharePoint site column types are available; for example, names on the example cannot be mapped to the user-type column. After mapping is done, the list just needs a name and a description. Importing Excel spreadsheets as SharePoint lists is a good idea when there are requirements for automation, reporting, or viewing data in SharePoint pages.

Managing list and library settings

List and library settings are managed through the classic SharePoint experience. Common settings for both and key differences of usage in the modern SharePoint experience are gone through in this section. On lists, settings are accessed from the **Settings** menu by selecting **List settings**. On libraries, the **Library settings** option opens a quick settings panel where the library's name and description can be changed and a default sensitivity label for the library can be set. More library settings links will open a classic SharePoint library settings page to access more detailed configuration.

Common settings for both

The list name, description, and navigation settings allow changing the name of a list or library, adding a description, and adding a link to the list or library to site navigation.

On the **Validation settings** page, column values can be confirmed using validation formulas. If validation fails, a custom error message is shown to the user:

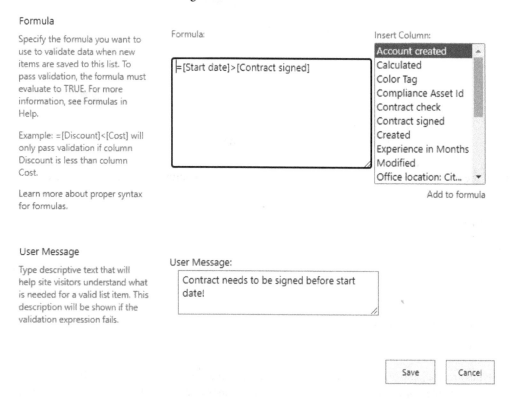

Figure 4.5 - List validation

- **Validations** are useful when, for example, a specific value difference between columns or a specific column value needs to be higher or lower than other columns, as in *Figure 4.5*, where the `Start date` must be higher than the `Contract signed` date. When validation fails, the list or library item cannot be saved. The user message should specify what is needed.

- **Audience targeting** of list items and documents can be enabled on the **Audience targeting** settings. Audience targeting enables list items and documents to be targeted to specific audiences. Targeting influences content aggregation, which can filter content based on the set target audience. For example, if the target audience is set to **HR Team**, only HR team members see content on aggregations.

- **Form settings** manage a SharePoint form or a custom form created with Power Apps used as default. On lists, there are still options for InfoPath available, but InfoPath itself is deprecated, and the end of life of the product is announced to be July 14, 2026. It's not recommended anymore to use InfoPath forms.

- **Permission settings** for lists and libraries are similar and are covered in *Chapter 3* of this book.

- The **Apply label to items in this list or library** setting enables adding a retention label automatically for items in this list. Retention labels can be used to manage the life cycle of list items and documents by setting up a label with specified settings. More details on retention labels are available at `https://learn.microsoft.com/en-us/purview/retention`.

List-specific settings

The versioning settings control the following:

- Content approval of submitted list items. Approval requires the **Approve** permission, which is automatically included in the **Site Owners** permissions.

- **Item Version History** defines how many versions of an item are saved, the maximum being 50,000, and a new version is created every time the item is saved. Lists only have major versions, such as 1.0, 2.0, and so on.

- **Draft Item Security** defines who can see draft items. Choices are **Any user who can read items**, **Only users who can edit items**, and **Only users who can approve items (and the author of the item)**.

The **Advanced settings** provide options to enable or disable various features of lists:

- **Are content types enabled?**
- **Can users add attachments to list items?**
- **Can users add comments to list items?**
- **Are users able to create folders?**
- **Is the list and list items included in the search index and are non-default list views indexed?**

The **Reindex list** button adds the list to the search indexing queue. This becomes handy when a list has major changes – for example, new site columns, which are required to be indexed as soon as possible.

With the **Item-level** permission, the behavior of read, create, and edit access can be controlled. For read access, options are **Read all items** or **Read items created by the current user**. For create and edit access, options are to create and edit all items in the list, edit items created by the user, or disable access by choosing **None**.

The **Rating** setting control can list items to be rated using either a star rating (1-5) or likes.

Library-specific settings

Versioning settings

On the versioning settings, the first setting is **Content Approval**. As with lists, libraries require the **Approve** permission, which is by default included in the **Site Owners** permissions. Libraries support two levels of versions, minor and major, which can be controlled with the **Document Version History** setting:

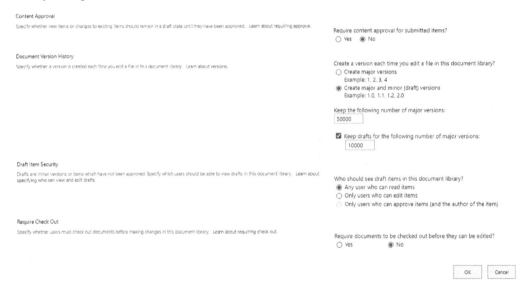

Figure 4.6 - Library versioning settings

When minor versioning is enabled, all saves increase the minor version number – for example, 1.3 to 1.4 – and the major version needs to be published separately from the context menu, which is opened from the three dots after the document name or second-clicking the document name:

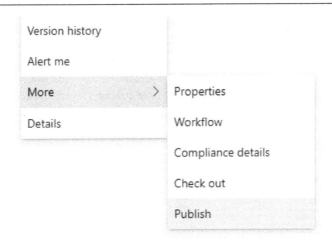

Figure 4.7 - Publishing a document: major version

The **Draft Item Security** setting is similar in lists.

The **Require Check Out** setting in SharePoint allows for the implementation of check-out and check-in policies for documents. This means that when a document is locked to a specific user, it must be checked out before any edits can be made and then checked back in once editing is complete before others can edit it. Check-out policies are particularly useful when formal management of documents, traceability, or version auditing is needed. However, it's important to note that enabling check-out policies disables the **Co-authoring** feature for documents in the document library.

Advanced settings

As with lists, library advanced settings enable content types, which are explained in *Chapter 5* in more detail, and allow users to create folders in a library. The library-specific document template, used for all created Word documents, can be changed. As with lists, library availability in the search index can be controlled and request reindexing of the library.

With the **Site Assets** library setting, the library can be set as the default library for images and other files uploaded to pages. In the modern experience, there is already a library named **Site Assets** for that purpose, and it's not recommended to add other libraries.

The **Quick Property Editing** setting can be used to disable editing library items using the information panel or in the grid view.

Column default value settings

Column default values for site columns can be set on libraries for a whole library or based on folder structure. This feature is nowadays rarely used, but it is still useful when metadata field default values differ on different folders or when centrally managed site columns are used, and default values are needed on the library.

Columns section on list and library settings

In the **Columns** section, all columns added to a list or library can be edited. Column settings are changed on the list or library level, and changes do not affect site columns:

Figure 4.8 - Columns section on settings

New columns can be created from the view. Newly created list columns are available only in the specific list or library. Existing site columns can also be added from the view. Nowadays, it's more common to add new columns and change settings from the modern list or library view directly, but sometimes it's still needed to change column settings using the list or library settings view.

Views section on list and library settings

The **Views** section displays all available views on a list or library:

Views

A view of a list allows you to see a particular selection of items or to see the items sorted in a particular order. Views currently configured for this list:

View (click to edit)	Default View	Mobile View
All Items	✓	✓
Group work by completed by date		✓
Group work by completion status		✓
Work to be completed		✓

▪ Create view

Figure 4.9 - Views section on settings

Users can access a certain view, select visible list columns, and change view settings such as grouping, sorting, or filtering.

New views can be created from the **Views** section, but it's recommended to use the modern experience to create new views. On recent modern views such as the **Calendar** or **Board** views, changes are made from the modern experience of lists.

Enabling the power of lists and libraries

The real power of lists and libraries comes when they are enhanced with site columns for describing the content, creating new, more compelling views, and customizing views for better visibility and structure.

List columns

When a blank list is created, just a title and a few default site columns, such as when the item was created or edited, and by whom, are automatically available. Adding more list columns to describe the content enhances the true potential of SharePoint lists. In the modern experience, adding a list column is simple: just click **Add column** on the list view. It is possible to choose from various column data types. These will be explained in more detail in the next chapter:

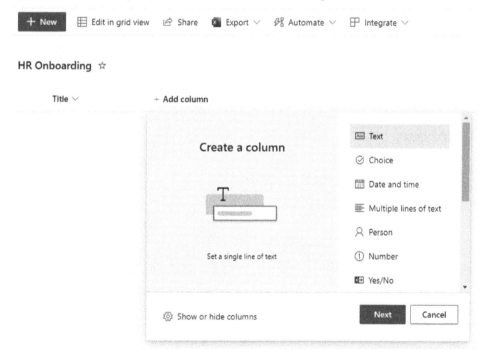

Figure 4.10 - Adding a site column

Let's add a couple of columns to the list:

- Rename title **New employee**
- **Start date**: date
- **Department**: text
- **Phone number**: text
- **Manager**: person
- **Account created**: **Yes/No**

When a new item is added to the list, all added metadata can be filled in:

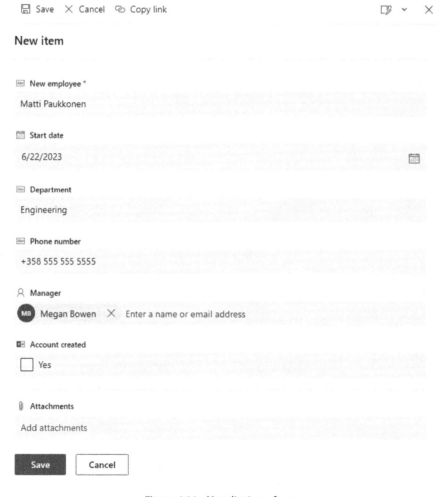

Figure 4.11 - New list item form

After the new item is saved, it's displayed as a row on the list:

Figure 4.12 - List item

Altering the list default view is simple. Columns can be reordered by dragging, and column widths can be narrowed or widened from the column edges or by opening the column context menu by clicking the column title, opening the **Column** setting, and selecting **Widen column** or **Narrow column**.

Columns can be renamed, and column settings can be changed. The **Title** column can also be renamed with a more descriptive name if needed. Notice that each column will have an internal name, which is automatically created during column creation, and a display name, which is visible to users. An internal name is required, for example, when customizing list views or when using specific columns with search. The internal name of a column is visible in the `sortField` query parameter when ordering a list based on columns, or when column settings are opened via list or library settings:

Figure 4.13 - Column internal name on URL

List and library views

Views supply a powerful and flexible way to show and visualize list and library content. A view can have a defined set of site columns visible, certain layouts, and visual effects, such as row or column coloring based on site column values. A list or library can have 50 views in total. New views can be created and changed from the view menu in the top-right corner of the view:

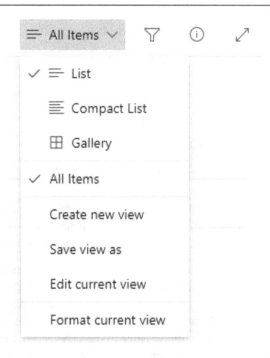

Figure 4.14 - The view menu

Depending on a list view layout, it's possible to use alternative layouts; for example, the default view can be shown as a compact list or gallery view. The menu also displays available views and states which is the active view. A new view can be created either by saving the current view with a new name or by creating a different view. The **Edit current view** choice opens the classic settings of the view. This is sometimes needed, for example, to show site columns that are not visible on the modern site column settings.

Creating and editing views

List views can be created and edited from the top-right corner of the list or library view. By default, there is an **All Items** view with three different layout options:

- **List, default row and column** layout
- **Compact list**, which makes row height smaller
- **Gallery**, which shows list items as cards

New views can be created easily by just selecting **Create view** and choosing from four different layout options: **List**, **Calendar**, **Gallery**, or **Board**:

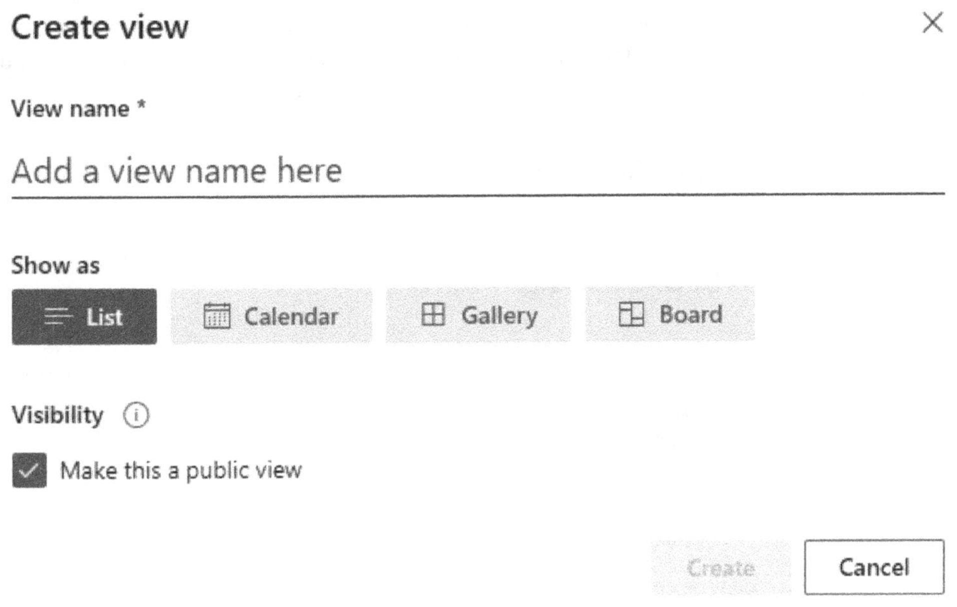

Create view   ✕

View name *

Add a view name here

Show as

[≡ List]   [📅 Calendar]   [⊞ Gallery]   [⊞ Board]

Visibility ⓘ

[✓] Make this a public view

[Create]   [Cancel]

Figure 4.15 - Creating a new view

- **List** view is a traditional column and row-styled view, as the default view.

- **Calendar** view can display list or library items in a month or week calendar layout. This view requires columns for the start and end date and a column for the event title. The same site column can be used for the start and end dates. These settings can be changed later by editing the view. Users can switch between weekly and monthly views from the view menu. **Calendar** view includes a **View event** panel located on the right side of the view. The panel includes the current day's events and items that don't have a start date set.

- **Gallery** view displays items as cards. Cards can be designed with a **Card Designer** tool found from the view menu by selecting **Format current view**. On the **Card Designer** editor, you can select which site columns are visible and reorder columns, preview specific columns shown, and make column names visible. Only columns that are set visible to the view can be shown. In libraries, the tool is called **Document Card Designer**, but the functionality is similar to the **Card Designer** tool. The only major difference is the preview of the document:

HR Onboarding ☆

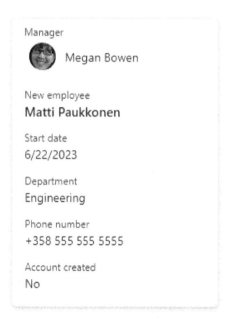

Figure 4.16 – Item card on Gallery view

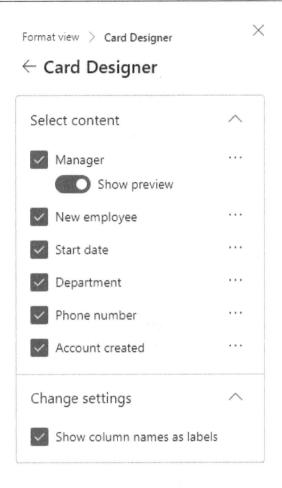

Figure 4.17 - Card Designer

- The **Board** view is only available with SharePoint lists. The **Board** view places list item cards in buckets based on a choice column; for example, **Status**. Items can be dragged between buckets, and the linked site column value will automatically update. An **Unassigned items** bucket is automatically generated and includes all items that don't have a linked site column value set. The **Unassigned items** bucket cannot be hidden:

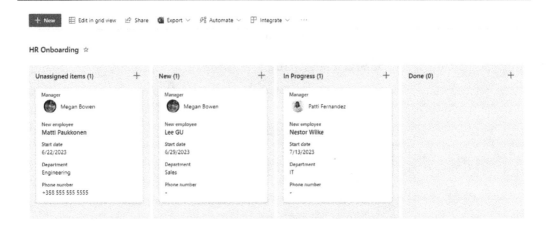

Figure 4.18 - Board view

View formatting

With view and column formatting, it is possible to add visual effects to a view based on conditions and site column values. Conditions rely on site column values and can have multiple rules. Visual effects include background color, font settings, border settings, and styles. Each view type has different options for view formatting:

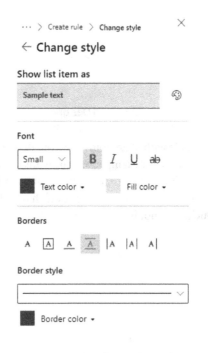

Figure 4.19 - List formatting styles

On the **List** view, rows can have alternate row colors for odd and even rows or use conditional formatting to design a style based on site column values. On the **Calendar** view, events can have different background colors based on conditions. The **Gallery** and **Board** views do not have choices for formatting views.

Column formatting

Each site column can have a format based on the column's value. Column formatting is displayed on top of view formats; for example, if the **Start date** column's background is formatted as red and on the view the row's background is set to green, the **Start date** column is displayed with a red background.

Views and columns can be formatted in **Advanced** mode, which enables customization of view or column HTML using specific JSON schema. More about advanced column formatting in *Chapter 15*.

Grid view

The grid view is an edit view for list items and documents where users can easily update and copy site column values on a grid-like format:

Figure 4.20 - Editing using grid view

Site column values can be updated for all visible rows and added to new columns and new list items. On document libraries, adding new documents is not available since it requires a file. One powerful feature of the grid view is the ability to duplicate column values from a specific row to multiple rows. This is done by grabbing the lower-right corner of the row and painting over the rows wanted:

HR Onboarding ☆

○	New employee ∨	Start date ∨	Department ∨
○	Matti Paukkonen	6/22/2023	Engineering
○	Lee GU	6/29/2023	Sales
	Nestor Wilke	7/13/2023	IT

Figure 4.21 - Copying items by dragging

Modifying new forms on lists

Columns and the layout of new and edited forms on lists can be edited directly from the form panel:

Figure 4.22 - Form customization menu

By editing columns, it's possible to show or hide specific columns, reorder columns, and use conditions to show a column based on the value of another column; for example, showing the **Manager** column when the **Status** column value is **In Progress**:

```
=if([$Status] == 'In Progress', true, false)
```

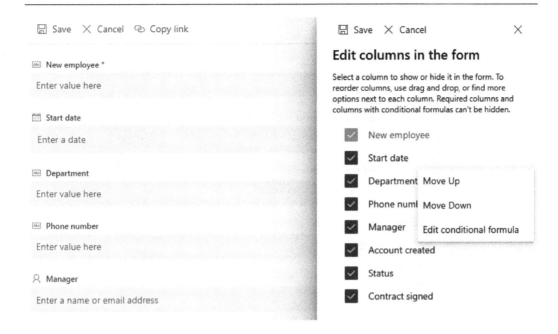

Figure 4.23 - Form column editor

The **Configure layout** choice allows you to create a customized header and footer and divide columns into titled sections:

Figure 4.24 - Column layout

Modifying list forms with Power Apps is explained in more detail in *Chapter 13*.

Microsoft Lists

Microsoft Lists is a separate application in Microsoft 365 for creating and accessing SharePoint lists found on users' personal OneDrive for Business or on SharePoint sites. Opening a list with Microsoft Lists focuses only on the specific list; for example, SharePoint site content elements are not available:

Figure 4.25 - Microsoft Lists

When opening the application, recently accessed lists and users' favorite lists are shown. Lists can be set as favorites by clicking a small star icon in the top-right corner of the list icon.

Creating a new list is basically the same as in SharePoint sites. It's possible to pick predefined templates, create a blank list, or import from an Excel or CSV file. The biggest difference is that it is possible to pick a location for the list either from recently accessed sites or by creating a list in users' personal OneDrive. Administrators can control the creation of lists in users' OneDrive, and **My lists** is not available for users:

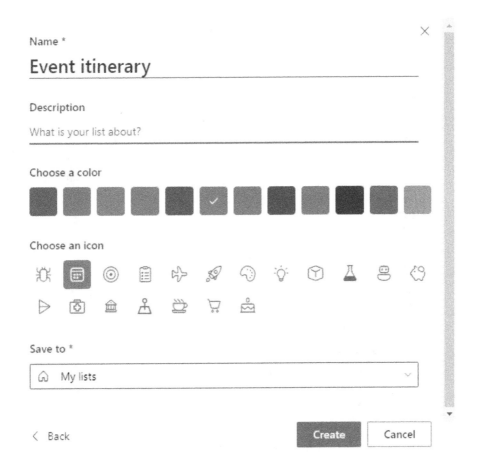

Figure 4.26 - Creating a new list

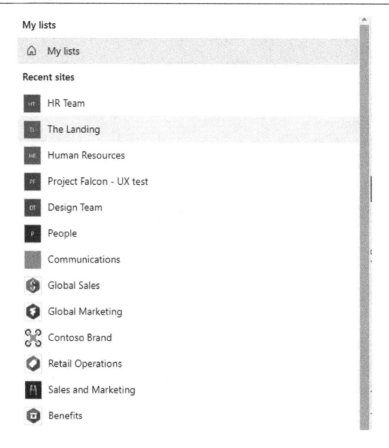

Figure 4.27 - Creating a new list

Microsoft Lists is a particularly useful application for accessing important and often updating lists that might be found on different sites. The Lists application is also available in Microsoft Teams where it enables bringing important SharePoint lists to tabs in Teams channels.

Summary

In this chapter, we learned what SharePoint lists and libraries are and what their main differences are. We saw how simple it is to create new lists and libraries and how to manage the most important settings.

We then observed how lists can be enhanced with site columns, how list views can be created and modified using simple browser tools, and how default forms can be customized.

Lastly, we had an overview of what Microsoft Lists is and how it relates to SharePoint lists.

In the following chapter, we will study more about SharePoint site columns and content types and how they can improve the information management capabilities of SharePoint.

5

Describing Content with Site Columns and Content Types

When managing large quantities of content, such as thousands of rows of data or tens of thousands of documents, metadata plays an important part in describing, sorting, and processing the content. In SharePoint, metadata is maintained in list or site columns, which can be added to lists and libraries. List columns are maintained at the list or library level. Site columns are reusable and available for all lists and libraries on a SharePoint site. A column can be, for example, a line of text, a number, a user or a group, or a centrally managed metadata term.

Different types of data in the same document library may require a different set of site columns, which is where content types come into play. A content type groups selected site columns together. In document libraries, a content type can also link to a document template, which is used when a new document is created with that specific content type.

Columns and content types can be created on a site or a list/library level, or they can be centrally managed using SharePoint admin center's Content type gallery.

Site columns and content types are a crucial part of the information architecture and require thorough planning. The information architecture plan should consider the following areas:

- Needed content types and content type inheritance
- Site columns and how they are mapped to content types
- Default and calculated values of columns

Centralized publishing of content types may become important when the same information architecture needs to be used on multiple sites.

In this chapter, we're going to cover the following main topics:

- Site columns
- Content types

- Using content types and site columns in lists and libraries
- Centrally managing and publishing content types and site columns

Site columns

SharePoint site columns can be thought of as reusable metadata for list items and documents that can be added to multiple lists and libraries. Site columns can be used to describe, group, sort, and filter items and documents. They can be used in search queries, templates, and refining and sorting search results. Site columns can be created at the site level. Columns created on the site level are reusable in all lists and libraries on the site. Site columns can be also published with centrally managed content types from the Content Type Gallery, which is accessed from the SharePoint Admin Center. Centrally published columns are created in a special site called Content Type Hub and copied to sites that use published content types.

There are 19 different data types in SharePoint; in this book, we will focus on column types that can be used in modern user experience. Each column requires a name, optional description, column group, and may require a value, as well as specific settings depending on the column type.

On the site, site columns are created from the **Site settings** page using the SharePoint classic experience:

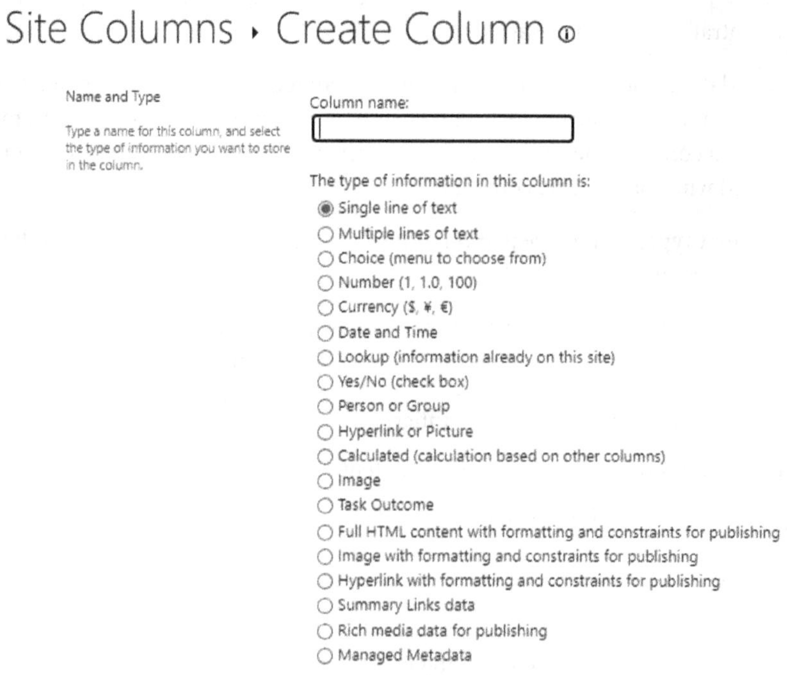

Site Columns ▸ Create Column ⓘ

Name and Type

Type a name for this column, and select the type of information you want to store in the column.

Column name:

The type of information in this column is:
- Single line of text
- Multiple lines of text
- Choice (menu to choose from)
- Number (1, 1.0, 100)
- Currency ($, ¥, €)
- Date and Time
- Lookup (information already on this site)
- Yes/No (check box)
- Person or Group
- Hyperlink or Picture
- Calculated (calculation based on other columns)
- Image
- Task Outcome
- Full HTML content with formatting and constraints for publishing
- Image with formatting and constraints for publishing
- Hyperlink with formatting and constraints for publishing
- Summary Links data
- Rich media data for publishing
- Managed Metadata

Figure 5.1 - Creating a new site column

On lists and libraries, list columns are created by adding new columns to the view using the modern experience or adding a column from the list settings:

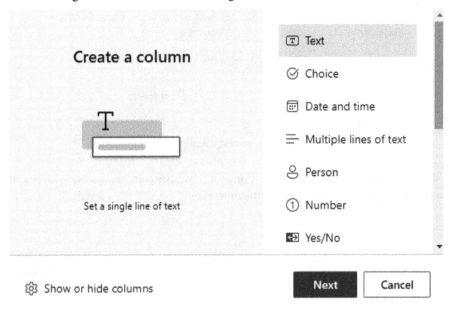

Figure 5.2 - Creating library columns

Column types

In this section, we will look at the various column types available in SharePoint.

Text columns

A **single-line-of-text** column can hold 1 to 255 characters; the limit can be set in the column settings. The default value can be set, or you can use a calculated value. Unique values can be also enforced.

Multiple-lines-of-text columns are used for freeform text. Columns can also hold rich text formatting including pictures, tables, and hyperlinks. Currently, list view formatting does not support rich text formats correctly and may cause issues. This column type can be set in append mode, which appends changes to the column value to existing text with user and timestamp information:

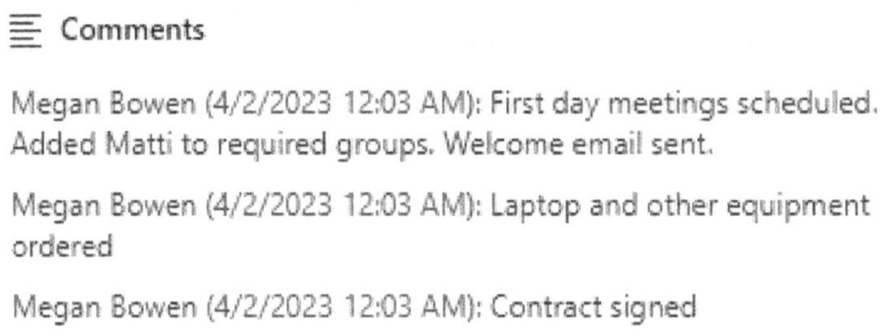

Comments
Megan Bowen (4/2/2023 12:03 AM): First day meetings scheduled. Added Matti to required groups. Welcome email sent.
Megan Bowen (4/2/2023 12:03 AM): Laptop and other equipment ordered
Megan Bowen (4/2/2023 12:03 AM): Contract signed

Figure 5.3 - Multiple-lines-of-text column in append mode

The append mode stores each change as a version, but when the column is accessed from another application (for example, a Power App), only the most recent change is displayed.

Choice

Choice columns are used to supply single or multi-select options. Each choice is text and can be 255 characters long, although keeping choices simple and short is a good practice. Choice columns also support reusable fill-in choices from users.

Choices can be shown as a drop-down menu or as radio buttons. Multi-select choices are shown as a list picker:

Benefits
Phone benefit
Lunch benefit
Type to filter
Company car
Sports vouchers

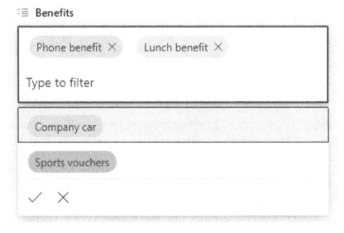

Figure 5.4 - Multi-select picker on the modern list experience

Date and time

Date and time columns can hold just a date and, if needed, include the time. The column value can be either shown in a date format or in a friendly format, such as "March 22, 2023" or "2 minutes ago." The date format depends on the site's language and regional settings.

Person

Person columns enable adding persons and groups to a list item or a document. A column can be limited to include just persons. Persons can be only retrieved from **Microsoft Entra ID (ME-ID)**. Group retrieval includes AAD groups and SharePoint site groups. The column type is linked to a persona card. A small card opens when hovering over the column value, and a large card opens when clicking the item. The persona card displays basic profile information from AAD enriched with insights such as organization charts, files, and LinkedIn profile information:

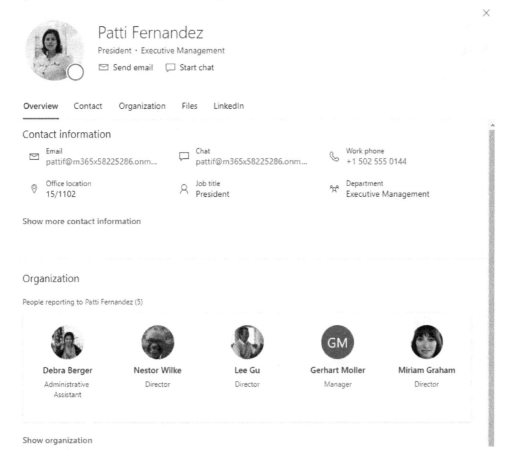

Figure 5.5 - Large persona card

Number and Currency

Number and Currency column types have quite similar settings. Both allow the setting of minimum and maximum allowed values, enabling/disabling thousands separators, and setting the number of decimals. On a Number column, it's possible to add a custom symbol or a short text visible with the value, and with a Currency column, it's possible to select a currency. Both field types can be used to calculate totals from all (filtered and grouped rows on the list). The column total can be any of the following:

- **Count**
- **Average**
- **Maximum**
- **Minimum**
- **Sum**
- **Std Deviation**
- **Variance**:

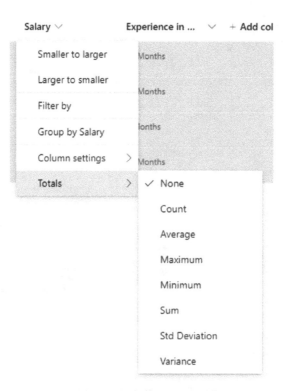

Figure 5.6 - Column totals

Yes/No

A Yes/No column type is just a simple checkbox.

Hyperlink

A hyperlink column includes a URL and an alternative text.

Location

Location columns can be used to pinpoint a specific location or an address. Locations and addresses are retrieved from Bing Maps. The column displays the location in textual format. On the column settings, automatically extracted linked columns can be enabled. Linked columns can include street address, city, state, country or region, postal code, coordinates, and name of the place.

Image

Image columns add an image to a list item or document.

Lookup

A Lookup column is a special column type that allows using another list as a data source for a column. The Lookup column refers to an item of a list set as a source based on a column. Site columns on the source list need to be created on the site level since they need to be reusable throughout the site. The Lookup column displays the value of the defined list item column and acts as a link to the selected list item on the source list of the lookup. Lookup columns do not support Person, Calculated, or Hyperlink columns.

Use Lookup columns carefully since they may cause performance issues when using large lists are a source. The source list must live on the same site. A list can hold a maximum of 12 Lookup columns. The Lookup column is not a two-way relation, and shouldn't be considered a similar relation as in relational databases.

Managed metadata

Managed metadata is a special column type that links the column to a managed metadata term set and a term hierarchy. The term set can be managed either globally on the tenant level or on the site. Term hierarchy can be seven levels deep. The column shows the name of the selected term, or the term and all parent terms from the hierarchy. The column can be set for users to enter new terms – for example, keywords. The underlying term set in managed metadata needs to also be set to allow new terms.

Users can search values in the column by typing the name of a term or selecting from the term hierarchy.

Managed metadata columns are quite often used when column values need to be centrally managed and all changes need to reflect for all sites.

Calculated column

Calculated columns can be used to calculate a value based on another column's value or condition or to calculate a value based on date and time. Calculated column values cannot be changed by users, and the column value is recalculated when an item is saved. The ID column value cannot be used as part of the calculation. A list can include a maximum of 20 calculated columns. The data type can be selected from five options:

- **Single line of text**

- **Number**

- **Currency**

- **Date and Time**

- **Yes/No**:

Name and Type	Column name:
Type a name for this column.	Contract check
	The type of information in this column is:
	Calculated (calculation based on other columns)
Additional Column Settings	Description:
Specify detailed options for the type of information you selected.	

Formula: Insert Column:

=DATEDIF([Contract signed], [Start date],"m")

Account created
Calculated
Compliance Asset Id
Contract signed
Created
Experience in Months
Modified
Office location: Cit...
Office location: Cou...
Office location: Nam...

Add to formula

The data type returned from this formula is:
- ⦿ Single line of text
- ○ Number (1, 1.0, 100)
- ○ Currency ($, ¥, €)
- ○ Date and Time
- ○ Yes/No

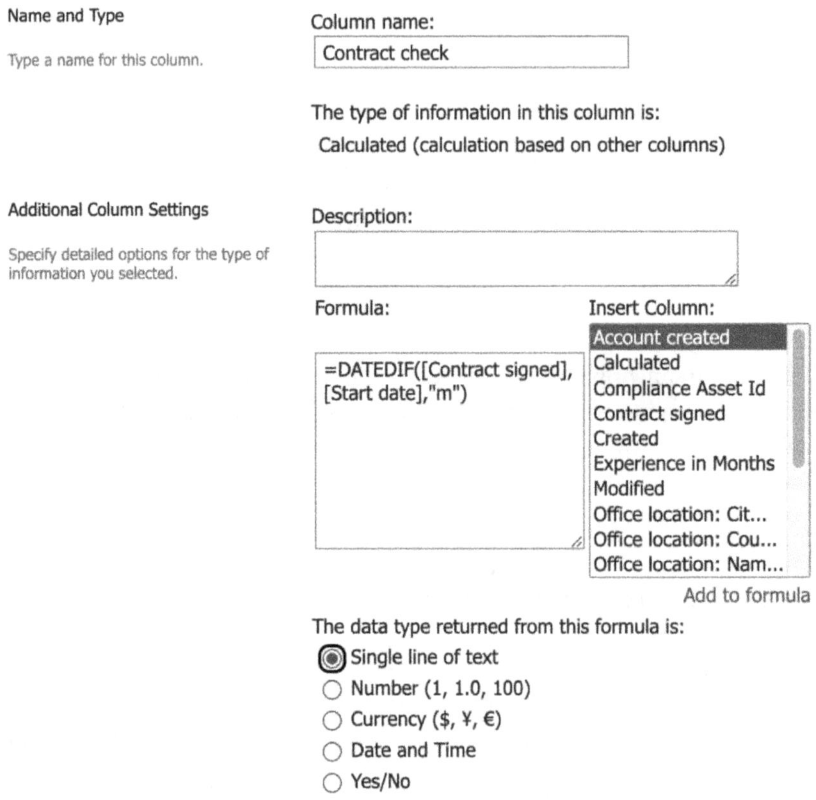

Figure 5.7 - Calculated column

> **Formula examples**
>
> To check that a contract is signed before a new employee starts, run the following code:
> `=IF([Contract signed]<=[Start date],"OK","Contract needs to be signed before start date")`
>
> Calculated column formulas are prone to errors. Make sure to test them thoroughly, especially when handling dates over different years.
>
> Calculated columns are created and managed using the classic SharePoint experience.

Default column values

A default value for a column can be added manually (for example, by entering a number or text) or be chosen from choices or a managed metadata term set. On datetime typed columns, the default value can be either the selected date or today's date. Users can override the default value by editing the column value:

Default value

| None | ∨ |

| None |
| Today's date |
| Select a date and time |

Figure 5.8 - Datetime column's default value

The calculated default value can be used to format datetimes – for example, showing just a year. The calculated default value cannot be referenced to other columns of the item; a calculated column needs to be used for that.

Here's an example:

For the year when a list item was created, run the following: `=TEXT(TODAY(),"yyyy")`

Column validation

Column validation can be used to ensure that users are adding correct values – for example, the start date needs to be later than today or the phone number column needs to include more than eight characters. Unlike calculated columns, column validation formulas cannot refer to other column values.

Content types

SharePoint content types are used to manage site columns, item or document behavior, and templates linked to a document. Every item and document is linked to a certain content type. On a list, the default content type is **Item**, which includes just an editable **Title** column and SharePoint's default columns, such as **Created**, **Modified**, and **Modified By**.

On a document library, the default content type is **Document**, which includes a name (linked to a filename), a title, and SharePoint's default columns. The **Document** content type is inherited from the **Item** content type. All content types derive from these basic content types by inheriting columns and settings. The content type ID visualizes the inheritance since the parent's ID is always included. This is very handy when you want to search over a content type and its descendants.

Here's an example of how a content type ID is structured when content types are inherited from each other:

Item: 0x01

Document: 0x0101

Contract: 0x0101003C509B9764D45E409E5759550D7D5EA8

Employment contract: 0x0101003C509B9764D45E409E5759550D7D5EA801

Content type settings

For a list content type, the settings are simple. The content type can be set as read-only, and you can choose for changes made to the content type to be updated to all content types inherited from that specific content type.

For document library content types, there is also a setting for document templates:

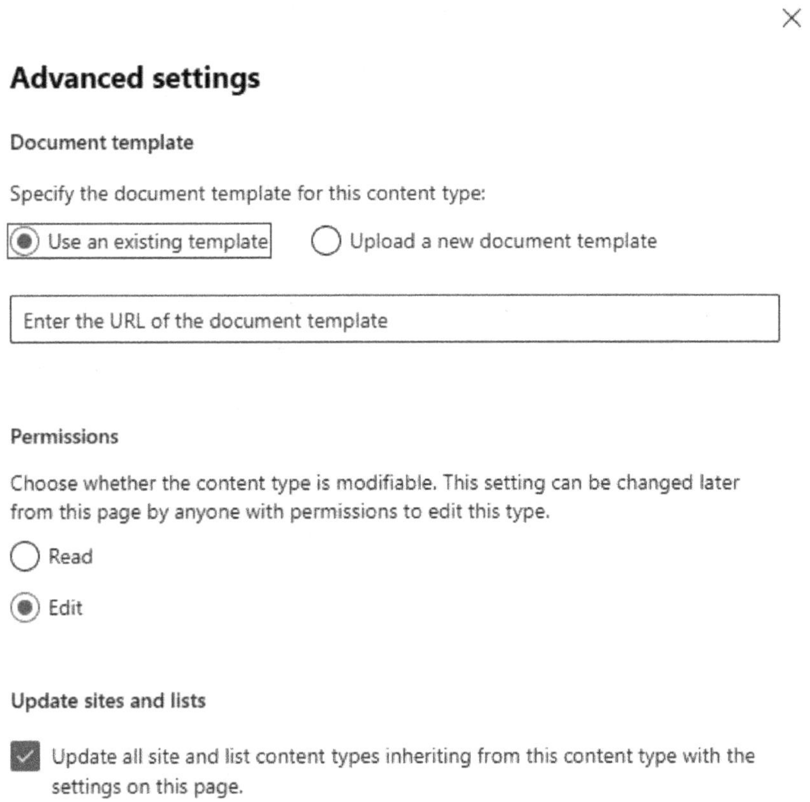

×

Advanced settings

Document template

Specify the document template for this content type:

⦿ Use an existing template   ◯ Upload a new document template

> Enter the URL of the document template

Permissions

Choose whether the content type is modifiable. This setting can be changed later from this page by anyone with permissions to edit this type.

◯ Read

⦿ Edit

Update sites and lists

☑ Update all site and list content types inheriting from this content type with the settings on this page.

Figure 5.9 - Document-based content type settings

Creating new content types

Content types are always created on the site level from **Site settings** or from the Content Type Gallery on SharePoint Admin Center. To navigate to **Site settings** on modern sites, open the **Settings** menu from the cog on the top-right corner and select **Site information**. On the **Site Information** panel, open **View all site settings** and pick **Site content types** from the **Web Designer Galleries** section. Select **Create content type**, which opens a panel on the right.

An added content type requires a name that needs to be unique within the site. A category can be created or picked from a previously created one. A good practice is to create a custom category for all custom content types, and then the category can be used to filter and group content types on the gallery. The parent content type choice defines which content type the added content type is derived from. Make this choice carefully since all changes to the parent content type might be reflected in the added content type:

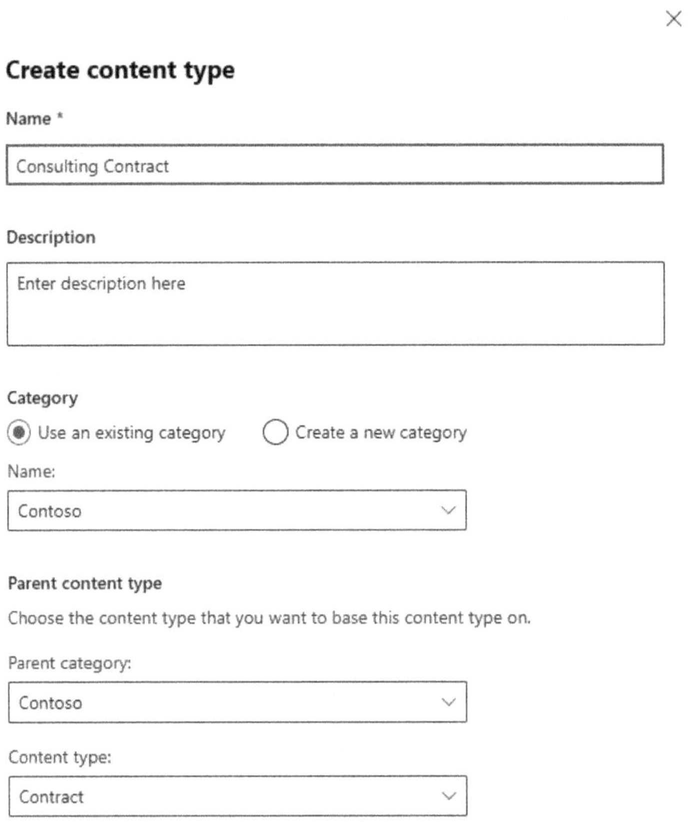

Figure 5.10 - Creating a new content type

When a content type is created, site columns can be added. On a content type level, a site column can be set as visible/hidden and optional/required, and it is updated to all site and list content types when the parent content type is updated. The actual site column settings are changed by editing the site column; the column settings panel includes a direct link at the bottom.

Special content types

Let's look at a couple of special content types and how to configure them.

Folder

As the name suggests, the **Folder** content type represents a folder in lists and libraries.

Document Set

A document set is like a folder, but it can have site columns attached to it, which are then inherited by the documents added to the document set. The **Document Set** content type limits which content types can be added or uploaded to a document set:

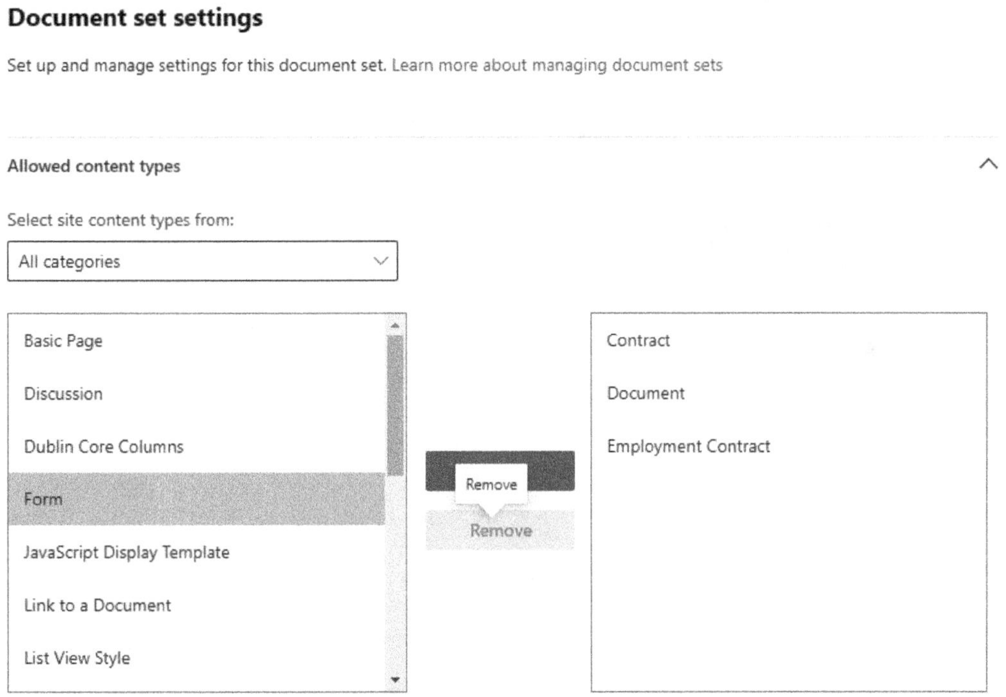

Document set settings

Set up and manage settings for this document set. Learn more about managing document sets

Allowed content types ⌃

Select site content types from:

All categories ⌄

Basic Page		Contract
Discussion		Document
Dublin Core Columns		Employment Contract
Form	Remove	
JavaScript Display Template	Remove	
Link to a Document		
List View Style		

Figure 5.11 - Document set settings

Document Set enables the automatic creation of specified documents and folders when a new document set is created in the document library. This is a handy feature when certain mandatory documents are always needed. Empty folder structures cannot be created, but as a workaround, it's possible to upload a simple text file to a folder.

Shared columns are automatically synchronized from the document set to added files. Files can also have dedicated site columns based on the content type.

The welcome page can show selected site columns when the document set is opened:

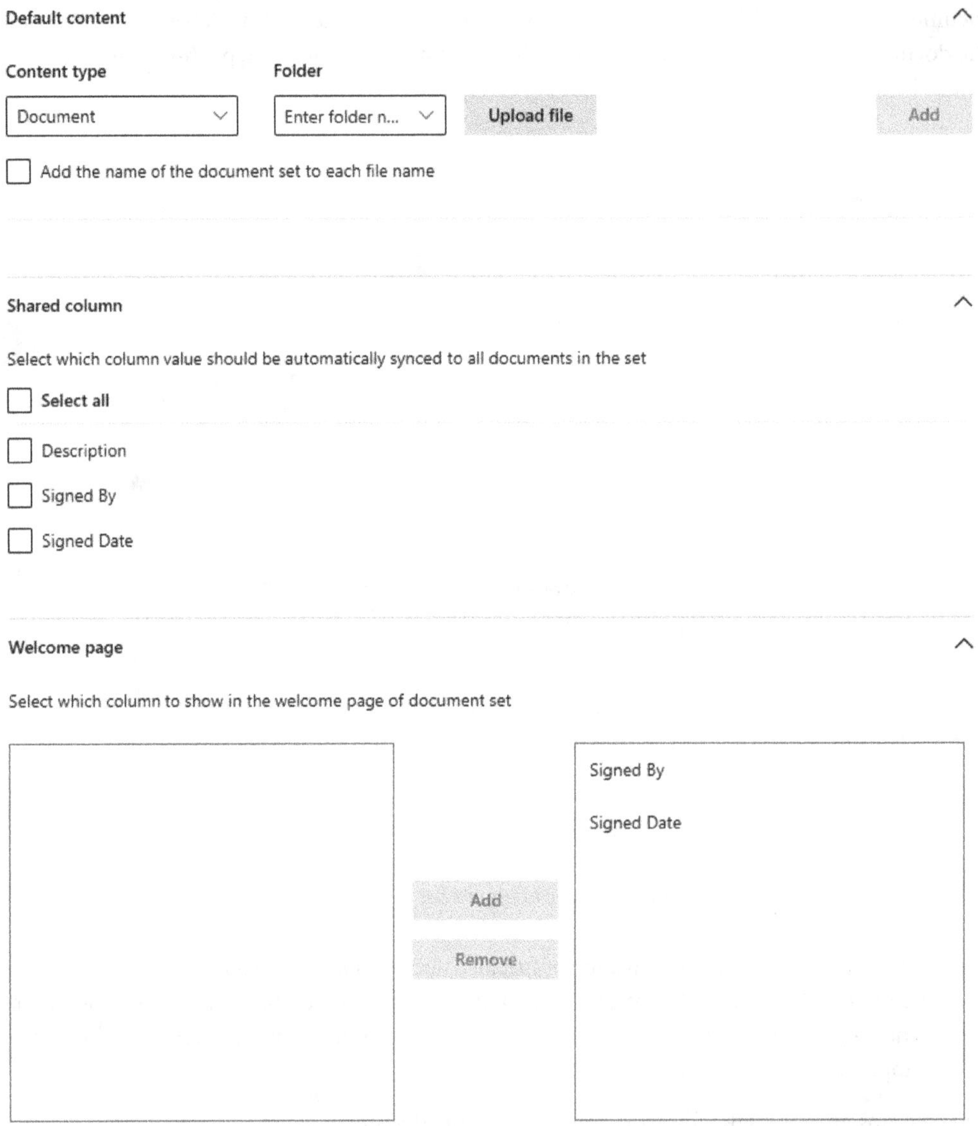

Default content   ∧

Content type   Folder

| Document ∨ | Enter folder n... ∨ | Upload file | Add |

☐ Add the name of the document set to each file name

Shared column   ∧

Select which column value should be automatically synced to all documents in the set

☐ Select all

☐ Description

☐ Signed By

☐ Signed Date

Welcome page   ∧

Select which column to show in the welcome page of document set

Signed By

Signed Date

Add

Remove

Figure 5.12 - Document set settings

When document sets are used, especially with custom site columns, it's important to plan and map site columns that are used on the document set and file level.

Document sets are useful when a document consists of multiple separate files – for example, a contract that holds an actual signed PDF document and several separate annexes.

Using content types and site columns in lists and libraries

Adding a new column to a list or libraries is simple. Click **Add column** at the end of a column, select the column type, and fill out the necessary information:

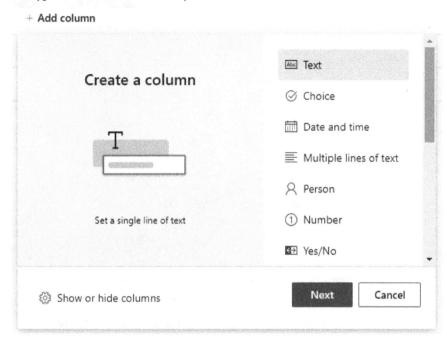

Figure 5.13 - Creating a column

Adding an existing site column to a list or library is done from **List settings**. Click **Add an existing site column** at the bottom of the columns list. Select needed columns and define columns updated to all content types and added to the default view. Adding columns to content types doesn't update site-level content types; it just manages content types on the list:

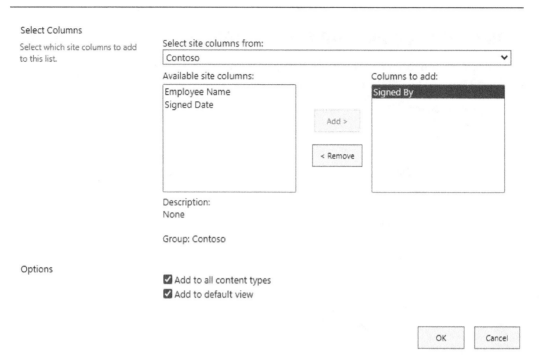

Figure 5.14 - Adding an existing site column to a list

Adding and managing content types on lists and libraries

Published content types can be added directly from the **Add column** view by scrolling to the bottom, selecting **Add a content type**, and selecting content types as needed. Content types need to be enabled first from the advanced list or library settings:

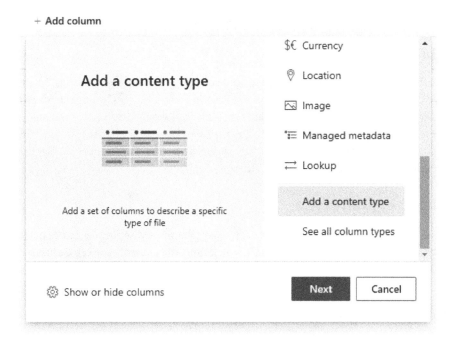

Figure 5.15 - Adding a published content type to a list

Published content types, which are managed on the Content Type Gallery, can be removed from the same view. Site content types are added from the **List settings** or **Library settings** view. The default content type and the setting for which content types are available on the **New** button are also managed on the list or library settings. On the **Change New Button Order** screen, view owners can choose visible content types and define the order, the first being the default content type:

Figure 5.16 - New button order view

Removing a content type is done by opening the content type from the content type list and selecting **Delete this content type**. This removes the content type from the list and doesn't affect the site-level content type. Content types that are used on list items or documents cannot be removed.

Centrally managing and publishing content types and site columns

The Content Type Gallery hosts centrally managed content types and site columns. The Content Type Gallery can be accessed from the SharePoint Admin Center in the **Content services** section. The user experience is similar to the site content type gallery; the only difference is the publishing of content types. The Content Type Gallery itself lives on a special SharePoint site that can be found at `https://<your-tenant>.sharepoint.com/sites/contenttypehub`. Don't use this site for anything other than content-type publishing.

Publishing a content type

Once the content type is ready, including all necessary site columns and settings, it can be published by clicking **Publish** from the content type toolbar. The first time, the content type can be just published:

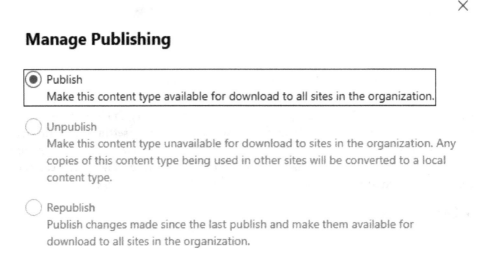

Figure 5.17 - Publishing a content type

After publishing, the content type is not automatically visible on SharePoint sites. In the modern content-type publishing experience, published content types are added directly to lists or libraries. When a content type is added to the list or library, it's also copied as a site content type.

Updating a published content type

The published content type is updated on the Content Type Gallery, and once updates are done, the content type can be republished. As with the publishing of a content type, republishing updates the content type to sites with a delay. Updating a published content type can be done manually from the site content type gallery:

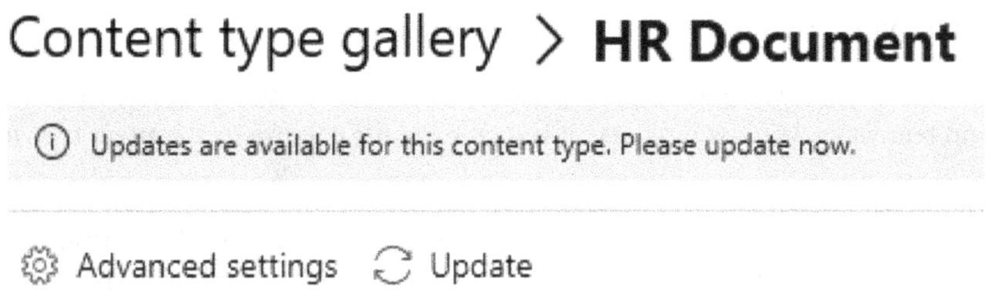

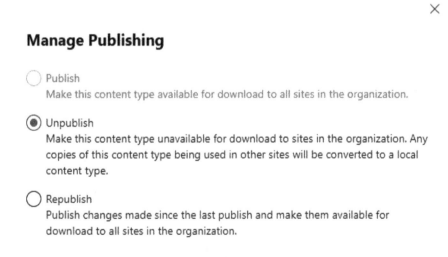

Figure 5.18 - Updated content type

Unpublishing a content type

To unpublish a content type, select the content type and click **Publish** from the toolbar. On the **Manage Publishing** panel, select **Unpublish**:

Figure 5.19 - Unpublishing a content type

Unpublishing a content type makes it unavailable to be used on sites. If the content type has already been used, it's converted as a local content type on sites where it's in use and needs to be removed when the content type is published again. Content-type publishing also requires planning and thorough testing. Publish content types in read-only mode to avoid conflicts when someone accidentally or without better knowledge edits the content type on sites.

Summary

In this chapter, we learned how site columns and content types can be used to describe and classify list items and documents. We learned about commonly used site columns in the modern SharePoint experience and how easy it is to create and manage columns.

Next, we were introduced to content types and how they are used to manage site column settings, behavior, and templates. We saw how easy it is to apply a site column or a content type to a list or a library.

In the last section, we learned how content types can be managed from the centralized Content Type Gallery, how content types are published and updated, and what happens when content types are unpublished.

In the following chapter, we will focus on modern SharePoint pages and how they can be used to create informative and stunning content.

6

Creating Informative and Stunning Content with Modern SharePoint Pages

SharePoint has a long history of being a platform for informative portals used with a web browser, commonly called intranets. The modern experience brought a huge change to content authoring, mobile friendly and responsive by nature. It has some limitations, such as strictly defined styles, fonts, and page structure. Customization of the look and feel is fairly limited to theming and icons, but the focus should in any case be the content itself, enriched with the organization's own images and graphics.

The modern authoring canvas is simple and intuitive to use. The page is structured in sections with different column layouts. The actual content is produced with web parts, which can be freely added and organized within columns, and move between columns and sections just by dragging. The content author sees the changes in real time when web parts are changed or content is added.

In this chapter, we're going to cover the following main topics:

- Creating your first SharePoint content page
- Aggregating content using web parts
- Targeting pages and documents
- Managing page templates
- Using SharePoint pages in Microsoft Teams

Creating your first SharePoint content page

Content pages live on the **Site Pages** library. Each site has a dedicated Site Pages library. Creating a new page starts by opening a site where the page needs to be published and shown to users. The easiest way is to navigate to the home page of the site, click + **New** from the toolbar, and select **Page** or **News post**, if the page is a news article:

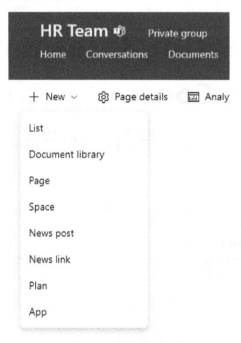

Figure 6.1 - Creating a page

Pick a template and select **Create page** from the bottom-right corner. The preview shows an overview of the template:

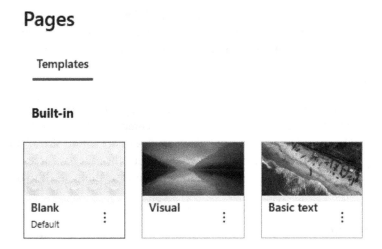

Figure 6.2 - Default page templates

The page itself consists of a header section and an authoring canvas.

Header section

The header section includes the title of the page, the author's name (which can be changed or hidden), the published date, and – depending on the header style – a background image. An optional text block above the title can be used for visually categorizing pages. The optional text block is limited to 40 characters. A pen icon for opening the **Settings** panel, as well as image editing tools, can be found on the top. The header settings panel opens to the right. On the settings panel, the author can change the layout of the header and alignment of the title, edit and hide text block text, and hide the published date:

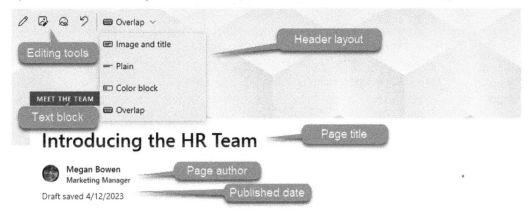

Figure 6.3 - Header section

When using the **Image and title** header layout, make sure that the title text is visible and that there is enough contrast between the title text and the background image. Text color is automatically set based on the background image, and sometimes, text may become hard to see from the background image.

Adding a background image to the header section

A background image for the header can be selected from images uploaded earlier to the site's libraries, picked from the user's OneDrive, or uploaded from the user's computer or from a link. Microsoft also provides thousands of ready-made stock images, which are free to use within SharePoint content. If an image is picked from OneDrive, make sure that users accessing the page have access to the image; otherwise, they will see just an empty image placeholder. The same thing needs to be considered when using linked images.

Authoring canvas

The authoring canvas is structured using sections with different predefined column layouts. New sections are created from the plus sign on the left sidebar:

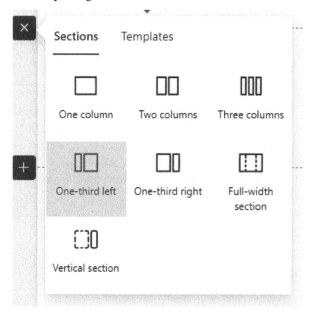

Figure 6.4 - Column layouts

Here's what you can see in the previous screenshot:

- The first five column layouts (**One column**, **Two columns**, **Three columns**, **One-third left**, and **One-third right**) are available when editing the section.

- **Full-width section** is only available during section creation. The full-width column supports only a few default web parts, and content is displayed in the width of the page.

- **Vertical section** is a special section type that creates a full-height section on the right side of the page. There can be only one vertical section on the page. When a vertical section is used, it is not possible to add full-width sections and vice versa.

Section settings

In the **Section** settings, the column layout, section background, and section collapse settings are set:

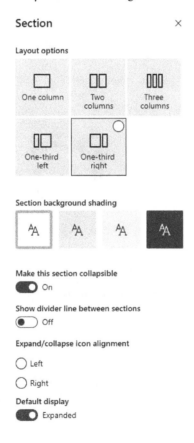

Figure 6.5 - Section settings

When the column layout of the full-width section is changed, it cannot be changed back to the original setting other than by creating a new full-width section or using **Undo** from the page toolbar.

The vertical section supports changing the background color and selecting the section displayed first or last when the user is accessing the page with mobile or other narrow-screen devices.

Collapsible sections

A section can be set as collapsible, which allows users to open or close the section by clicking the section header or the small arrow icon on the left or right side when viewing the page. Authors can set the title of the section and placement of the arrow icon and can define the section collapsed by default. Here is a screenshot of a collapsed section:

Employee Benefits   ∨

Figure 6.6 - Collapsed section

And here is a screenshot of the same section when expanded:

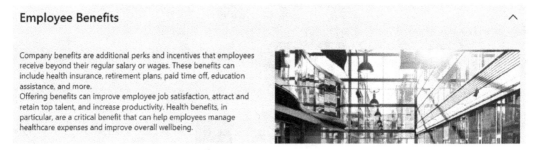

Figure 6.7 - Same section uncollapsed

Collapsible sections are useful for long pages – for example, FAQs, manuals, and team information.

Web parts

The content of the page is authored using different web parts. With the modern SharePoint experience, every content block on the page is a web part. A web part is added to a section by selecting a plus icon appearing when hovering on the section. Web parts are picked from the web part picker:

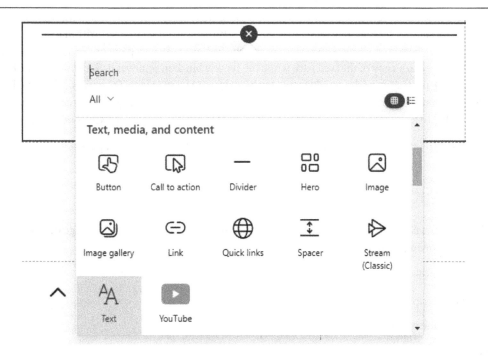

Figure 6.8 - Web part picker

SharePoint Online offers a few dozen web parts. Each web part has a toolbar in the top-left corner:

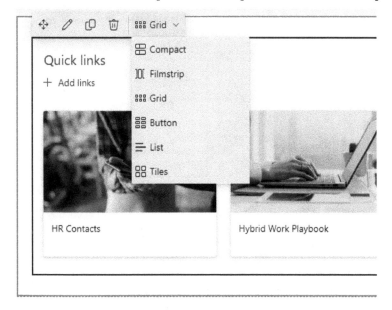

Figure 6.9 - Web part

The web part can be dragged between sections, and its order can be changed within a section by using the arrow icon. The pen icon is used to open the web part settings pane on the right. The two squares icon creates a copy of the web part, while the recycle bin icon removes it. Some web parts may have quick settings, such as the quick layout settings shown in *Figure 6.9*. The content displayed in the web part settings pane may vary depending on the type of web part. To ensure accessibility, it is recommended to add a title to web parts having textual content. The title can be set from the title row.

The best way to learn how web parts work and look is to create a test site or a page and try out the web parts.

Page details

The **Page details** pane opens from the **Page details** button on the page toolbar. The **Page details** pane allows the following to be changed:

- The thumbnail image
- The description
- The name of the page file

It also allows you to do the following:

- Add metadata to the page (in *Figure 6.10*, under **Department**)
- Delete the page:

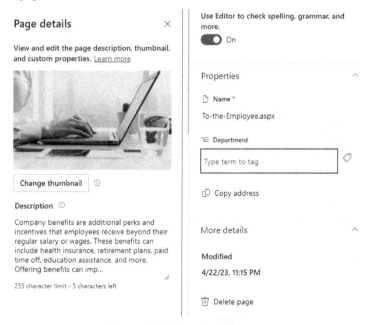

Figure 6.10 - Page details pane

In some cases, disabling the editor is needed – for example, when having multilingual pages with a lot of content. An example of that kind of page is having certain phrases, keywords, or terms published in different languages on the same page.

Drafts and publishing of pages

A page can be saved as a draft version. Drafts are, by default, available for all users with editor permissions. The recently launched Private drafts feature allows selecting users, who can edit the draft or keep it private. Private drafts are enabled on the page creation dialog.

Once a page is finished, it can be published by clicking **Publish** in the top-right corner. After the first publish, a promotion pane opens, which allows adding the page to site navigation, promoting the page as a news article, emailing or posting it to Viva Engage, and saving the page as a page template. Promotion can be done afterward by clicking the **Promote** button from the page toolbar. Notice that once a page is promoted as a news article, the operation cannot be reverted.

When a published page is changed, it can be saved as a draft and republished.

Now that you know how to create and publish pages, let's move on to make pages more dynamic with aggregation web parts.

Aggregating content using web parts

SharePoint Online offers a range of web parts for aggregating pages, news, documents, list items, events, and sites to a page. The source for aggregated content can be set as the current site, from all sites linked to a hub site, pre-selected sites, or recommended for the user. The recommended selection will aggregate content from users the current user is working with, the top 20 sites the user is following, and the most recently visited sites. Options vary between different web parts. Each web part also includes different layout options for viewing aggregated content items. When content is aggregated from other sites, queries are made against the search index, which is not updated in real time, and it may take some minutes to see recently added items.

News

The news web part is focused on aggregating news from various sources with predefined layout options:

Figure 6.11 - News web part layouts

Options for displayed information vary between different layout options. In the filtering options, news articles can be filtered with a word in the title, by whether they were recently added or recently changed, based on who created or modified the article, or based on page properties or managed properties added to the page.

With the **Organize** feature, certain news articles can be manually reordered by dragging them to the wanted placeholder on the list:

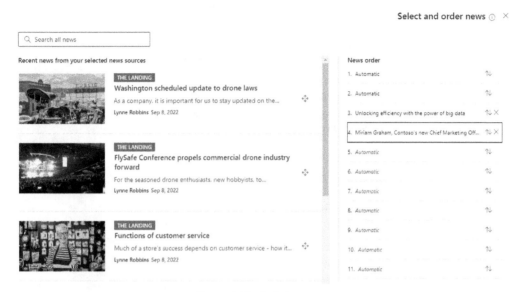

Figure 6.12 - Ordering news

Manually selected news articles stay in their selected placeholders, and automatic items change based on web part settings.

Highlighted content

The highlighted content web part can be used to aggregate different content types, such as documents, pages, news, videos, or links, from different content sources. The web part includes the same filtering options as the news web part and different layouts.

Custom search queries can also be used with the highlighted content web part:

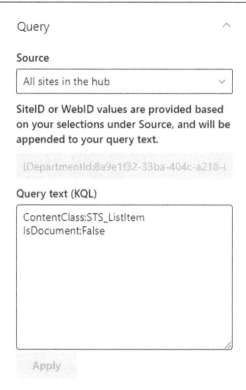

Figure 6.13 - Search query option in highlighted content web part

This is useful when content needs to be filtered more specifically than available in default filtering or when focusing on a specific list, folder, or document library. The source choice allows focusing the search query on specific content, such as just all sites linked to a hub site. The search query is added to the query text field. All search query features are available. More about search queries in *Chapter 7*.

Events

The events web part is used to aggregate events from a specified event list on a site, all events on a site, all sites in the hub, all sites in the tenant, or specific sites. The event category can be used as a filter, and the date range can be selected from predefined choices such as **Next two weeks** or **All upcoming events**, or you can pick a date range manually:

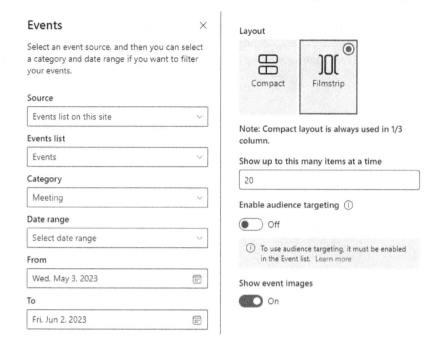

Figure 6.14 - Events web part

Again, the best way to learn how these aggregation web parts work is to add them to a page and try different settings and layout options.

Targeting pages and documents

Audience targeting allows aggregated content to be personalized based on user group memberships. Audience targeting needs to be first enabled from the library settings. In the modern experience, select **Enable audience targeting**, which supports mail-enabled groups, Microsoft 365 groups, and individual email addresses on Microsoft Entra ID. Classic audience targeting is not covered in this book:

Figure 6.15 - Audience targeting

Once targeting is enabled, target audiences can be set on the info panel on list items and documents, and in the page properties panel on pages and news articles. In the following screenshot, the content author has added the **HR Team Members** group as a target audience and is searching for sales-related groups to add:

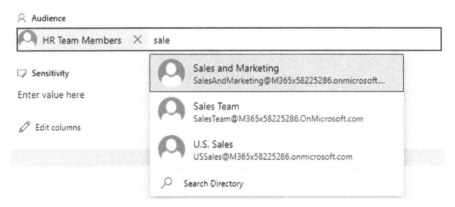

Figure 6.16 - Picking target audiences

Audience targeting needs to be enabled on the aggregation web part to use the feature; otherwise, all items are displayed to all users. When targeting is enabled, targeted items are viewed by users who are members of specified target groups. Audience targeting is not changing permission but is commonly used to personalize content.

When enabling audience targeting, plan the target groups carefully. It is a clever idea to have a clear naming policy for audience target groups since the audience picker returns all mail-enabled groups from AAD. Also, provide clear guidance to content authors who are using the feature.

Managing page templates

Page templates are useful for guiding content authors to use certain section layouts, web parts, and content elements on new pages to ensure a uniform look and feel. A page template can be created from any of the content pages or by creating a new page. The page is saved as a template by selecting **Save as template** from the page toolbar:

Figure 6.17 - Saving a page as a template

All sections, web parts, and metadata in page details will be copied to the new template. All sections and web parts are available for page templates. It's also a clever idea to create a guidance text element for the template to advise content authors on how the template is used. If the template contains more than one text web part, it is also a good idea to include a short intro text for all text elements to make them easier to find on the page:

Figure 6.18 - Page template with guidance

When a template is final, it can be saved by clicking **Save page template** from the top-right corner.

Page templates can be displayed on the new page dialog (*Figure 6.18*) or by accessing the Site Pages library, where page templates are added to a `Template` sub-folder:

Figure 6.19 - Page templates

On the new page creation dialog, the template can be set as default or removed from the site. The template can also be removed from the Site Pages library's templates folder.

Notice that page templates are only available on the site they are created, and there is no out-of-the-box distribution mechanism for page templates. When templates are needed on multiple sites, they need to be created per site or distributed using Power Automate workflows or PnP PowerShell, which is an open source module developed by the SharePoint Patterns and Practices community, cmdlets, and provisioning templates.

Using SharePoint pages in Microsoft Teams

SharePoint pages are useful for bringing important content to tabs on Microsoft Teams channels. Pages can be used to introduce a project or a team, bring in important news or events, create wiki pages, or create visual link lists to important content. All section and web part capabilities are available. Teams' tabs do not support SharePoint's navigation, so navigation needs to be figured out with tab titles.

Adding a page to the Teams channel is simple. Just click the + icon from the tab bar and search for SharePoint. The same tab can also bring in lists and document libraries:

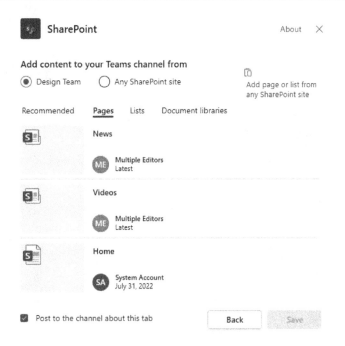

Figure 6.20 - SharePoint tab in Teams

By default, the tab discovers pages, lists, and libraries from the site linked to the opened team, but with linking, it's possible to add content from other sites as well. When linking a tab to content on another site, the users need to have permission on that specific site to see the content.

Summary

In this chapter, we learned how to create pages, how pages are structured, and how web parts are used to create content. Since SharePoint has several dozens of web parts, the best way to learn is to try out how they work and look. We also learned how page drafts and publishing work and how pages can be promoted.

Next, we discovered the power of aggregation web parts and audience targeting, which can be used to bring in content from various sources, with a choice to use a personalized view.

Finally, we were introduced to page templates and how they are used to create uniform content.

In the following chapter, we will move to backend services and focus on SharePoint's search engine and search features in detail.

Part 2:
Enhancing the
SharePoint Content

In this part, you will get an overview of SharePoint Online's back-end services, such as search and managed metadata. In addition, you will also learn to utilize Microsoft Syntex for document processing and simplifying discoverability. You will also learn basic app management tasks and integration between SharePoint and Teams using Viva Connections.

This part has the following chapters:

- *Chapter 7: Search in SharePoint*
- *Chapter 8: Managed Metadata*
- *Chapter 9: Understand Information with Microsoft Syntex*
- *Chapter 10: Bring SharePoint Content to Teams with Viva Connections*
- *Chapter 11: App Catalog and SharePoint Store*

7
Search in SharePoint

SharePoint's search is a powerful tool for discovering, sorting, and filtering content added to SharePoint sites. Search can index pages, lists, libraries, and even access the content of supported documents and extract search terms from the document content. In addition, SharePoint's search index can be used to create different content aggregations and, as an example, out-of-the-box news web parts utilize the search index to aggregate content from different locations in SharePoint. SharePoint search includes sophisticated features such as promoting or ranking important search results.

In the modern SharePoint, as well as many other Microsoft 365 services, Microsoft Search is the default search experience. Microsoft Search brings together data across Microsoft 365, from SharePoint, Microsoft Teams, People, Power BI reports, and customized locations such as company CRM, Wiki platform, or public websites. Microsoft 365 utilizes Microsoft Graph to query the information from Microsoft 365, and it's used as a backend for many content aggregations across services. Microsoft Search is also incorporated with Microsoft's Bing search engine, which can be used to search publicly available content and organization content on Microsoft 365 using the same search box experience.

In this chapter, we're going to cover the following main topics:

- The search experience in the modern SharePoint
- Search schema and schema management
- Using query rules
- Microsoft Search and search in Microsoft 365

Search experience in the modern SharePoint

The search box is located on the Microsoft 365 suite bar or header bar across different services and Microsoft 365 applications, such as Word, Excel, or Microsoft Teams. Depending on the location, the search box offers different types of results. In SharePoint, when the search box is accessed, it already displays some relevant content to the user:

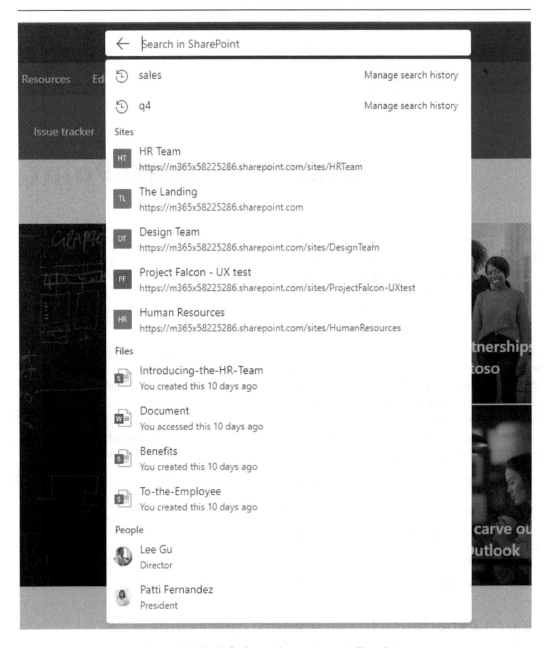

Figure 7.1 - The default search experience in SharePoint

As shown in *Figure 7.1*, the search box displays the history of used search terms, recently accessed and relevant sites, recently accessed files and pages, and relevant people. Relevant sites are based on users' membership and what sites users are following. Relevant people are discovered based on collaboration patterns and connections in the organization. When the user starts typing in a search term, the search box results are refined:

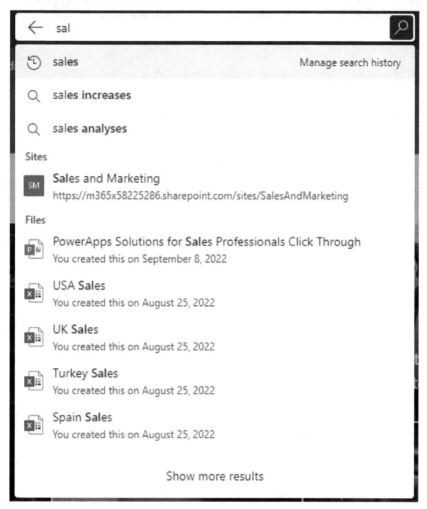

Figure 7.2 - Refined search box results

Upon hitting the *Enter* key, the user is directed to a page displaying the search results:

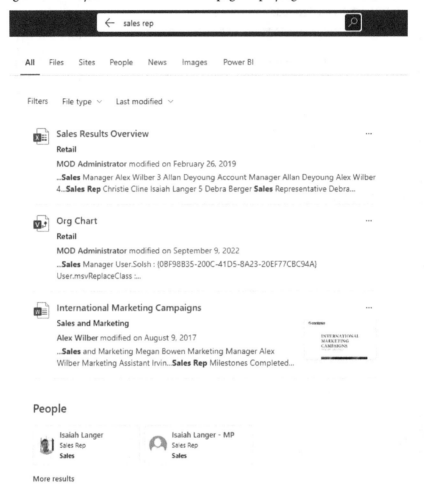

Figure 7.3 - Search results page

On the results page, the user can filter results with search verticals (**Files**, **Sites**, **People**, and so on, as shown in *Figure 7.3*) and by file type or last modified time. On new sites, the default search context is the current site and the search experience includes a search breadcrumb, which can be used to widen the search context. When the site is connected to a hub site, the hub site is included in the search breadcrumb (**Global Sales** in *Figure 7.4*) and the search context can be widened to the hub level, which then includes all sites connected to that hub site. If the hub site is connected to another hub, the parent hub will be also displayed on the search breadcrumb:

Figure 7.4 - The search experience on a site linked to a hub

Managing site-specific search settings

By default, the search box in the suite navigation bar is targeted to the specific site, and if it is a hub site, also to connected sites. The search box settings can be changed using PnP PowerShell, which is an open source SharePoint Patterns and Practices community module, commands:

```
Set-PnPSearchSettings -SearchScope Tenant
```

The preceding example targets the search box so that it includes results from the whole tenant. In other words, results are displayed at the organizational level. Other options are Site, which is the default settings, and Hub, which targets the search box to the site's parent hub site.

The search box can be also hidden at the site level, such as when a custom search box is added to the page content:

```
Set-PnPSearchSettings -Scope Site -SearchBoxInNavBar Hidden
```

The search box can be made visible with the following command:

```
Set-PnPSearchSettings -Scope Site -SearchBoxInNavBar Inherit
```

Customizing the default search experience

The default search experience can be customized in several ways. This includes new verticals for returning a more specific set of results, customizing available verticals for specific needs, and result types for formatting the result layout.

Adding new search verticals

New search verticals can be added at the tenant level or the site level. Tenant-level search verticals are visible in the whole tenant-wide search results and at the site-level or the hub-level search results if the site is promoted as a hub site.

As an example, let's create a new **Events** vertical at the site level. Site-level search settings can be accessed from **Search insights**, while the configuration can be accessed from the **Site settings** page. On the **Verticals** tab, it is possible to add, remove, and edit custom verticals and out-of-the-box verticals. To create a new vertical, select **Add**. For vertical settings, do the following:

1. Enter a name for the vertical. The name is visible on the search results page.

2. For **Content source**, select **SharePoint**.

3. On the query, enter `ContentType:Event` as a **Keyword Query Language** (**KQL**) query. This will return all events.

4. In the **Filters** section, add `CategoryOWNCHCHS` as a filter property. This enables filtering using **Event category**.

5. On the **Review** page, set the vertical to **Enabled**:

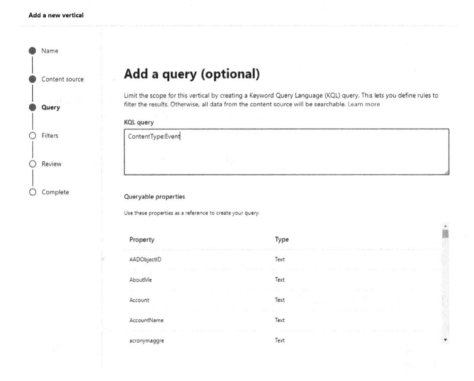

Figure 7.5 - Creating a site-level vertical

6. Changes to the verticals will take effect with a few hours' delay. To make changes available at once, add the `cacheClear=true` query parameter to the end of the URL of the search results page – for example, `https://tenant.sharepoint.com/_layouts/15/search.aspx?cacheClear=true` – to get the following result:

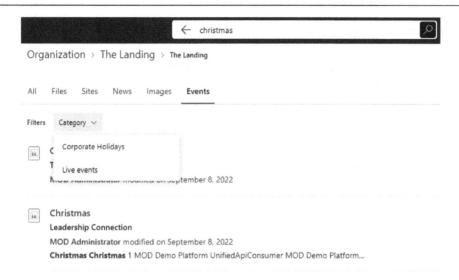

Figure 7.6 - Events vertical results

Verticals can also be created and configured at the tenant level by going to the **Search & intelligence** settings area in the Microsoft 365 admin center.

Managing the search result layout with a result type

As seen in *Figure 7.6*, the layout of event results is not adequate since the results are missing dates and times and are not visually attractive. With result types, the layout of a specific search result can be customized using Adaptive Cards technology.

> **Adaptive Cards**
> **Adaptive Cards** are platform-agnostic user interface elements that are authored as JSON to define the structure and content of the card. The target app adds needed visual elements and styles around the card.

Result types can be created at the site level and the tenant level. To create a new result type at the site level, access **Search insights** and **Configuration** from the **Site settings**, open the **Result types** tab, and select **Add**. For a result type configuration, do the following:

1. Give it a name.

2. Select a content source – in this case, **SharePoint and OneDrive**.

3. For **Type of content**, select the **SharePoint** list item and set **ContentType** equal to **Event** as a rule (*Figure 7.7*).

4. Build your layout with the layout designer or some other tool that supports Adaptive Cards.

5. Click **Create result type**:

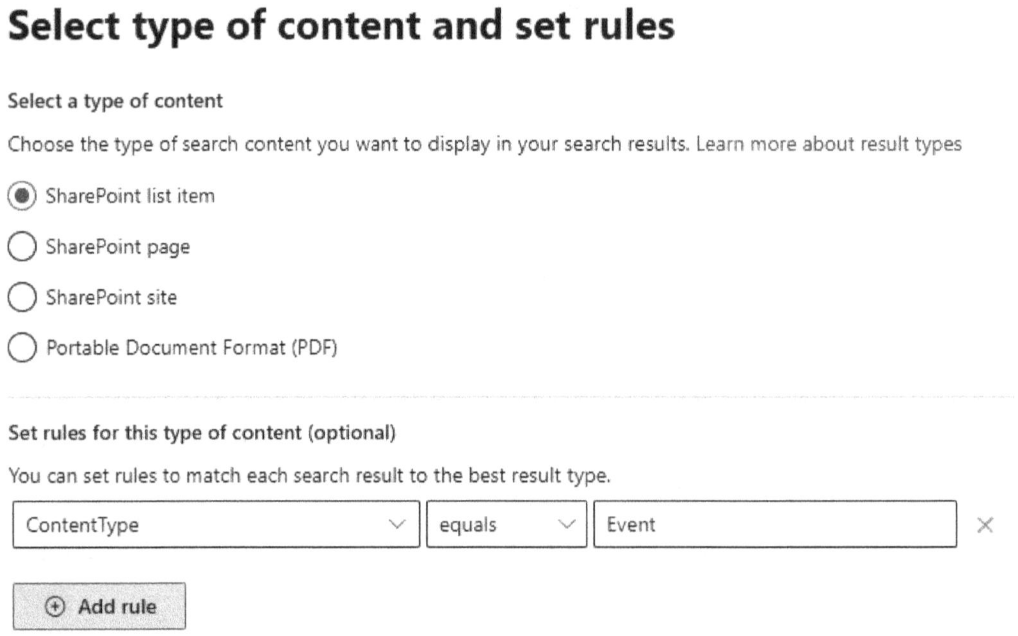

Select type of content and set rules

Select a type of content

Choose the type of search content you want to display in your search results. Learn more about result types

- ⦿ SharePoint list item
- ◯ SharePoint page
- ◯ SharePoint site
- ◯ Portable Document Format (PDF)

Set rules for this type of content (optional)

You can set rules to match each search result to the best result type.

| ContentType ⌄ | equals ⌄ | Event | ✕ |

⊕ **Add rule**

Figure 7.7 - Result type rules

After a while, *Result type* should appear in the search results.

The following code is part of Adaptive Cards and defines the column layouts with event start time and end time texts. You can find the full Adaptive Card layout example at Packt Publishing/ Customizing-and-Extending-SharePoint-Online: Customizing and Extending SharePoint Online, published by Packt (github.com):

```
"columns": [
{
    "type": "Column",
    "width": "stretch",
    "items": [
    {
        "type": "TextBlock",
        "text":
        "Starts{{DATE(${EventDateOWSDATE},SHORT)}}",
        "weight": "Bold","size": "Medium","wrap": true,
        "maxLines": 3
    },
    {
```

```
        "type": "TextBlock",
        "text":
        "Ends: {{DATE(${EndDateOWSDATE},SHORT)}}",
        "weight": "Bold","size": "Medium","wrap": true,
        "maxLines": 3
}
]}]
```

The event search result using the Adaptive Card layout looks like this:

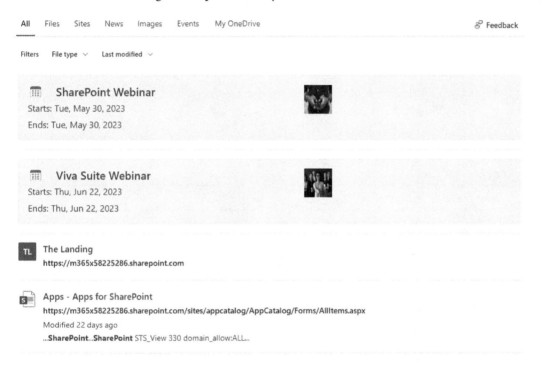

Figure 7.8 - Custom result type for events

Tenant-wide search experience settings

Microsoft Search supports several tenant-wide experience settings that can be curated to help users discover important content about the organization. With answers, search results can be enriched with curated acronyms, bookmarks, locations, and Q&A.

Almost every organization has at least some **acronyms**, which are not always clear to users. Acronyms can be added to the search for users to discover. To add a new acronym, navigate to the **Answers** section of the **Search & intelligence** settings, which can be found underneath the **Settings** group in the Microsoft 365 admin center or by navigating to `https://admin.microsoft.com/Adminportal/Home#/MicrosoftSearch`. When creating a new acronym, you must explain what it stands for and provide a description, which is displayed in the search results, and an optional link to more resources:

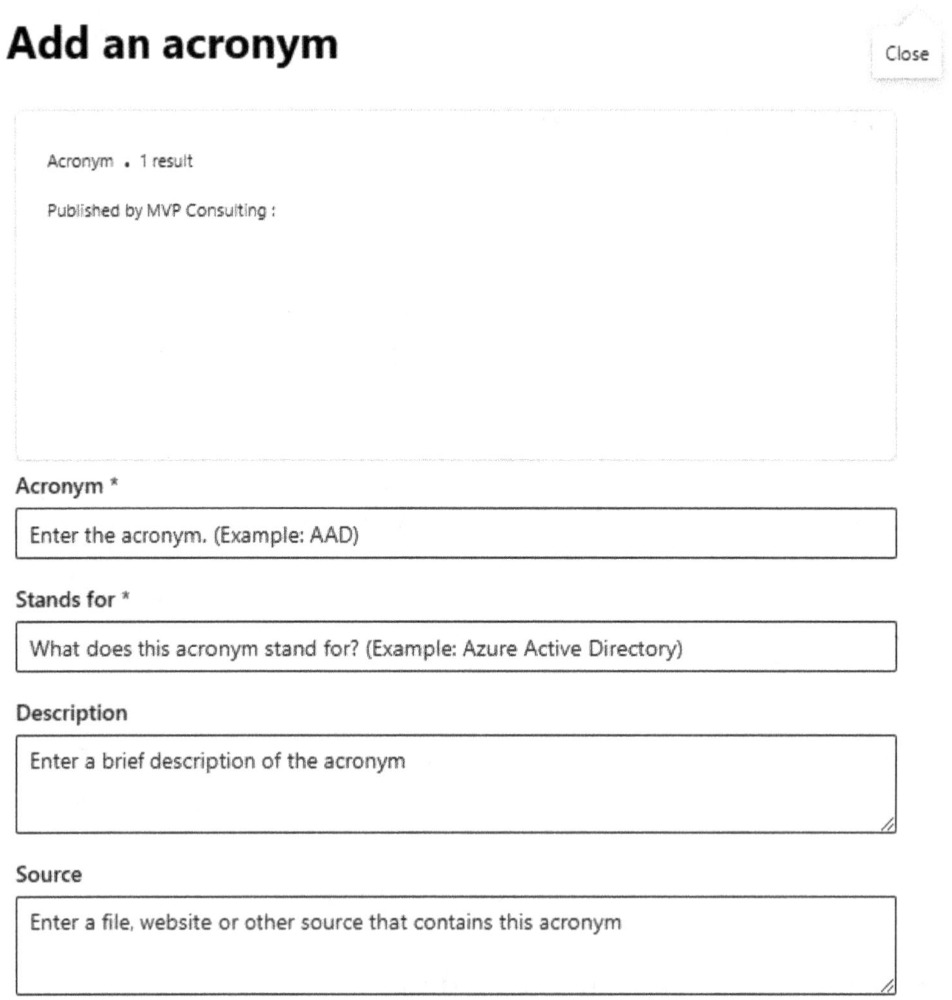

Add an acronym

Close

Acronym . 1 result

Published by MVP Consulting :

Acronym *

Enter the acronym. (Example: AAD)

Stands for *

What does this acronym stand for? (Example: Azure Active Directory)

Description

Enter a brief description of the acronym

Source

Enter a file, website or other source that contains this acronym

Figure 7.9 - Adding an acronym to search

Bookmarks enable organizations to promote important links, pages, or other content in search results that match specific keywords. Keywords can also be reserved for specific bookmarks. A bookmark can be targeted based on country or region, specific groups, and devices with specific operating system versions:

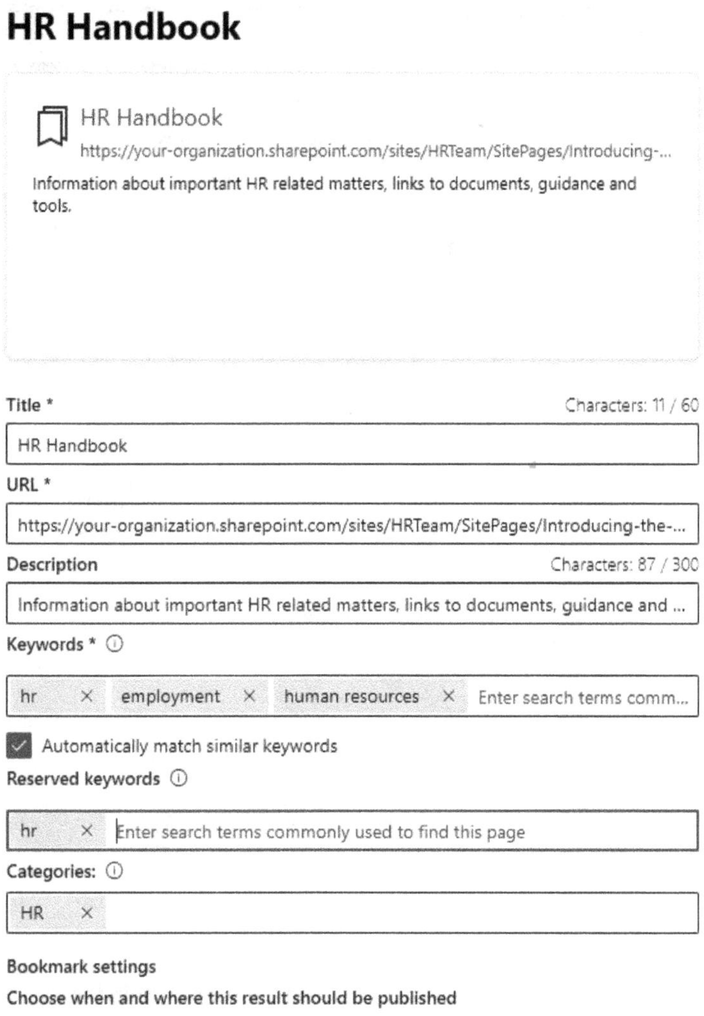

HR Handbook

📑 HR Handbook
https://your-organization.sharepoint.com/sites/HRTeam/SitePages/Introducing-...

Information about important HR related matters, links to documents, guidance and tools.

Title *   Characters: 11 / 60

HR Handbook

URL *

https://your-organization.sharepoint.com/sites/HRTeam/SitePages/Introducing-the-...

Description   Characters: 87 / 300

Information about important HR related matters, links to documents, guidance and ...

Keywords * ⓘ

hr ✕   employment ✕   human resources ✕   Enter search terms comm...

☑ Automatically match similar keywords

Reserved keywords ⓘ

hr ✕   Enter search terms commonly used to find this page

Categories: ⓘ

HR ✕

Bookmark settings

Choose when and where this result should be published

Figure 7.10 - Creating a bookmark

In the search results, published bookmarks are added to the top of the search results:

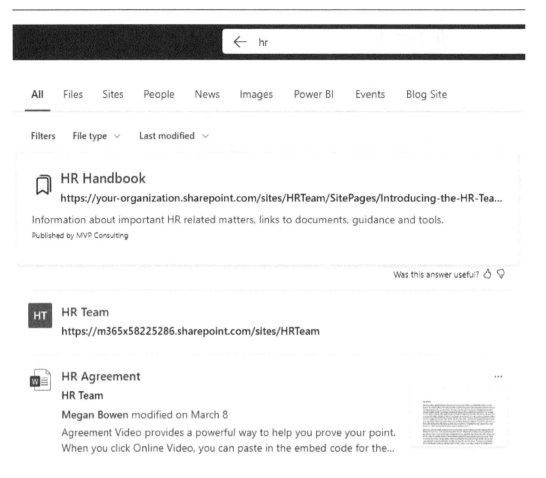

Figure 7.11 - Bookmark in search results

Q&As can be used to provide answers to the most common questions within the organization. Q&As act similarly to bookmarks, but rather than providing a link to the information, the Q&A element provides the answer directly.

Like in bookmarks, a Q&A answer has a title, a link to an intranet page, for example, for more information, an answer description, which is displayed alongside the search result, and keywords:

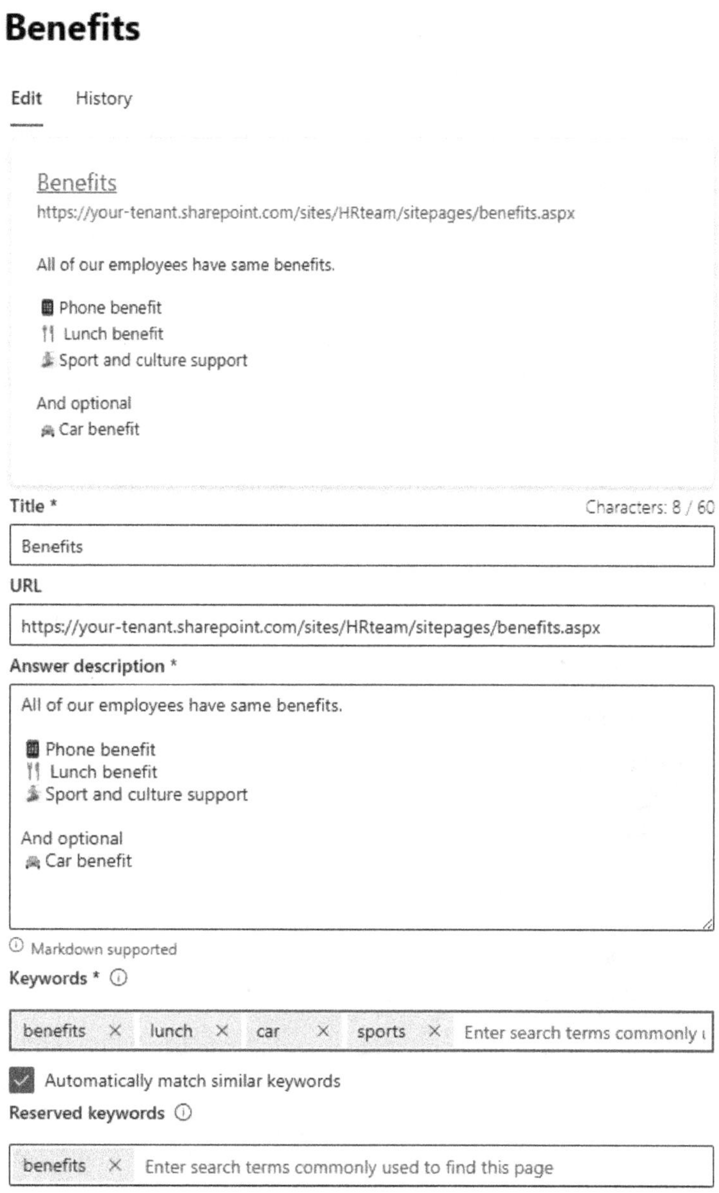

Benefits

Edit   History

Benefits
https://your-tenant.sharepoint.com/sites/HRteam/sitepages/benefits.aspx

All of our employees have same benefits.

📱 Phone benefit
🍴 Lunch benefit
🏋 Sport and culture support

And optional
🚗 Car benefit

Title *   Characters: 8 / 60

Benefits

URL

https://your-tenant.sharepoint.com/sites/HRteam/sitepages/benefits.aspx

Answer description *

All of our employees have same benefits.

📱 Phone benefit
🍴 Lunch benefit
🏋 Sport and culture support

And optional
🚗 Car benefit

ⓘ Markdown supported

Keywords * ⓘ

benefits ✕   lunch ✕   car ✕   sports ✕   Enter search terms commonly (

☑ Automatically match similar keywords

Reserved keywords ⓘ

benefits ✕   Enter search terms commonly used to find this page

Figure 7.12 - Q&A answer

Q&A answer settings can be used to control when the Q&A is available in the search results, as well as how it's targeted. The answer can be targeted to specific countries, groups, and devices. It's also possible to have a different answer to the same keywords for different devices and countries:

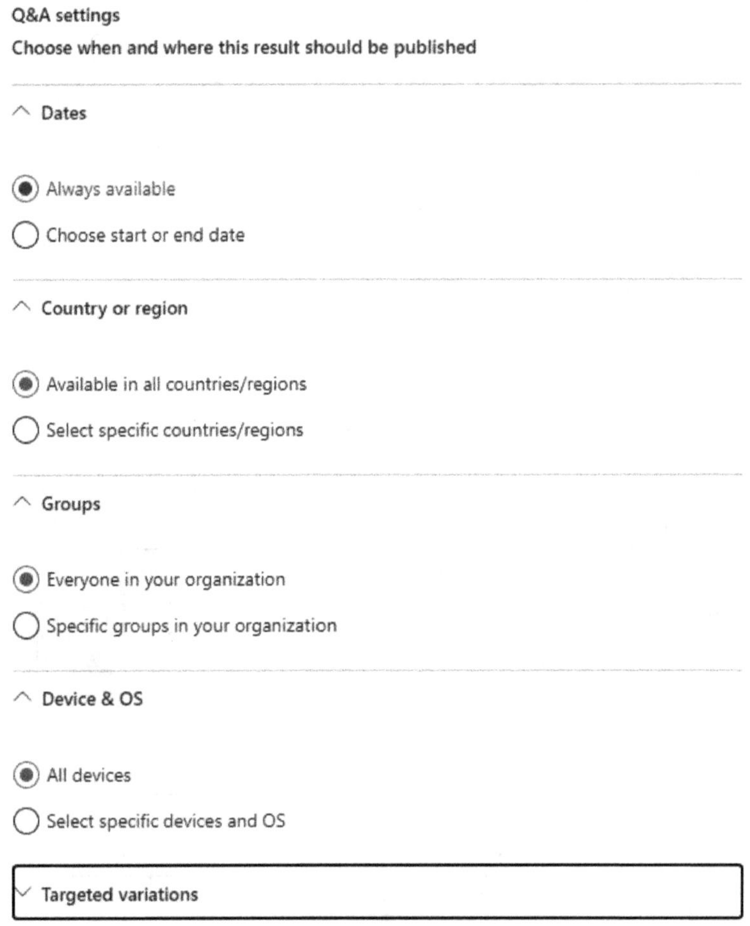

Q&A settings
Choose when and where this result should be published

⌃ Dates

◉ Always available

◯ Choose start or end date

⌃ Country or region

◉ Available in all countries/regions

◯ Select specific countries/regions

⌃ Groups

◉ Everyone in your organization

◯ Specific groups in your organization

⌃ Device & OS

◉ All devices

◯ Select specific devices and OS

⌄ Targeted variations

Figure 7.13 - Q&A answer settings

Locations can be used to include, for example, office locations with an address and a map to search results:

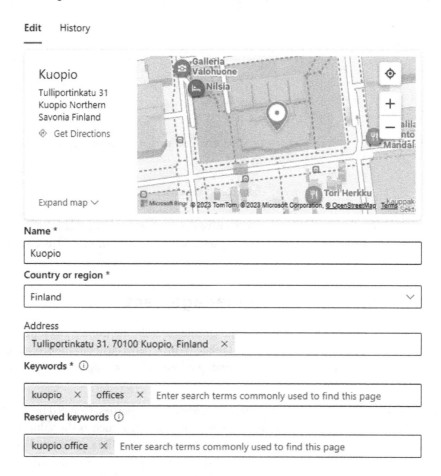

Kuopio

Edit   History

Name *

Kuopio

Country or region *

Finland

Address

Tulliportinkatu 31, 70100 Kuopio, Finland   ✕

Keywords * ⓘ

kuopio ✕   offices ✕   Enter search terms commonly used to find this page

Reserved keywords ⓘ

kuopio office ✕   Enter search terms commonly used to find this page

Figure 7.14 - Adding a location to search results

Locations are displayed at the top of search results when keywords are matched:

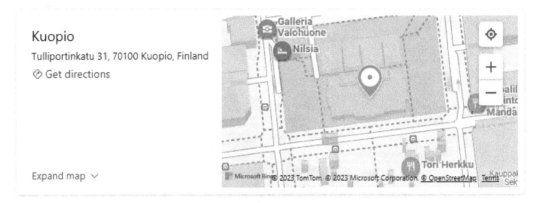

Figure 7.15 - Location in search results

Acronyms, bookmarks, Q&As, and locations improve the discovery of valuable information and content for users. Bookmarks can be used like a campaign, such as for publishing guidance for holidays near summertime.

Search schema and schema management

The search schema is a crucial part of SharePoint Online's search functionality as it defines how information is indexed and queried in SharePoint Online. With schema customization, organizations can tailor the search results for specific needs – for example, by enabling sorting or refining capabilities to specific indexed site columns.

The search schema is built on crawled properties and managed properties. Crawled properties are pieces of information that are taken from the content that is indexed, such as the value of the site column on a list item or a part of a document content on a document library. Crawled properties are created automatically when the content is crawled – for example, a value of the Salary column is linked to a crawled property called **ows_Salary**. All the columns with the same name are linked to the same crawled property. Managed properties are used to define how content can be retrieved, queried, or searched from the search index. A managed property mapping is always needed for the crawled property to be available for search, querying, and retrieving. Managed properties also control sorting and refining based on crawled properties. A managed property can be mapped to one or more crawled properties at a time.

The search schema can be controlled at the tenant level or the site level from site settings. Tenant-level schema settings can be found by going to **Search Administration**, which can be accessed from the **More feature** section in the SharePoint admin center or by navigating to `https://tenant-admin.sharepoint.com/_layouts/15/searchadmin/TA_SearchAdministration.aspx`.

Tenant-level changes affect all sites at the tenant and site level for the specific site. Site-level settings are useful when building a site-specific solution that relies on a search index or developing or testing a solution that requires search schema changes. Also, regular users typically do not have access to the SharePoint admin center, which requires a SharePoint Administrator managed role, and cannot alter the search schema at the tenant level.

Property mapping

Mapping a crawled property to a managed property can be done by editing either one of them. On crawled properties, only mappings to managed properties can be managed. To add a new mapping to a crawled property, open **Search schema settings** from the site settings. Alternatively, from the search settings in the SharePoint admin center, select the **Crawled Properties** tab and search for a property to edit. On the **Crawled Property** settings page (*Figure 7.16*), select **Add a Mapping**:

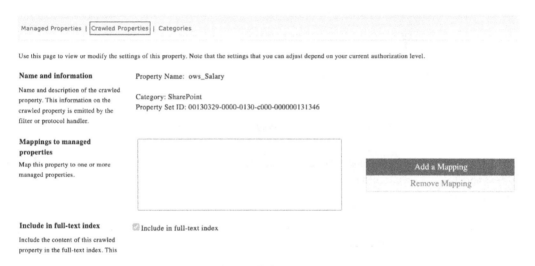

Figure 7.16 - Crawled property settings

On the **Add mapping** dialogue, search for a managed property the crawled property should be mapped to. The crawled property can have multiple mappings, which means that its values can be used via multiple managed properties.

Creating a managed property

Managed properties are used to retrieve data from the search index and can be configured for whether they can be used in search results, queried against properties, or used for sorting and refining search results.

Managed properties are not created automatically for crawled properties. It's possible to use existing managed properties for property mapping, but quite commonly, a new property is needed.

Creating a new property is simple. Again, open the search settings from the site settings or tenant-wide search settings from the SharePoint admin center, depending on which context property is created. On the **Managed Properties** tab, select **New Managed Property**:

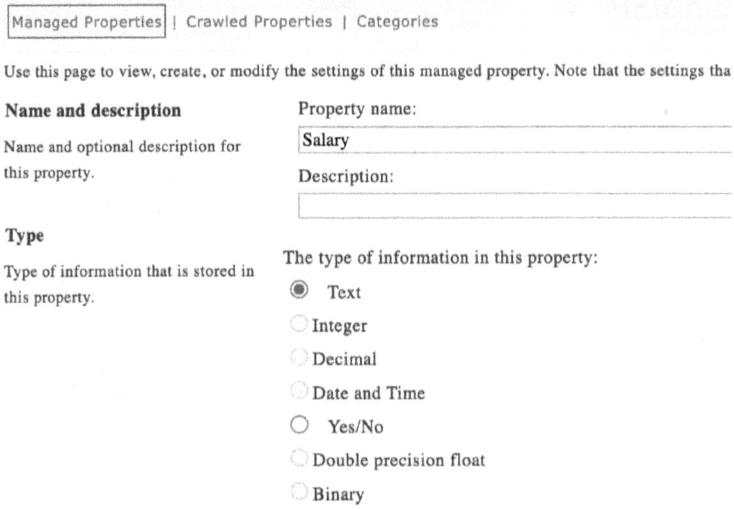

Figure 7.17 - Creating a new managed property

The new property requires a name and optional description. When creating new managed properties, only **Text** and **Yes/No** are allowed types. The behavior of the managed property can be managed with the following settings:

- **Searchable**: When enabled, search queries are run against the property in the full-text index. If the property contains a search term, it is returned.

- **Queryable**: The property can be queried by a property name, such as `JobTitle:Engineer`, which returns all items when `JobTitle` contains the `Engineer` value.

- **Retrievable**: This defines the values of the property that are returned as a search result.

- **Allow multiple values**: When enabled, it stores individual values. For example, on multi-value user fields, it separates each user as a separate value.

- **Refinable**: This defines when the property can be used as a search filter. This setting is only available for specially managed properties, as explained in the next section.

- **Sortable**: This defines whether the property can be used to sort the search results. This setting is only available for specially managed properties, as explained in the next section.

- **Alias**: This defines an alternative alias for the property to be used in search queries.

- **Token normalization**: When enabled, it ignores letter casings and diacritics in the search query.

- **Complete matching**: When enabled, only values that completely match the search query are returned.

- **Finer query tokenization**: This improves partial matching when the property has separators such as dashes or dots.

Under **Property mappings** (*Figure 7.18*), all mapped crawled properties are displayed:

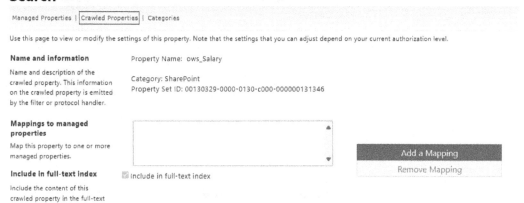

Figure 7.18 - Property mappings

The order of the properties is important when **Mappings to crawled properties** is set to **Include content from the first crawled property that is not empty, based on the specified order**. In the preceding example (*Figure 7.18*), the value is returned from the ows_JobTitle property, which is linked to a list column. If it is empty, the value is returned from the SPS-JobTitle user profile property.

Refinable and sortable properties

When creating a new managed property, refinable and sortable settings are grayed out. It's not possible to create new managed properties with these settings. If a new or existing crawled property needs to be refined or sorted on search results, or there is a requirement for integer, decimal, date, and time, double or binary data types, which cannot be set on custom managed properties, SharePoint search offers pre-configured managed properties.

These properties are named starting with the term Refinable, data type, and are followed by sequential numbering – for example, RefinableString100. These properties are handy when you're building solutions around search, such as with PnP Search Web Parts, which offer a search box, results, filters, and verticals to be used in SharePoint pages.

Organization search results in Bing.com

When a user is logged into Bing.com with a work account, it can be used as a search engine as well. Bing's work results supply similar search verticals and use some of Microsoft Search's features, such as bookmarks and locations. Result types don't work with Bing.com search results:

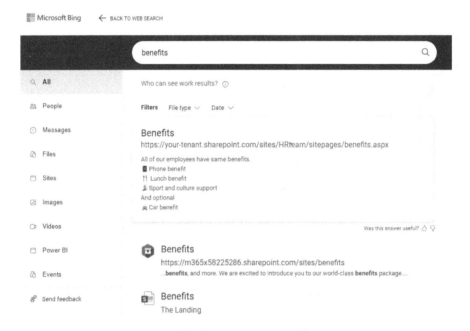

Figure 7.19 - Search results in Bing

It's important to educate users about Bing.com's search since it might cause confusion that important documents and content are visible at the top of the public search engine. The public Bing search engine does not have access to and does not index the content of the organization's Microsoft 365; rather, it uses a signed-in user to access available APIs to supply results.

Summary

In this chapter, we discovered the user experience of searching in modern SharePoint sites and pages.

Next, we introduced how to customize search results with search verticals and result types, and Microsoft Search tenant-wide features such as acronyms, Q&As, bookmarks, and locations.

Then, we took a deep dive into the search schema and schema management, and how to create refinable or sortable search-managed properties. Finally, we introduced how Bing.com can serve an organization's search results.

In the next chapter, we will learn how to use SharePoint's managed metadata services.

8
Managed Metadata

Managed metadata on SharePoint online provides a formal and controlled way to classify content using hierarchical collections of terms, grouped by term sets, which can be used as metadata and keywords on SharePoint content. Centrally managed metadata ensures consistency across SharePoint sites and helps with the discoverability, sorting, and filtering of content using search. Enabling the Enterprise keywords feature on the library or list level provides a simple way to consume managed metadata terms. Another way is to create a managed metadata column and attach a term set to it on the list or library level.

A term set is a collection of terms, for example, products, which can either be a flat list hierarchy or be a maximum of seven levels deep. Term sets can either be controlled and centrally authored taxonomies or act as a folksonomy where users can add new terms.

Term sets can be published either from the central term store in the SharePoint admin center or using a site-level local term store. Local term stores nowadays are only used for special cases, for example building a local document repository. For reusability's sake, it's better to use the centralized term store.

In this chapter, we're going to cover the following main topics:

- Managed metadata and the term store
- Term groups, term sets, and terms
- Built-in term sets
- Metadata terms in SharePoint content

Managed metadata and term store

Managed metadata in SharePoint online is made up of three core structures:

- **Term groups**: These can be used to create logical groups of term sets, for example, all term sets about human resources metadata would be in a term group called HR. A term group also creates a management layer for allowing specific people to manage all term sets and terms within a term group.

- **Term sets**: These hold term hierarchies of some specific metadata or topic, for example, department or location.

- **Terms**: These are the actual metadata values and can be used in site columns to describe documents, list items, or other SharePoint content.

The hierarchy can be seen in the following figure:

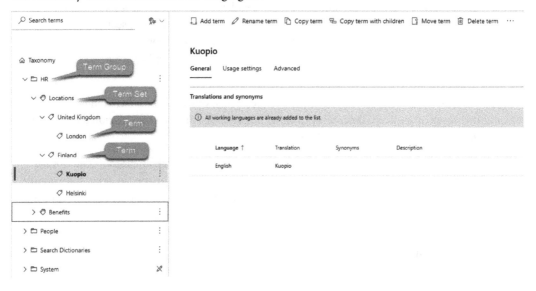

Figure 8.1 - Term hierarchy

A Microsoft 365 tenant can have one million global terms, including terms published on site collections, 1,000 global term groups, and 1,000 global term sets.

Global term groups, term sets, and terms are managed on the term store, which can be accessed in the SharePoint admin center or at `https://<tenant-name>-admin.sharepoint.com/_layouts/15/online/AdminHome.aspx#/termStoreAdminCenter`.

Term groups

A term group can be thought of as a folder for term sets. Term sets within a term group are managed by users who have been assigned the group manager role. Group managers can manage the term groups they are assigned to, create and manage term sets, and create and manage terms. Users who have been assigned the term group contributor role can create and manage term sets and terms.

Term groups are created on the term store level by selecting the **Add term** group from the three dots after Taxonomy. Creating a term group requires the term store admin role:

Figure 8.2 - Creating a new term group

On the site level, there can be only one term group, which needs to be created before the site level term set can be created.

Term sets

A term set is a collection of specific terms. A term set can be either local, i.e., created on a site collection level and only used on that specific site collection, or global, i.e. created on a term store found within the SharePoint admin center and used on all sites in a tenant.

Term set owners maintain the term set. A term set owner can be a single person, a Microsoft 365 group, or a security group. Term group contributors and managers can also manage term sets in the specified term group.

Term set stakeholders are users who are accountable for the term set and added terms. Stakeholder is a governing role. Stakeholders cannot maintain the term set but are rather notified of major term set changes.

On the term set usage settings, the term set can be either closed or open in terms of submission policy. Users can add new terms themselves when the term set is set as open:

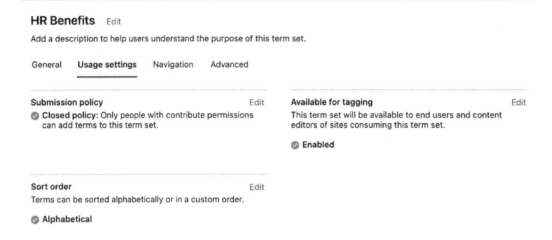

HR Benefits   Edit

Add a description to help users understand the purpose of this term set.

General   **Usage settings**   Navigation   Advanced

Submission policy   Edit
✓ **Closed policy:** Only people with contribute permissions
   can add terms to this term set.

Available for tagging   Edit
This term set will be available to end users and content
editors of sites consuming this term set.

✓ **Enabled**

Sort order   Edit
Terms can be sorted alphabetically or in a custom order.

✓ **Alphabetical**

Figure 8.3 - Term set usage settings

When available for tagging is enabled, the term set can be used to classify and tag content within a SharePoint list or library. Term set terms can be sorted alphabetically or manually.

On term set navigation settings, term set can be enabled for site and faceted navigation. These features are not currently available on modern SharePoint.

If there are multiple languages in an organization, especially when using multi-lingual content, term set translation can be used to translate terms to those languages. Term set terms can be automatically translated using machine translation, which is available for all languages supported by the term store. The term set translation settings are available on the **Advanced** tab:

←   ×

Machine translation

What terms do you want to translate?

● All terms

○ Only the terms updated since the last translation

Translate from

| English   ∨ |

Translate to

| Swedish   ∨ |

Figure 8.4 - Term set machine translation

The term set custom properties can be used to store detailed information about the term set. Custom properties are quite commonly used with customized solutions that use the term store term sets.

Importing term sets

Terms set can be imported to term groups using either CSV or **Simple Knowledge Organization System (SKOS)**, which is a **World Wide Web Consortium (W3C)** recommendation for representing taxonomies and other structured vocabularies. Example files for both can be downloaded from the term set import panel, which can be opened by selecting **Import term set** from a term group.

In the CSV format, the term set and each term are represented as a separate line. A term's parent hierarchy is presented on the line, and parent terms should exist before creating child terms. The SKOS format is more enhanced, allowing the application of term translation, synonyms, and settings.

Terms

Terms can be used for adding metadata and tagging SharePoint content.

Terms are organized as a hierarchical structure, at a maximum of seven levels deep. A single term always belongs to a specified term set, but terms can be pinned, reused, or merged to be available on another term set. A pinned term and its child terms can be edited only on the original term, and all changes made are synchronized to other term sets. Pinned terms are marked with a pushpin icon on the term hierarchy. In *Figure 8.5*, the term **Finland** from the **Locations** term set is pinned to the **Offices** term set:

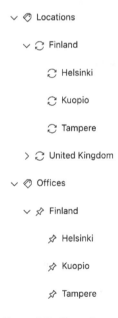

Figure 8.5 - Pinned terms

For multilingual content, terms can be translated either manually or using machine translation on the term set level. Terms can also have synonyms, which are useful when using terms as keywords:

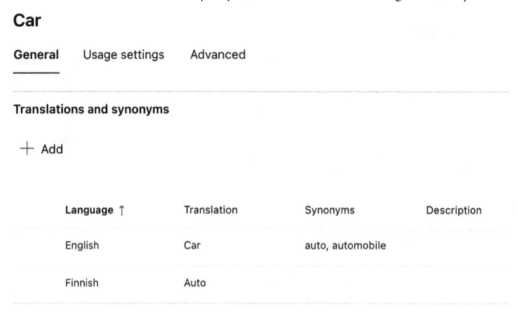

Figure 8.6 - Term translations and synonyms

Merging terms will copy translations, synonyms, and custom properties from a source term to the destination. Both terms are updated when changes are made to either of them.

In short, select pin when a term and its child terms are maintained in the source term, select reuse when the term itself must be linked to another term set and child terms can be different, and select merge when two terms need to be in sync.

Term deprecation can be used to disable tagging while keeping child terms usable. Deprecated terms also stay in SharePoint content. Deprecation is useful when terms become outdated.

Terms can also be copied and moved inside of the term store hierarchy.

Built-in term sets

The term store in SharePoint online includes several built-in term sets, which are automatically created. These term sets can be used and managed similarly to other term sets.

Term sets in the search dictionaries term group are not available on SharePoint online and are not covered in this book.

People

Underneath the people term group, there are three term sets whose terms are automatically provisioned based on user profiles:

- **Job title**: Terms are created from the user's job title property in Azure Active Directory.

- **Department**: Terms are created based on the user's department property in Microsoft Entra ID.

- **Location**: Terms are created automatically based on Office location in the user's profile in SharePoint. Users can edit and add new values to the term set by editing their profile. These values are not synchronized with Azure AD.

Term set administrators and group managers can manage these term sets in the term store. When a term is removed from the term set, for example, "engineering" from the department term set, the value will be automatically added back to the term set when a new user has the department value "engineering" or an existing user's department value is updated to "engineering". Terms are not automatically removed from these term sets.

These term sets can be used to query and refine search results, for example, department refiner is useful when building a people search solution using SharePoint search.

Keywords

Keywords is a global, non-hierarchical term set that can be used to manage organization-wide keywords. By default, the term set is set as open, so users can add new keywords using the Enterprise keywords column in SharePoint content. Term store administrators and system term group managers can set the term set as closed if the organization wants to centrally manage its keywords.

Enterprise keywords are enabled on lists and libraries from **Enterprise Metadata and Keywords Settings** on list or library settings.

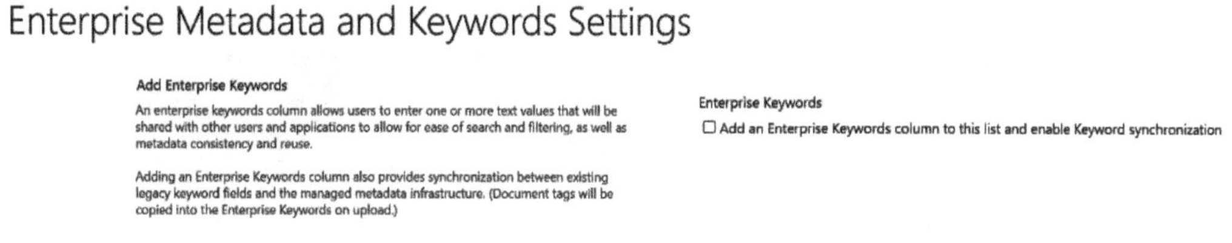

Enterprise Metadata and Keywords Settings

Add Enterprise Keywords

An enterprise keywords column allows users to enter one or more text values that will be shared with other users and applications to allow for ease of search and filtering, as well as metadata consistency and reuse.

Adding an Enterprise Keywords column also provides synchronization between existing legacy keyword fields and the managed metadata infrastructure. (Document tags will be copied into the Enterprise Keywords on upload.)

Enterprise Keywords

☐ Add an Enterprise Keywords column to this list and enable Keyword synchronization

Figure 8.7 - Apply Enterprise keywords to all content types

The Enterprise keywords column on lists and libraries allows users to add terms from all term sets available for tagging, for example, the user can add two keywords from the keywords term set and a term from the job title term set to a document. All terms will be stored in the Enterprise keywords column.

Using managed metadata in SharePoint content

Managed metadata terms are added to SharePoint content using managed metadata-type site columns. Managed metadata can be used on both lists and libraries.

When a term is added to a site column, it is referenced with the term's unique ID, so if the term changes, the link to SharePoint will remain intact.

Using terms in pages, documents, and list items

On the information panel on lists and libraries, there are two ways to add terms to list items or documents. Users can search for a term and the column will begin suggesting matching terms as shown in *Figure 8.9*:

Figure 8.8 - Adding a term on the information panel

Another way is to open a term set browser (*Figure 8.9*) from the small tag icon on the right side of the column (*Figure 8.8*):

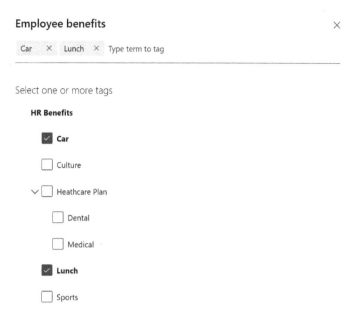

Figure 8.9 - Term set browser

If the column is set as multi-valued, users can search for more terms or select desired terms on the term set browser as shown in *Figure 8.9*. Once terms are applied, they are automatically updated to the list item or the document.

Terms can also be added and changed using the grid view edit mode by searching or using the term set browser.

Enable adding terms from SharePoint

To enable users to add terms, the term set must be set as open policy and you must enable **Allow users to type new values** on the site column settings.

In the modern SharePoint experience, adding a new term in the information panel is not so intuitive for users. Users need to open the term set browser and select **New Term** from the three dots after term set or term title. This allows users to create nested terms:

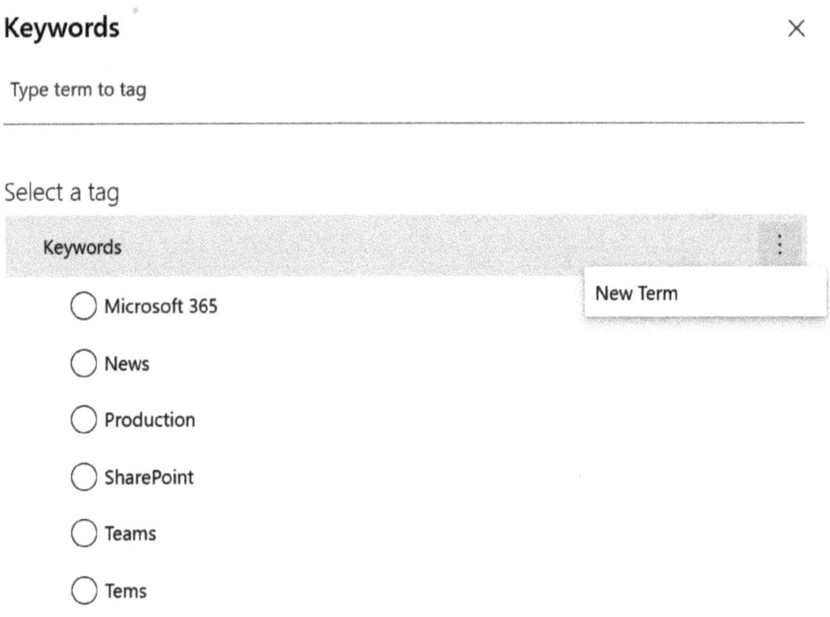

Figure 8.10 - Adding a new term to open term set

Using Terms for filtering SharePoint content using out-of-the-box web parts

News and highlighted content web parts can use managed metadata for filtering. This requires that the managed metadata site column is mapped to a managed property set as refinable on the search schema. Managed properties on the search schema are explained in more detail in *Chapter 7*.

On the news web part, the **Filter** is set as **Managed property**, and property is searched for and picked from the list:

Figure 8.11 - Managed property filtering on the news web part

The example in *Figure 8.12*, will only return news articles that have a managed metadata-type site column with the value **HR**. The site column needs to be mapped to department-managed property on the search schema.

Possible filtering options are equals, does not equal, begins with, contains, and does not contain. The value needs to be added manually.

On the highlighted content web part, the experience differs a little, but the result is basically the same. The highlighted content web part also supports sorting based on managed properties. Sorting requires that the used property is set as sortable on the search schema.

To use a custom-managed metadata term set for filtering and sorting in out-of-the-box web parts, it needs to be planned well and changes to the search schema need to be handled. When managed metadata-enabled site columns are mapped to a managed property within SharePoint's search schema, it takes some time to reflect the changes in the search index. As a rule of thumb, it's good to wait at least 24 hours for changes to update. Remember to use the enforced reindexing found under the list and library advanced settings.

Summary

In this chapter, we first learned the basic concepts of managed metadata in SharePoint online.

Next, we learned how to manage managed metadata term groups, term sets, and terms. We looked through built-in term sets and how they can be managed. In the last part, we discovered how to use managed metadata terms in SharePoint content and how they can be used to filter content with out-of-the-box web parts.

In the next chapter, we will cover Microsoft Syntex.

Understand Information with Microsoft Syntex

Microsoft Syntex is a bundle of services for intelligent document processing, content understanding, and compliance for SharePoint, Teams, OneDrive, and Exchange. The Microsoft Syntex product family also includes premium taxonomy services and advanced management capabilities for SharePoint. Syntex is an add-on and it's licensed separately based on used capabilities.

Intelligent document processing can automatically generate documents such as contracts, extract information, tag images, and **optical character recognition** (**OCR**) in printed and handwritten documents.

Taxonomy services contain term set imports using SKOS-format, which is a W3C recommendation for representing taxonomies and publishing content types to a hub site and all child sites including new lists and libraries.

SharePoint Advanced Management includes features such as restricted access controls, conditional access policies, and content life cycle management.

In this chapter, we're going to cover the following main topics:

- Setting up Microsoft Syntex
- Intelligent document processing capabilities
- Creating repetitive files using modern templates
- Image tagging and OCR
- Premium taxonomy features
- eSignatures on SharePoint
- Microsoft 365 Archive and Backup
- Licensing and pricing of Syntex capabilities

Setting up Microsoft Syntex

To set up the intelligent content processing capabilities of Microsoft Syntex, a Microsoft Azure subscription is needed. Microsoft Syntex requires a resource group in a subscription. Earlier Syntex also included per-user licensing, but it was deprecated on July 1, 2023.

> **Important note**
> The Microsoft Syntex service will be renamed as SharePoint Premium in the near future.

The billing and settings of Syntex are managed on the **Use content AI with Microsoft Syntex** section in the Microsoft 365 admin center.

The setup starts by linking the Azure subscription and a resource group for billing:

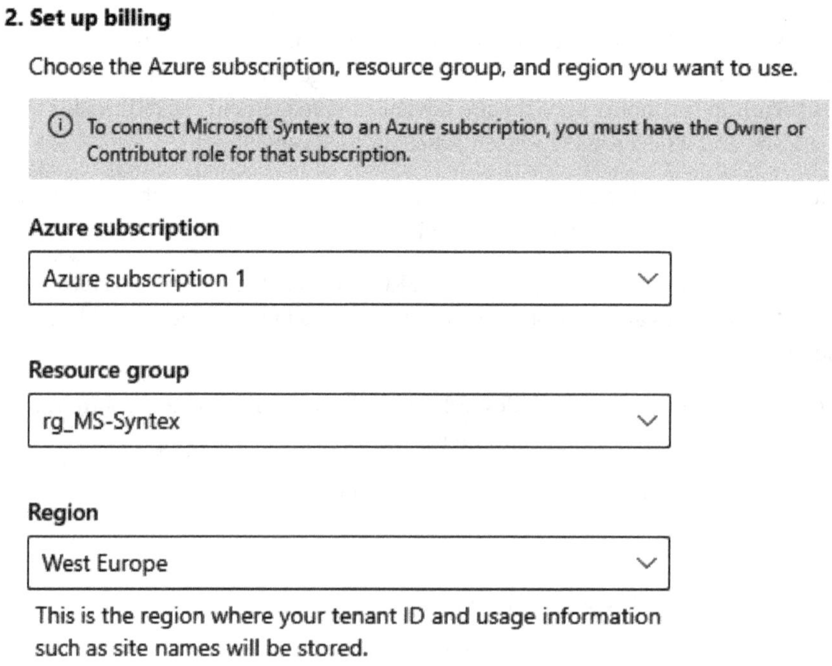

2. Set up billing

Choose the Azure subscription, resource group, and region you want to use.

ⓘ To connect Microsoft Syntex to an Azure subscription, you must have the Owner or Contributor role for that subscription.

Azure subscription

Azure subscription 1	⌄

Resource group

rg_MS-Syntex	⌄

Region

West Europe	⌄

This is the region where your tenant ID and usage information such as site names will be stored.

Figure 9.1 - Set up Syntex billing

When billing is configured, the next step is to set up a content center, which is a special SharePoint site created during the setup process and a location for creating and managing content processing models:

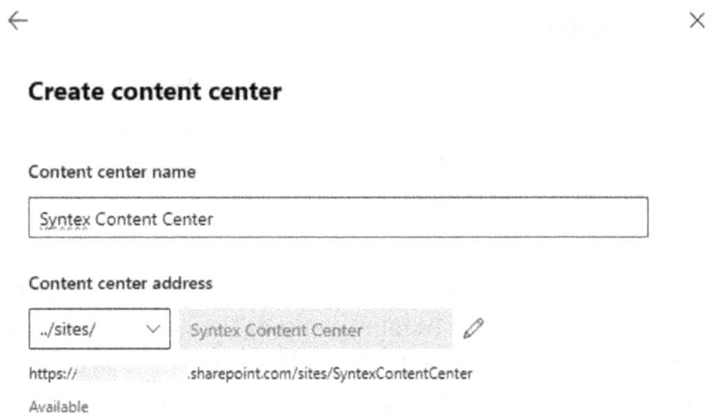

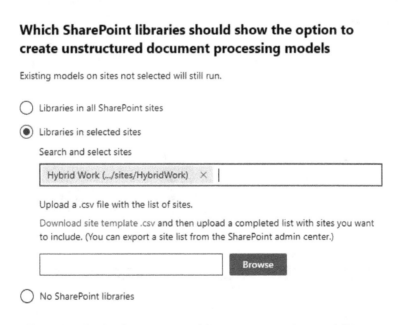

Figure 9.2 - Create a Syntex content center

When the content center is created, administrators can select sites where document processing, OCR, image tagging, and content assembly features are activated. Choice can be all sites, selected specific sites, or not enabled on any site. If Syntex features are used for specific document processing purposes or a limited set of users, it's reasonable to activate features only for sites used for document processing purposes. Costs are also something to be taken care of since every processing transaction is billed, even if processing is unsuccessful.

Figure 9.3 - Setting for unstructured document processing capabilities

Document processing capabilities

The document processing capabilities of Microsoft Syntex include prebuilt document processing models for contracts, invoices, and receipts. These models are pretrained to process common business use cases and for structured documents. Prebuilt models use OCR and deep learning models to extract data from structured documents. Prebuilt models are a good method to start automating document processing and content extraction.

Custom document processing models support structured, freeform, and unstructured documents. The difference between these models is the training method. The structured model uses the layout method where the model creator trains the model by marking the content fields from the document. On the freeform model, the model is trained by selecting the content for extraction anywhere on the document. On unstructured documents, the model is trained by teaching the model. Freeform and structured models are created and trained using the Microsoft Power Apps AI Builder feature.

All document processing models are managed on the content center site.

Setting up a prebuilt model

Creating a new model starts in the content center by selecting **New** on the content center homepage:

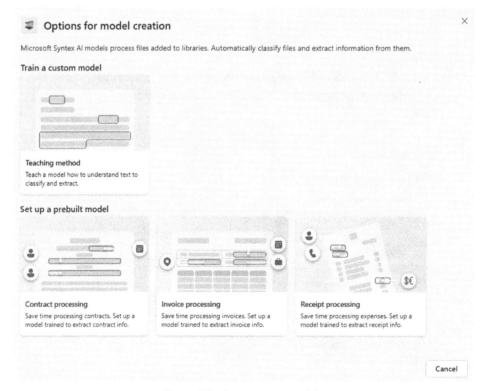

Figure 9.4 - Create a new model

Model creators can choose to train a custom model or start from prebuilt models. On prebuilt models, several languages are available. If the language is not supported on a prebuilt model, a custom model should be used. A new model requires a name and a description in the creation phase. For this example, let's pick the invoice processing model and name it the invoice model. After the model is created, the next step is to add files for analysis and extractor setup. Files are selected from the training document library and can be uploaded to the library during selection. When files are added, the model automatically identifies extractors from the file content. An extractor is an entity inside of the document, such as a customer address, date, or invoice number. Each element that we want to extract from the document requires an extractor:

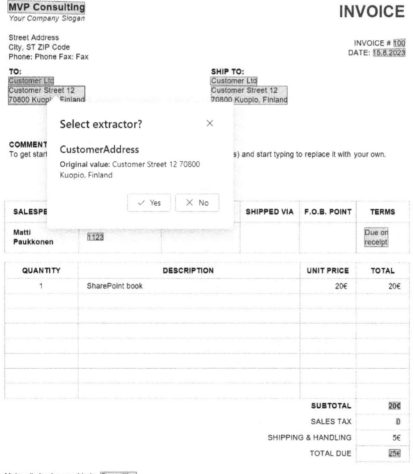

Figure 9.5 - Identified extractors

Discovered extractors are mapped as site columns. The model creates new to site columns by default and adds them to the library. Extractors can be renamed, which requires synchronizing the model changes to libraries where it's applied. Site columns already created by the model are not automatically removed. An extractor can also be mapped to an existing or new site column, which is a better practice for keeping the solution more consistent across different libraries:

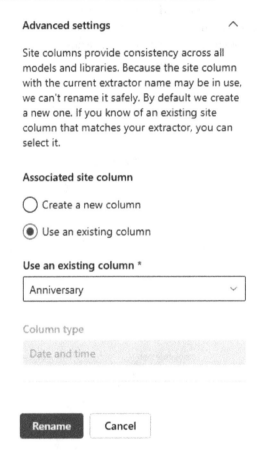

Figure 9.6 - Mapping the extractor to an existing site column

The model can also apply a sensitivity label and a retention label to analyzed documents. These are set in **Model settings**:

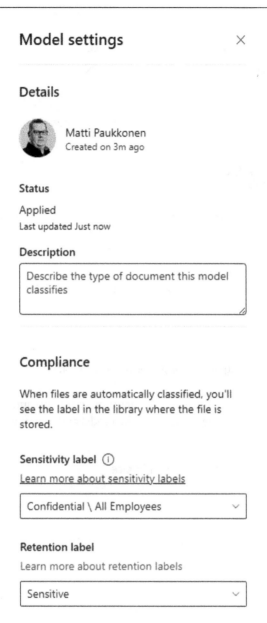

Figure 9.7 - Setting up automatic labeling of analyzed files

Finally, the model is applied to libraries on the SharePoint site:

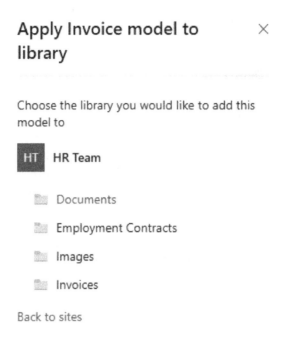

Apply Invoice model to library   ✕

Choose the library you would like to add this model to

HT   HR Team

    📄 Documents

    📄 Employment Contracts

    📄 Images

    📄 Invoices

Back to sites

Figure 9.8 - Apply the model to a library

Changes to the model, such as renaming an extractor or setting up automatic labeling, need to synchronize to libraries. This is done by opening the model and selecting **Sync all** in **Where the model is applied on this site**:

Where the model is applied on this site

When files are added to these libraries the model will process them.

+ Apply model   🔄 Sync all   — Remove

⌄ Name	Modified date
⌄ Testisivusto	
Documents	8m ago

Figure 9.9 - Synchronizing model changes to libraries

When a new file is uploaded to a library where the model is applied, the model will process it and save values from found model extractors to site columns in the library. Existing files can be processed by selecting the file and selecting **Classify and extract** from the ribbon. The process isn't instantaneous and can take up to 30 minutes to complete.

Figure 9.10 - Analyzed invoice

Created models can be found in the Models library in the Syntex content center.

Setting up a custom model

A custom model for unstructured document processing can be created from the Syntex content center. Setting up a custom model starts like with prebuilt models, but on the **Option for model creation** dialog, the **Train a custom model** option is chosen (*Figure 9.4*). On advanced model settings, the content type model uses, sensitivity, and retention labels can be set automatically. The content type is either created with the model or associated with an existing content type:

Figure 9.11 - Advanced custom model settings

The model requires at least five positively matching example files and at least one negatively matching example file for training the model. In complex scenarios, it is reasonable to have more examples to improve the accuracy of the model. Each file is labeled as a positive or negative match. Once example files are labeled, the model is ready to be trained. For training, some explanations for identifying content are required. An explanation can be based on a phrase list or regular expression, and accuracy again improves with more explanations:

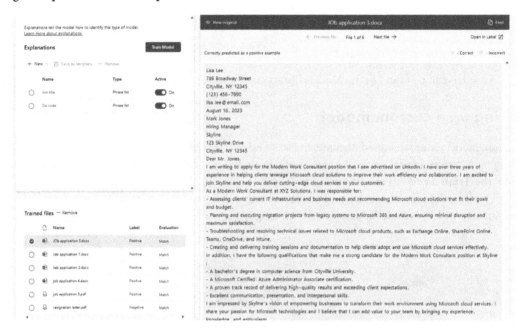

Figure 9.12 - Custom model training

The next phase is testing the model with example files. Added files are labeled as positive or negative matches using the trained model. After the training is completed, the next step is to create extractors for automatically extracting content to site columns. First, example files are labeled with the content to be extracted – in this example, an email address. Labeling is made by highlighting the content on an example document. If the content – in this case, an email address – is not found, the file is marked as **No label**. In the training phase, again, explanations for finding the content are needed. In this example, an explanation for the email address is created from a predefined template:

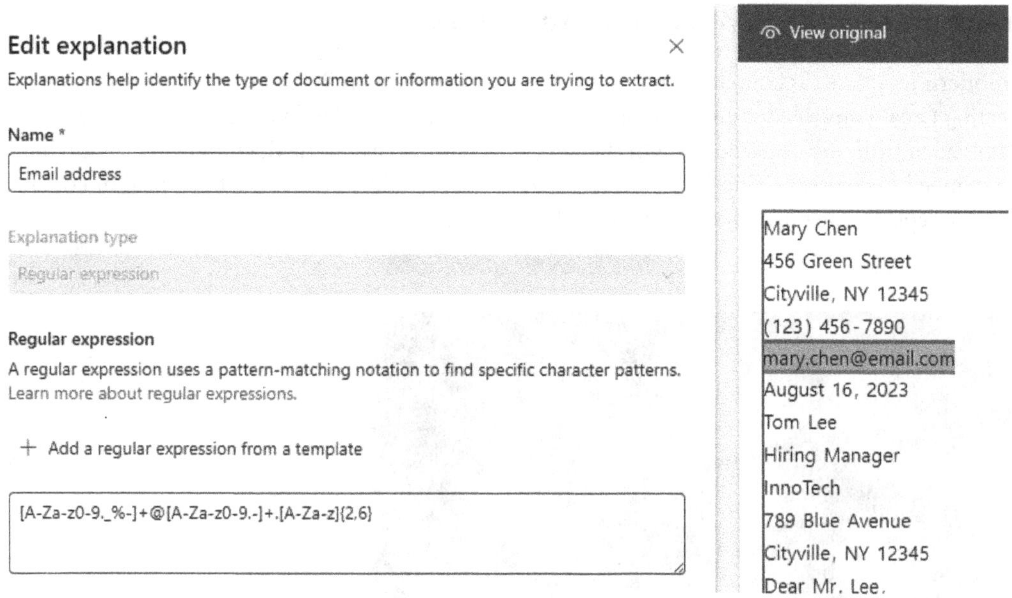

Edit explanation   ✕

Explanations help identify the type of document or information you are trying to extract.

◎ View original

Name *

Email address

Explanation type

Regular expression   ⌄

Regular expression

A regular expression uses a pattern-matching notation to find specific character patterns.
Learn more about regular expressions.

+ Add a regular expression from a template

[A-Za-z0-9._%-]+@[A-Za-z0-9.-]+.[A-Za-z]{2,6}

Mary Chen
456 Green Street
Cityville, NY 12345
(123) 456-7890
mary.chen@email.com
August 16, 2023
Tom Lee
Hiring Manager
InnoTech
789 Blue Avenue
Cityville, NY 12345
Dear Mr. Lee.

Figure 9.13 - Email address explanation

Once explanations are created, the model training starts and results are visible in the Trained files section with an evaluation of success. The model accuracy is visible in the top-right corner, and once the level of accuracy is on an adequate level, the testing phase can be started. After testing, the model can be published to document libraries.

Finding an email address from an unstructured file is simple. In more complex scenarios, creating good explanations for identifying files and extracting content to site columns is important. Training might also need more example files to improve accuracy.

Creating repetitive files using modern templates

Content assembly enables the creation of generic, repetitive documents such as contracts, agreements, or letters. Content assembly is based on Microsoft Word documents that are deployed as templates for content assembly. Fields are mapped to placeholders on the template. When the document is filled, placeholders are automatically filled with field values on the content assembly form. Fields can also be mapped as library columns, and filled values are automatically extracted. A template is currently only available in the document library where it's created and cannot be copied to other document libraries.

Creating a modern document template

A modern template for content assembly is added to a document library from the **New** menu by selecting **Create modern template**. A template file is selected from document libraries in SharePoint or uploaded from the user's device. On the template, setup areas on the document are highlighted and mapped to corresponding fields, which are required. A field can be just a form field or content field that replaces the highlighted content on the document.

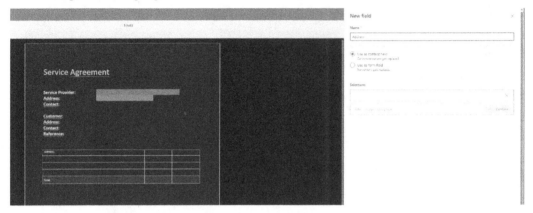

Figure 9.14 - Modern template editor

The type of the field can be selected from single or multiple lines of text, number, date, email, or hyperlink, or bring choices from a list column or managed metadata term set. Once all required fields are mapped, the template can be published. During the publishing of the template, the mapped fields can be added to site columns in the library:

Publish template   ✕

Publish so you can create a new file from this template. Find the template in the **New menu**.

Template name

Service Agreement

Show fields as columns

Add fields to a custom view of the library.

Template fields   ✕ 7 selected

✔	Field ↓	Type
✔	Provider	Single line of text
✔	Address	Single line of text
✔	Contact	Email
✔	Department	Managed metadata
✔	Customer	Single line of text
✔	Customer Address	Single line of text
✔	Customer contact	Email

☑ Set the default view of the library

Figure 9.15 - Publishing the modern template

A document using the published content assembly template can be created from the **New** menu of the library, which opens the form editor:

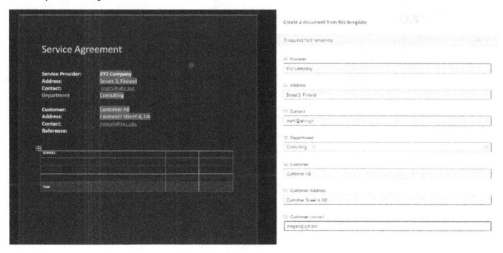

Figure 9.16 - Form editor

Filled fields are automatically added to the document content and also to site columns if they are created in the library:

Figure 9.17 - Created document with metadata in site columns

After the document is created, it can be edited normally using Word. Fields created in the modern template are not locked and can be changed as well, but site column values are not affected when the document is edited. Site column values can also be changed, which does not affect the document content.

Image tagging and OCR

Image tagging generates descriptive keywords to the special site column called **Image Tags**. The **Image Tags** column is a managed metadata column, and it also supports managing image tags manually. Image tagging uses AI to detect images, and it may take from five minutes to 24 hours to automatically tag the images. Image tagging is only supported for newly added images after the feature is activated in a document library.

OCR extracts printed or handwritten text from images and PDF documents. The text is extracted as words, text lines, and paragraphs. Currently supported image types are JPG, JPEG, PNG, BMP, and TIFF, and OCR supports over 150 languages. Added images are analyzed automatically after OCR is activated. The extracted text is added to the **Extracted Text** site column.

Premium taxonomy features

Microsoft Syntex includes a couple of premium taxonomy features.

Support for importing taxonomy term sets using W3C recommended SKOS-formatted enables possibilities to import term sets to SharePoint from other SKOS-supported systems.

The SKOS-formatted term set is imported on the Term store like csv-formatted term sets. A sample file can be downloaded from the **Import new term set** pane:

Import new term set

Import a term set using either the CSV format or the new import format based on SKOS. Learn more

Download one of the following templates to create your import file

* sample-metadata.csv
* sample-metadata.ttl

Import the completed file to create a new term set

Target term group

Test Group

File format

SKOS (*.ttl)   ⌄

Browse   Selected file: None

Figure 9.18 - Importing a SKOS-formatted term set

Another premium extension is the ability to push published content types to a hub and all associated sites. Content types are automatically added to lists and libraries, also libraries created after the settings are applied. Content types derived from the default document content type are automatically added to libraries, and content types not derived from the document content type to lists.

Push is enabled per content type basis in the Content Type Gallery in the SharePoint admin center:

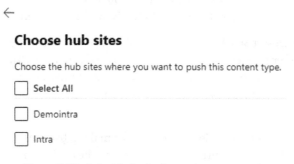

←

Choose hub sites

Choose the hub sites where you want to push this content type.

☐ Select All

☐ Demointra

☐ Intra

Figure 9.19 - Select hub site for content type push

eSignatures on SharePoint

eSignatures on SharePoint provides a simple way to share and get signatures onto documents. Currently, the service only supports signing PDF documents. The service is enabled on Syntex settings in the Microsoft 365 admin center, and it can be done after pay-as-you-go billing is activated.

> **Note**
> SharePoint's eSignatures feature is available only in the US market at the time of writing this book. The feature will be available in other regions in 2024.

The signing process starts with a PDF document, where the user can select Get signatures. Next, the people who need to sign the document are chosen. They can be either internal users or external users. The number of signees is limited to 10.

The next step is to add signature placeholders to the documents for all signees. After that, signature requests are sent.

The signee receives the invitation to sign the document via email. The signee needs to log in with their account to get access to the document to be signed. The signature is typed in as text, and the signee can change the font if needed. Other required fields such as date or initials are also filled in as text. The signee can also decline the signing process.

Once all signees have signed the document, the signatures and the audit trail are appended to the PDF document. The signed document is then digitally signed by Microsoft.

Microsoft 365 Archive and Backup

Microsoft 365 Archive and Backup are recently published services on Preview.

Microsoft 365 Archive allows archiving of SharePoint sites by the SharePoint administrator. The archived site is removed from active sites, search, and cannot be accessed while in its archived state. Archived sites are visible on the separate Archived sites list in the SharePoint admin center.

An advantage of the Microsoft 365 Archive service is that it shows when a tenant's storage capacity has reached its limit; after that, every gigabyte will be priced separately. The price of storage for archived sites is about a quarter of the price of extra storage. Restoring an archived site is also priced separately. The costs of the archive service are billed on Syntex's pay-as-you-go model with a linked Azure subscription.

Microsoft 365 Backup allows the creation of policies for making backups of Exchange mailboxes and OneDrive and SharePoint sites. Currently, restoration can be made for mailbox items and whole OneDrive and SharePoint sites; for example, restoring a single file is not currently supported. OneDrive and SharePoint sites can be restored to a different location for inspecting and looking for specific items. Using backup policies specific mailboxes, OneDrive and sites can be included in the backup.

Pricing of the backup is per gigabyte for data currently stored in the backed-up entities. It's worth noting that deleted data will be charged for 365 days; after that, it's removed from the backup.

Both of these services will be in production during the year 2024.

Licensing and pricing of Syntex capabilities

Document processing, content assembly, image tagging, and OCR features are billed based on pay-as-you-go licensing, which requires an Azure subscription for billing. Operations are transaction-based, and a transaction is a page in a document, an Excel sheet, or an image file – for example, extracting content from a 10-page Word document counts as 10 transactions. Detailed pricing can be found in the Microsoft Syntex documentation.

On a cost basis, setting up Syntex's intelligent document modeling capabilities requires thorough planning, since each processing operation is billed, even unsuccessful ones. Publishing intelligent models to be available on all SharePoint sites and libraries may lead to uncontrolled costs on an Azure subscription. When Syntex features are implemented, it's a good practice to monitor costs on the linked resource group in Azure.

Summary

In this chapter, we learned about the intelligent document processing capabilities of Microsoft Syntex. First, we learned how to set up Microsoft Syntex billing, create a content center, and configure different services.

In the next section, we delved into document processing capabilities with examples of using prebuilt and custom models.

After that, we were introduced to the content assembly feature, which simplifies the creation of generic, repetitive documents.

Next, we covered how image tagging and OCR work in SharePoint document libraries.

And finally, we were introduced to Syntex's premium taxonomy features.

In the next chapter, we will look into how Viva Connections can be used to bring SharePoint content to Microsoft Teams.

10

Bring SharePoint Content to Teams with Viva Connections

The use of Microsoft Teams for communication and collaboration has grown rapidly, reaching over 320 million monthly active users in 2023, and it has become the most important application for information workers. The Microsoft Viva suite, the new employee experience product line launched in 2021, brings capabilities for communications, goal setting, knowledge management, and learning, Viva Connections being one of these experiences. Viva Connections enables experiences in both Teams and SharePoint, which enables users to fluently access important content such as news, videos, links, and articles without leaving Teams. Viva Connections also brings relevant conversations from the Viva Engage social platform (previously known as Yammer) to the same context.

Viva Connections is a landing experience for accessing SharePoint content. It can be thought of as an intranet landing page. Viva Connections and the SharePoint home site experience come together in a dashboard, which acts as an important gateway to important links, applications, quick information, a feed that gathers relevant and personalized news, conversations, and videos to the user, and Viva Home, which is a personalized view of Teams and provides access to the dashboard, the feed, global SharePoint navigation, and other Viva Suite products.

In this chapter, we're going to cover the following main topics:

- Building blocks of Viva Connections
- How to curate content for the Viva Connections feed
- How to manage the Viva Connections dashboard
- How to enable and customize Viva Connections in Teams

Building blocks of Viva Connections

The Viva Connections home experience is built on a couple of components that are used to curate and bring content from SharePoint and other Microsoft 365 services to Teams. The Viva Connections home experience is a landing page that brings important news, recent conversations and videos, a curated dashboard, and links to different curated resources via navigation and what users have been using or following recently:

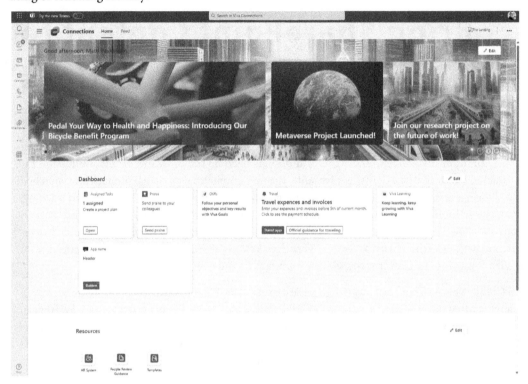

Figure 10.1 - Viva Connections home experience

The landing page is opened when a user accesses the Viva Connections app from the left rail menu in Teams. **Feed** brings curated, important content to users based on interest and the user's role. **Dashboard** is used to view relevant links, content, applications, and quickly accessible information in a card-like format. **Resources** is a curated list of important resources and can be managed by users who have edit permissions for the Viva home experience:

Figure 10.2 - Managing resources

Users can easily access other enabled Viva Suite services such as Engage, Learning, and Insights from the top-left corner of Viva Home view and open the SharePoint home site portal from the top-right corner.

On Teams Mobile, the Viva Connections home experience is divided into three main tabs – **Dashboard**, **Feed**, and **Resources**:

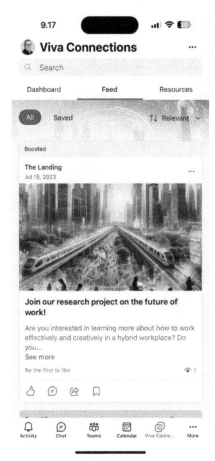

Figure 10.3 - Viva feed on Teams Mobile

The dashboard is what opens to the user first, so it's important to have relevant and up-to-date information available. Also, the global navigation structure is another crucial element to plan so mobile users can easily access needed information.

The feed can also be used as a web part on SharePoint pages. The feed web part has a couple of layout options and a choice between a fixed number of items displayed or a dynamic number determined by the page height:

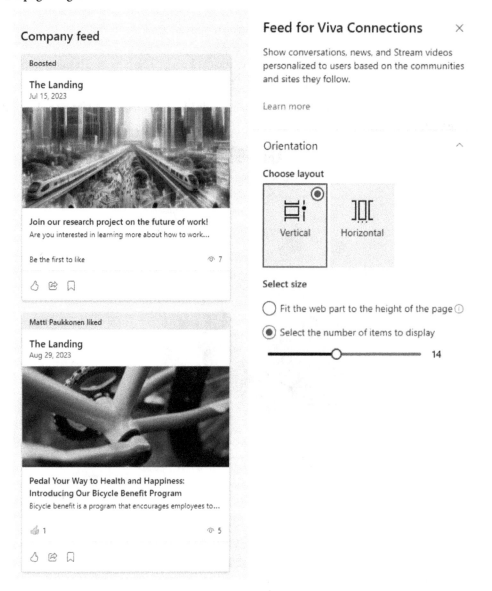

Figure 10.4 - Feed web part and settings

The feed web part can be used to bring company news feed visible to other important SharePoint sites.

The dashboard can be used as a web part as well, but only on the SharePoint home site, since it relies on the dashboard page hosted on the home site:

Figure 10.5 - Viva dashboard on the SharePoint page

The dashboard scales automatically based on the number of columns it uses, and the author can choose how many cards are displayed based on the order of the cards on the dashboard management page.

Setting up Viva Connections

Viva Connections settings are managed in the Microsoft 365 admin center. The settings can be accessed by opening Viva from the **Settings** group in the left menu and then opening Viva Connections, or by navigating to https://admin.microsoft.com/#/viva/connections. Viva Connections home experiences can be created and modified in **Create and manage Viva Connections experiences**. The settings allow enabling the home experience on a new SharePoint or connecting the experience to an existing site. The SharePoint home site configuration and enabling of the Viva Connections home experience are done automatically.

A global administrator or SharePoint administrator role is required for managing Viva Connections.

> **Note**
>
> A prerequisite for Viva Connections is that the SharePoint home site is configured. The configuration of the SharePoint home site is gone through in detail in *Chapter 2* of this book.

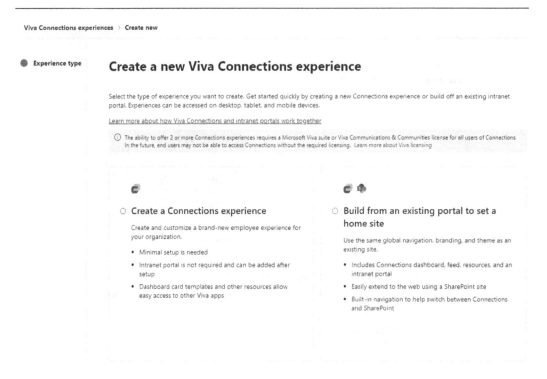

Figure 10.6 - Set up the Viva Connections experience

The **Create a Connections experience** option creates a new communications site and enables Viva Connections features there. **Build from an existing portal to set a home site** enables Viva Connections on an existing site, such as an intranet landing site.

Setting up and managing multiple Viva Connections experiences

For organizations with Viva Suite or Viva Employee Communications and Communities licenses, it's possible to create up to 10 Viva Connections home experiences. Creating an additional Viva Connections experience starts similarly to creating the organization's default experience. It's possible to create a new experience with a new site or connect to an existing site (*Figure 10.6*). New experiences are first created with a draft status and are not visible to users.

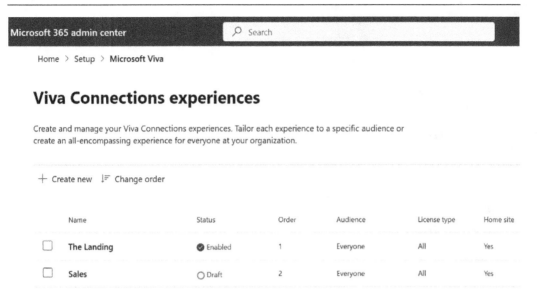

Figure 10.7 - Viva Connections experiences in the admin center

Administrators can assign site ownership of a specific experience to users who manage the content of the experience.

Targeting the experience to audiences

Each experience can be targeted based on a user's license type and group membership. Choices for license types are **Frontline worker** and **Information worker**. The frontline worker license type includes users with Microsoft 365 F-series licenses (Microsoft 365 F1 and F3). The information worker license type includes users with other licenses.

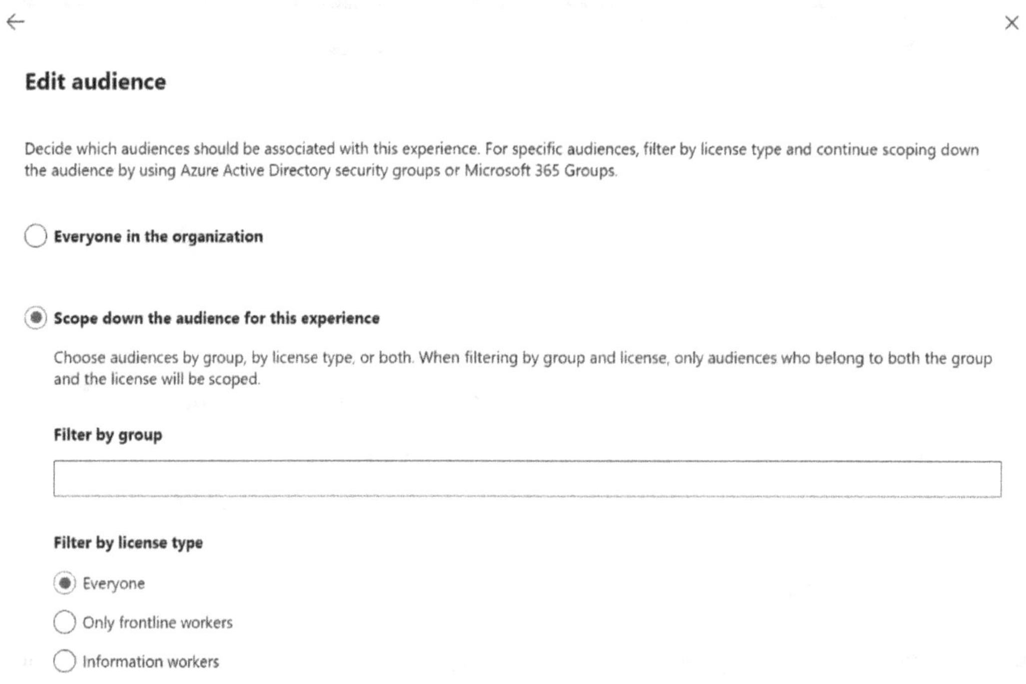

←   ×

Edit audience

Decide which audiences should be associated with this experience. For specific audiences, filter by license type and continue scoping down
the audience by using Azure Active Directory security groups or Microsoft 365 Groups.

◯ **Everyone in the organization**

◉ **Scope down the audience for this experience**

Choose audiences by group, by license type, or both. When filtering by group and license, only audiences who belong to both the group
and the license will be scoped.

Filter by group

```
[                                                                                                         ]
```

Filter by license type

◉ Everyone

◯ Only frontline workers

◯ Information workers

Figure 10.8 - Managing Viva Connections experience audiences

With groups, the experience is available for selected groups. License type and group targeting can also be combined.

The order of the experiences is important, especially when users may have more than one experience targeted to them. The order appoints the default experience for the user.

The last thing to do before enabling the new experience for users is to configure the Viva Connections dashboard for that specific experience to support the target users' daily work. Once that is done, the experience can be enabled from the experience settings.

Beneficial use cases for additional Viva Connections experiences include the following:

- Supporting frontline workers and bringing their important tools to the dashboard
- Creating an experience for each official language of the organization, since the dashboard does not support translation
- Personalizing experiences for each division, department, or other organizational unit
- Accommodating different regulations or legal matters in an international organization

Personalization can also be done by targeting the dashboard cards to certain audiences.

Organizations with Office 365 or Microsoft 365 licenses are limited to just one Viva Connections home experience.

How to curate SharePoint content for the Viva Connections feed

The curation of the Viva Connections feed is automatic. It displays content published in specific locations and based on the user's choice. News articles are displayed from several personalized locations:

- Sites configured as organizational news sites
- Sites that the user is following and has recently visited
- Boosted news and audience-targeted news on organizational news sites
- News relevant to the user based on their interests

From Viva Engage, which is a Viva product for building communities and internal social media, the feed displays the following:

- Posts and announcements from the **All Company** feed
- Posts, Q&As, praises, and announcements on communities the user is following
- Storyline posts

All videos shared to the entire organization from SharePoint and OneDrive are displayed on the feed.

The content ranking of the feed is based on several factors such as content age, source, boosting, or highlighting. Content authors can prioritize content to the feed by using the news boost feature and publishing news on organizational news sites and SharePoint home sites, highlighting conversations on Viva Engage using featured conversations, and publishing videos from SharePoint using video news links. Content ranking automatically ensures a mix of content so all content types get a placeholder in the feed.

Customizing and personalizing the Viva dashboard

The Viva dashboard is one content area that needs constant care when Viva Connections is deployed. Current out-of-the-box features offer a few dashboard cards that personalize based on the user, such as **Top New**, **Assigned Tasks**, and **Viva Learning** content. Dashboard authors can design cards using a web links card, a Teams apps card, or a card designer to design more functional cards. There are also third-party applications for the Viva dashboard available on the SharePoint Store.

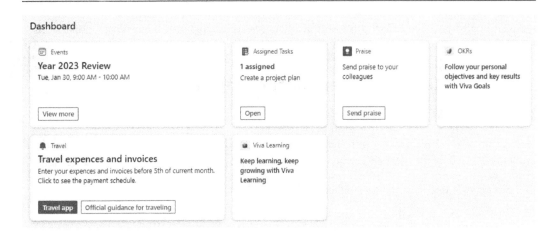

Figure 10.9 - Dashboard cards

The dashboard content can be customized from SharePoint or the Viva Connections app on Teams. The dashboard is hosted on a specific page, called `dashboard.aspx`, within the `Site Pages` library on the site to which Viva Connections is connected. On Teams, the dashboard can be edited directly from the Viva Connections home experience. When using multiple experiences, it's recommended to customize the dashboard using the Viva Connections home experience via Teams.

Editing the dashboard

Editing a dashboard is like editing a modern SharePoint page, but it only allows cards:

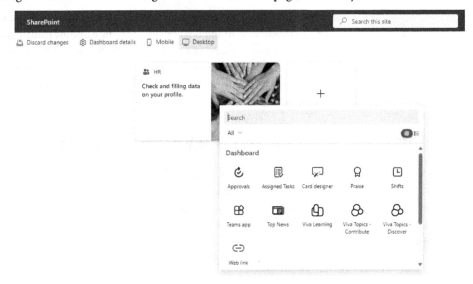

Figure 10.10 - Adding cards to the dashboard

Cards have two sizes: medium (which is a square card) and large (which is the width of two medium cards). In mobile view, a medium-sized card is half the width of the screen, and a large card is as wide as the screen. The layout scales automatically on different devices and screen sizes. This is something to consider when planning dashboards for mobile users. Use the preview to see how the dashboard looks in mobile view.

Cards have different properties based on the card type. Some cards have just layout and targeting settings, such as **Assigned Tasks**, **Praise**, and **Shifts**, and content cannot be changed at all. Web link cards allow the creation of visual links to content in Microsoft 365 or to external services or websites. Web link cards can be customized with a card logo, card title, image, and text content:

Figure 10.11 - Web link card

Teams app cards can be used to inform about important Teams apps the organization is using:

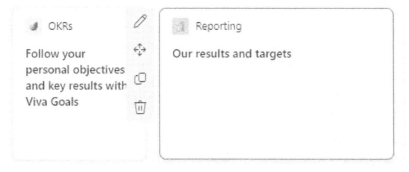

Figure 10.12 - Teams app cards

Create functional and custom cards with the card designer card

With the card designer card, authors can create more extended experiences with a quick view and buttons. On medium-sized cards, only one button is supported, and large cards can have either one or two buttons. Clicking a card or a button can open a link, open a Teams app, show your location or preset location, or open a quick view:

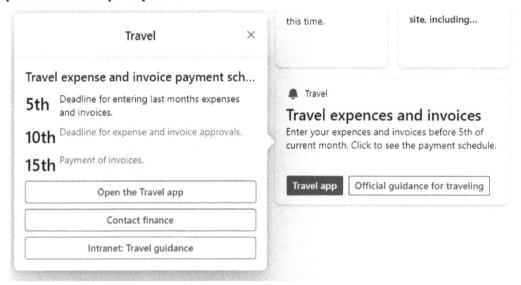

Figure 10.13 - Custom card with a quick view

A quick view (on the left in *Figure 10.13*) is a card extension that can display more information about the card's content. The quick view is created using Adaptive Cards JSON templating. An adaptive card template is a format for creating simple, card-like layouts that can have text, images, videos, basic input fields, and actions. The layout is designed with different components using specific settings. The actual visual styles such as fonts, colors, spacings, and card frames are generated by the app where the card is viewed. The same card may look different on Teams and the Viva Connections dashboard, but the content and structure remain.

The Viva Connections dashboard can be extended with custom cards called **Adaptive Card Extensions** (**ACEs**). Creating custom cards is explained in detail in *Chapter 19*.

Targeting cards

Each card on the dashboard can be targeted using the **Audience targeting** setting. A target audience is a mail-enabled group in Microsoft Entra ID, such as mail-enabled security groups, distribution lists, or Microsoft 365 groups. A card can be targeted to 50 separate target audiences:

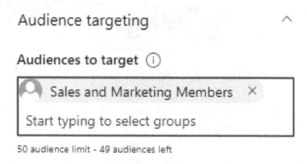

Figure 10.14 - Targeting a card to an audience

Audience targeting allows personalization of the dashboard based on the user's group memberships. When using audience targeting, it's crucial to plan and document audiences for dashboard authors and other authors who are using audience targeting in SharePoint, since the feature is looking for audiences from all supported Entra ID groups.

Audience targeting should be considered as a choice for creating multiple Viva Connections experiences.

Multilingual dashboards

Translations are supported in Viva dashboard content, which follows the language settings of the SharePoint site. Web links, Teams apps, and custom cards can be translated. The translated dashboard is accessed from the translation panel or by switching the site language in the **Language** menu.

The dashboard provides important content on Viva Connections and should be thoroughly planned. Mobile users should be prioritized since the dashboard is the first content they land on when opening Viva Connections.

Announcements in Viva Connections

Announcements is a premium feature of Viva Connections and is included in Viva Suite and Viva Employee Communications and Communities licenses. Announcements are a way to inform users about important issues, such as upcoming changes or service breaks. Published announcements appear at the top of the company feed on the Viva Connections home experience:

Figure 10.15 - Announcements

Users with edit permissions on the Viva home experience can create and manage announcements on the **Announcements** view. The view can be opened by clicking the three dots on the top-right corner of the Viva home experience and selecting **Manage announcements**. Another way to access the announcements is to navigate to the **Announcements** pages library in the SharePoint home site. All created announcements are visible in the **Announcements** view. Announcements in a draft state can be edited, but already published announcements can only be removed:

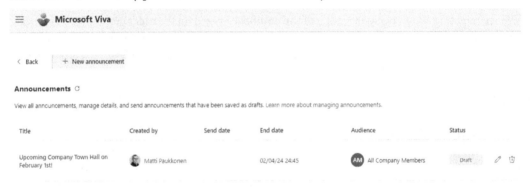

Figure 10.16 - Announcements view

Announcements are created from the **Announcements** view. An announcement requires a title, description, target audience, and end date for when the announcement will be hidden from the home experience. A target audience can be a Microsoft Entra ID group or a Microsoft 365 group. The announcement can also have a scheduled sending date and an optional link – for example, to an intranet page including more details.

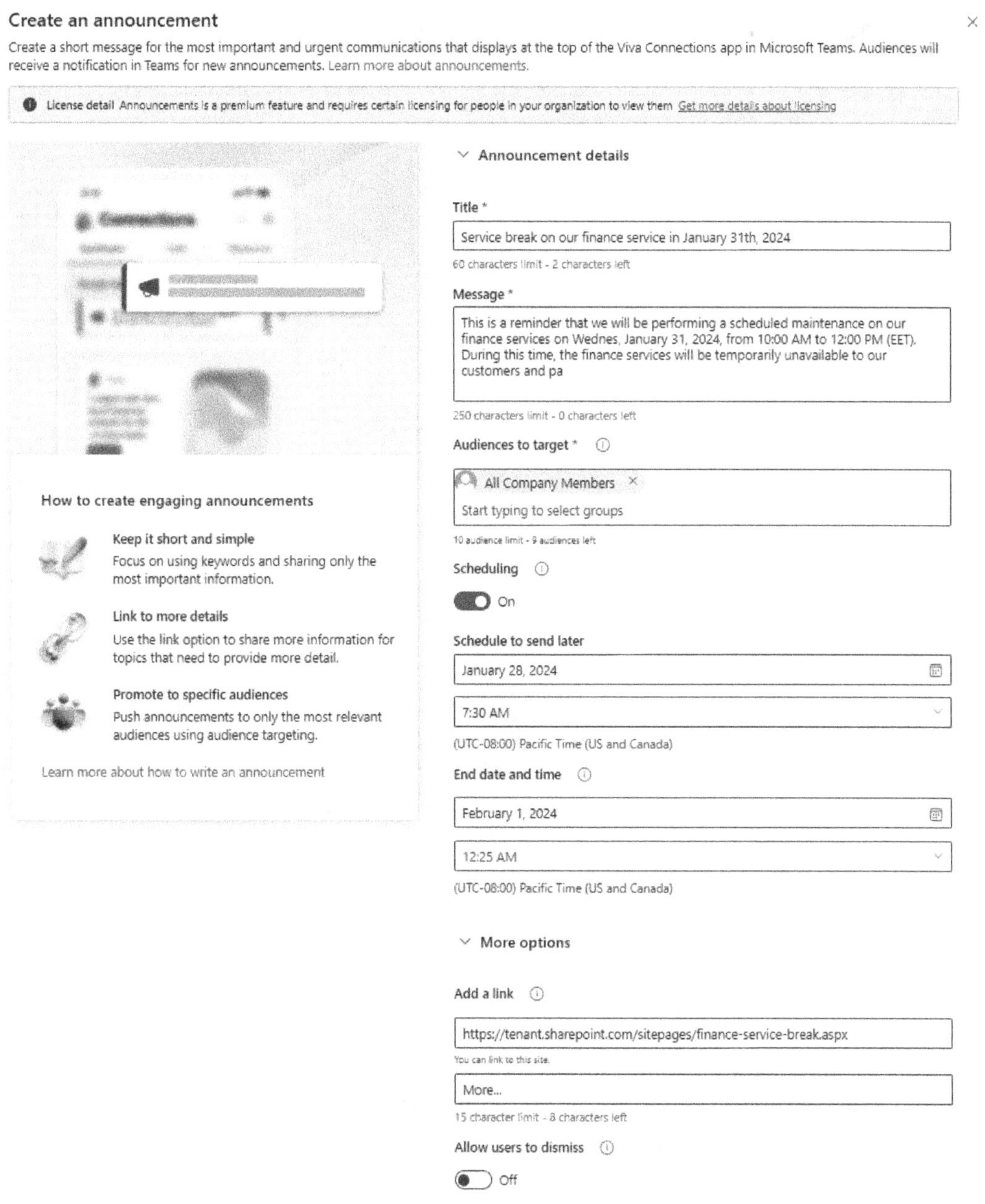

Create an announcement

✕

Create a short message for the most important and urgent communications that displays at the top of the Viva Connections app in Microsoft Teams. Audiences will receive a notification in Teams for new announcements. Learn more about announcements.

ⓘ License detail Announcements is a premium feature and requires certain licensing for people in your organization to view them Get more details about licensing

How to create engaging announcements

Keep it short and simple
Focus on using keywords and sharing only the most important information.

Link to more details
Use the link option to share more information for topics that need to provide more detail.

Promote to specific audiences
Push announcements to only the most relevant audiences using audience targeting.

Learn more about how to write an announcement

⌄ **Announcement details**

Title *

Service break on our finance service in January 31th, 2024

60 characters limit - 2 characters left

Message *

This is a reminder that we will be performing a scheduled maintenance on our finance services on Wednes, January 31, 2024, from 10:00 AM to 12:00 PM (EET). During this time, the finance services will be temporarily unavailable to our customers and pa

250 characters limit - 0 characters left

Audiences to target * ⓘ

All Company Members ✕

Start typing to select groups

10 audience limit - 9 audiences left

Scheduling ⓘ

🔵 On

Schedule to send later

January 28, 2024   📅

7:30 AM   ⌄

(UTC-08:00) Pacific Time (US and Canada)

End date and time ⓘ

February 1, 2024   📅

12:25 AM   ⌄

(UTC-08:00) Pacific Time (US and Canada)

⌄ **More options**

Add a link ⓘ

https://tenant.sharepoint.com/sitepages/finance-service-break.aspx

You can link to this site.

More...

15 character limit - 8 characters left

Allow users to dismiss ⓘ

🔘 Off

Figure 10.17 - Create an announcement

Viva Connections analytics

Viva Connections analytics show statistics on how the service has been used. Analytics can be accessed from the top-right-corner menu of the Viva home experience by selecting **View analytics**:

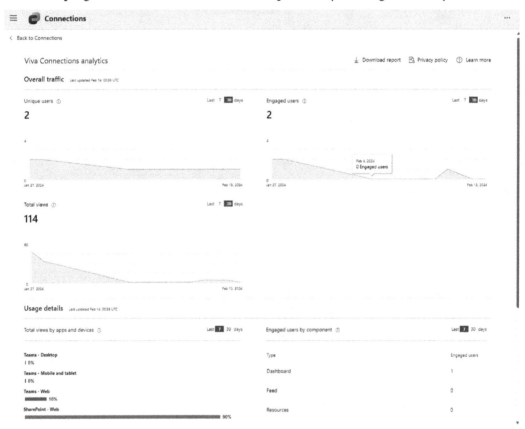

Figure 10.18 - Analytics on Viva Connections

Analytics show overall usage by unique and engaged users, total views, which apps users are using, and how users have engaged on different Viva components and dashboard cards. Analytics can be shown from a seven- or thirty-day period.

Enabling and publishing Viva Connections in Teams

Finally, when needed Viva Connections experiences are configured and targeted, curation of the feed is planned, and all dashboards are configured, the last step is to publish Viva Connections to users in Teams.

Microsoft has preinstalled the Viva Connections application to the Microsoft Teams app catalog. The Viva Connections application supports customization so that organizations can name the app and add descriptions and application logos. Customization is done by opening the **Manage apps** view from the Teams admin center and searching for Viva Connections:

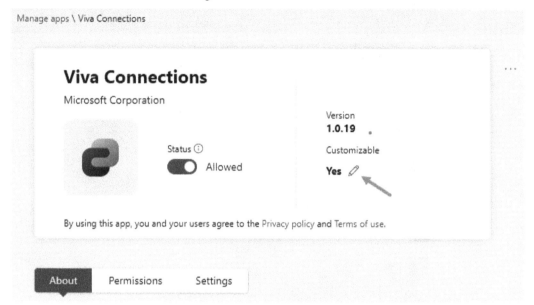

Figure 10.19 - Viva Connections application

Specific settings can be changed on the **Customize** panel. When changing logos, it's important to check the requirements for them, especially the **Outline** icon, whose requirements are quite detailed. When settings are updated, it may take several hours to see the changes on Microsoft Teams.

Publishing the Viva Connections application to the left rail menu on Microsoft Teams is done with Teams apps setup policies.

On the pinned apps section, the Viva Connections app is added and then dragged to the desired location. If the title of the application is changed from the application's settings, that name needs to be used when searching the application.

Making the Viva Connections app the first application on the list is recommended since the user will land on the app when Teams loses its context or when the user is signing in.

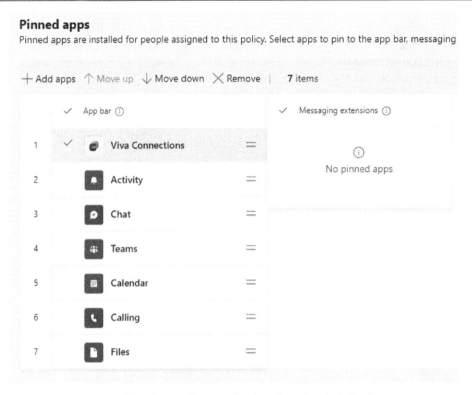

Figure 10.20 - Viva Connections application pinned to the left rail menu

After the changes are saved, it may take up to 24 hours for the application to appear on the user's left rail menu on Teams.

Summary

In this chapter, we learned how Viva Connections can be used to make content from SharePoint available on Microsoft Teams. First, we're introduced to the building blocks of Viva Connections, how Viva Connections is configured, and how organizations can create multiple Viva Connections experiences.

Next, we learned how the Viva Connections feed is generated, what content is displayed to users, and how authors can bring content to the feed.

The next section focused on the Viva Connections dashboard, and how to create content for the dashboard, target the cards, and translate the dashboard.

Finally, we delved into how Viva Connections is published to the left rail menu of Microsoft Teams for users.

In the next chapter, we will learn how to bring customized applications and third-party applications to SharePoint with SharePoint's app catalog and the SharePoint Store.

11

App Catalog and the SharePoint Store

SharePoint has always been an extensible platform that allows it to be customized in various ways over the product's lifetime. Mechanisms for deploying vary, from injecting code directly into SharePoint's HTML code and packaging apps as features to deploying applications through App Catalog. In modern SharePoint, applications and extensions are deployed via App Catalog or installed from the SharePoint Store. The tenant-wide app catalog is a special site created at the tenant level and is used to deploy customized apps and SharePoint store apps for the whole organization. SharePoint also supports site collection app catalogs, which can be enabled on a specific site collection for testing and developing apps or isolating apps for specific use.

The SharePoint Store is a marketplace for third-party application vendors. The store supports SharePoint full-page applications and web parts, but also Teams personal apps and tabs and Viva Connections Dashboard apps. What's common regarding these application types is that they are deployed via App Catalog. When an application is deployed from the SharePoint Store, it is placed in App Catalog and deployed to targets that the application supports. Organizations can also disable the Sharepoint Store or configure a request-and-approval mechanism for apps.

In this chapter, we're going to cover the following main topics:

- App Catalog in SharePoint
- Deploying apps to SharePoint
- Getting third-party apps from the SharePoint Store

App Catalog in SharePoint

The tenant-wide App Catalog can be accessed from the SharePoint admin center by opening **More features** and selecting **Apps**. The SharePoint Administrator or Global Administrator role is needed for the user to manage apps, App Catalog, and SharePoint Store-specific settings. To manage API access, which enables apps to use the Graph API and other Microsoft APIs, only the Global Administrator role is supported:

Figure 11.1 - App Catalog

All deployed apps are listed on the **Manage apps** page, which opens by default when accessing App Catalog. Administrators can see the basic details of apps, which platform the apps are available for, and whether apps can be used. The supported platforms for apps are SharePoint, Teams, and Viva Connections Dashboard.

On the left-hand side, administrators can access app requests, go to the SharePoint Store, and open the **API access management** page. From **More features**, administrators can access tenant-wide extensions settings (which control how extensions are deployed to SharePoint sites), list all app principals (which are used to supply access to SharePoint content), and manage SharePoint store settings.

Administrators can delegate the approval of users' app requests for non-admin role users by supplying site administrator permissions for approvers.

Deploying apps to App Catalog

New applications can be deployed to App Catalog by uploading an application package via the **Manage apps** page:

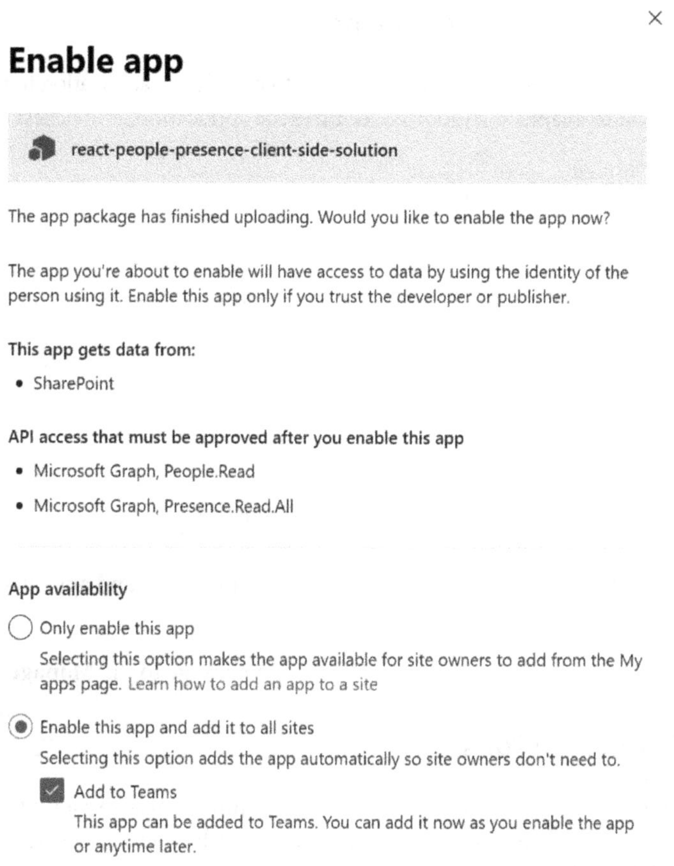

×

Enable app

 react-people-presence-client-side-solution

The app package has finished uploading. Would you like to enable the app now?

The app you're about to enable will have access to data by using the identity of the person using it. Enable this app only if you trust the developer or publisher.

This app gets data from:

- SharePoint

API access that must be approved after you enable this app

- Microsoft Graph, People.Read
- Microsoft Graph, Presence.Read.All

App availability

◯ Only enable this app

   Selecting this option makes the app available for site owners to add from the My apps page. Learn how to add an app to a site

◉ Enable this app and add it to all sites

   Selecting this option adds the app automatically so site owners don't need to.

   ☑ Add to Teams

      This app can be added to Teams. You can add it now as you enable the app or anytime later.

Figure 11.2 - Deploying an app to App Catalog

When an application is uploaded, it also needs to be enabled. Depending on the application's configuration, different settings can be controlled when enabling the application. The **Enable app** panel (*Figure 12.2*) displays where the application is hosted and which API permissions the application requires. The administrator can control the deployment of the application and enable it for all sites automatically or enable the application for site owners to deploy to a specific site. If the application supports deployment to Teams, it can be done at the same time and the application will be available to be used on Teams as well.

App details, settings, and updating apps

When an application is selected, administrators can choose to not add the application to new sites, choose to deploy the application to Teams, if supported, remove the application, and access the app's details:

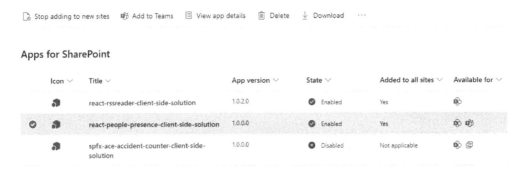

Figure 11.3 - App settings

The **App details** page shows more detailed information about the app, and apps deployed from the SharePoint Store also show user reviews.

You can update a custom app by uploading the updated app package to the **Manage apps** page.

Managing API permissions

If the application requires specific API permissions, the administrator must go to the API access management page during application deployment. Alternatively, they can decide to approve API permissions later from the API access page via the SharePoint admin center. The API access management page displays all the requested and approved API permissions, which application is requesting the permission, and when it was requested:

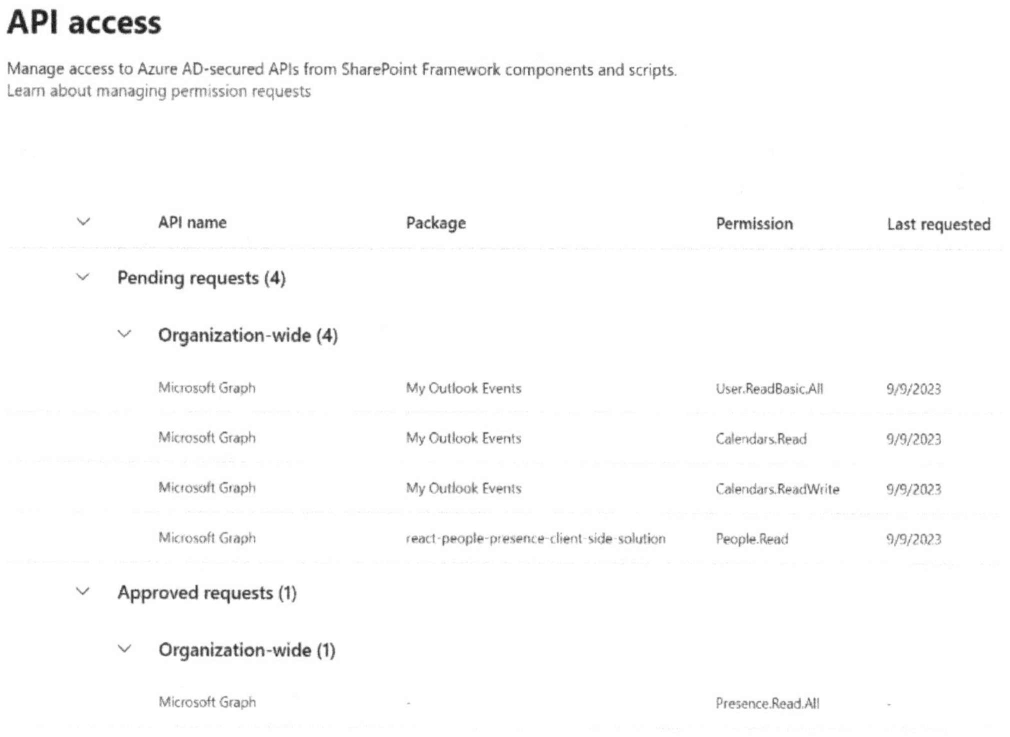

API access

Manage access to Azure AD-secured APIs from SharePoint Framework components and scripts.
Learn about managing permission requests

	API name	Package	Permission	Last requested
⌄	**Pending requests (4)**			
	⌄ Organization-wide (4)			
	Microsoft Graph	My Outlook Events	User.ReadBasic.All	9/9/2023
	Microsoft Graph	My Outlook Events	Calendars.Read	9/9/2023
	Microsoft Graph	My Outlook Events	Calendars.ReadWrite	9/9/2023
	Microsoft Graph	react-people-presence-client-side-solution	People.Read	9/9/2023
⌄	**Approved requests (1)**			
	⌄ Organization-wide (1)			
	Microsoft Graph	-	Presence.Read.All	-

Figure 11.4 - API access management

Note

Refer to the Microsoft Graph API documentation before approving the API permissions for an application to see which data the application has access to. For example, the `Calendar.ReadWrite` Graph API permission allows you to read, create, delete, and change the calendar events of the user who is using the application.

API permissions can also be managed using SharePoint Online Management Shell.

By using the `Get-SPOTenantServicePrincipalPermissionRequests` cmdlet, administrators can list app permission requests:

```
C:\code> Get-SPOTenantServicePrincipalPermissionRequests

Id                   : 52737abe-5ad6-48de-b7e9-12a074618e31
PackageApproverName  : Matti Paukkonen
PackageName          : My Outlook Events
PackageVersion       : 1.2.0.0
```

```
Resource      : Microsoft Graph
Scope         : User.ReadBasic.All
TimeRequested : 9.9.2023 3.41.27
```

Administrators can approve a permission request using `Approve-SPOTenantServicePrinc` `ipalPermissionRequest`, where `RequestId` is the ID of the request:

```
C:\code> Approve-SPOTenantServicePrincipalPermissionRequest -RequestId
52737abe-5ad6-48de-b7e9-12a074618e31
```

Administrators can also approve permissions to applications without a request on the applications package file by using the `Approve-SPOTenantServicePrincipalPermissionGrant` cmdlet. The `Resource` parameter defines which API resource the permission is granted, such as `"Microsoft Graph"`, while `Scope` defines the permission that was requested:

```
Approve-SPOTenantServicePrincipalPermissionGrant -Resource "Microsoft
Graph" -Scope "Mail.Read"
```

The preceding example grants Microsoft's Graph API access to read all users' emails.

> **Note**
>
> After granting this permission, all applications that use this specific permission can use the API without additional approval.

Deploying tenant-wide extensions

SharePoint Framework extensions such as **Application Customizer** and **ListView Command Set** can be deployed to sites using tenant-wide deployment. With tenant-wide deployment options, administrators can deploy extensions to lists or sites based on a list or site template. These settings are controlled in the tenant-wide deployment list via **Apps site**:

Figure 11.5 - Tenant-wide deployment list

Deploying to a specific type of site can be configured by modifying the Web Template property of the list item – for example, adding GROUP#0 to enable the extension for all Microsoft 365 group-connected team sites, including sites that are connected to a Teams team. An example of a Web Template property value for a modern communication site is SITEPAGEPUBLISHING#0. All classic site templates are also supported.

With lists, ListView Command Set is supported for lists that support the modern experience. At the time of writing, the recommended List Template values are 100 for Custom List and 101 for Document Library.

Site collection app catalog

With site collection app catalogs, administrators can decentralize the deployment of apps to specific sites. Site collection app catalogs are useful for development and testing purposes since administrators can delegate the management of apps to site collection administrators. It's also a good way to deploy apps for a limited audience and not affect the whole tenant at the same time. Apps that are deployed to the site collection app catalog are only available via that site collection.

Managing site collection app catalogs

Site collection app catalogs can be created using SharePoint Online Management Shell. A tenant-wide app catalog is required before you can create site collection app catalogs. The user who is creating a new site collection app catalog needs to have site collection administrator permissions to the tenant-wide app catalog and the target site:

```
Add-SPOSiteCollectionAppCatalog -Site https://tenant.sharepoint.com/
sites/hr-site
```

Administrators can see all site collections where the app catalog is enabled by looking at the SiteCollectionAppCatalogs list on the tenant-wide app catalog site:

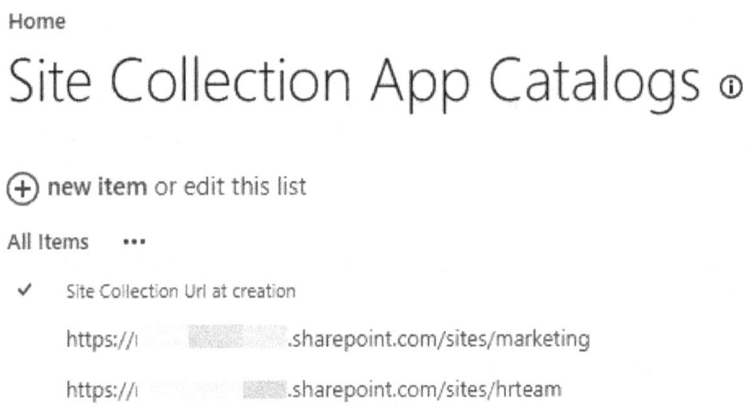

Home

Site Collection App Catalogs ⓘ

(+) **new item** or edit this list

All Items   •••

✓   Site Collection Url at creation

https://ı   .sharepoint.com/sites/marketing

https://ı   .sharepoint.com/sites/hrteam

Figure 11.6 - Site Collection App Catalogs

To disable the app catalog from a specific site, administrators can use this command:

```
Remove-SPOSiteCollectionAppCatalog -Site https:// tenant.sharepoint.
com/sites/hr-site
```

When the app catalog feature is disabled from a site, the Apps for SharePoint library remains, but it cannot be used to deploy apps.

It's crucial to educate users who manage approvals on the tenant-wide app catalog or the site collection app catalogs about the potential access apps may have to other sites and content based on user permissions.

Getting third-party apps from the SharePoint Store

The SharePoint Store is a public marketplace for third-party apps for Microsoft 365, as well as Dynamics 365, Microsoft's cloud platform for **customer relationship management (CRM)**, **enterprise resource planning (ERP)**, finance-related operations, and Power Platform. The SharePoint Store is enabled by default for users to get and request apps. Users can access and browse the SharePoint Store directly from sites:

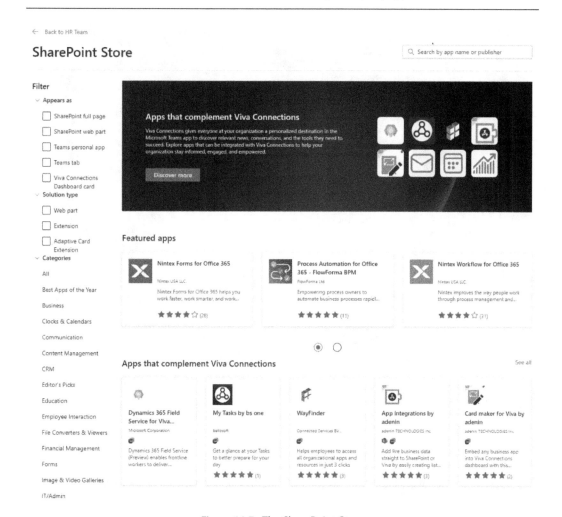

Figure 11.7 - The SharePoint Store

Administrators can control the SharePoint Store's settings on the tenant-wide app catalog by going to the **Configure store settings** page via the **More features** page. When the **App purchases** setting is set to **No**, users can still browse and request apps from the SharePoint Store.

App requests

Users can send app requests from the SharePoint Store underneath a specific app:

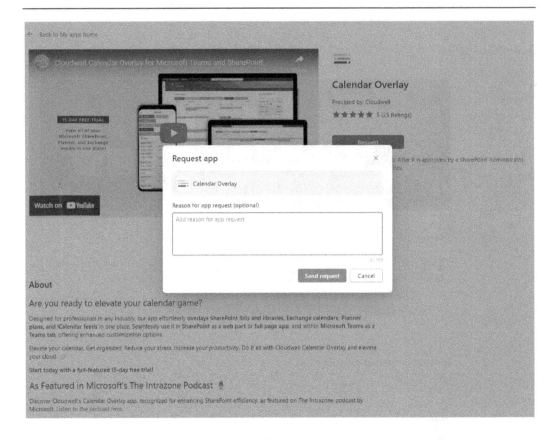

Figure 11.8 - Requesting an app

When a user sends an app request, it's added to the pending requests list on the **Apps site** view. Administrators can access it via the SharePoint admin center's app catalog:

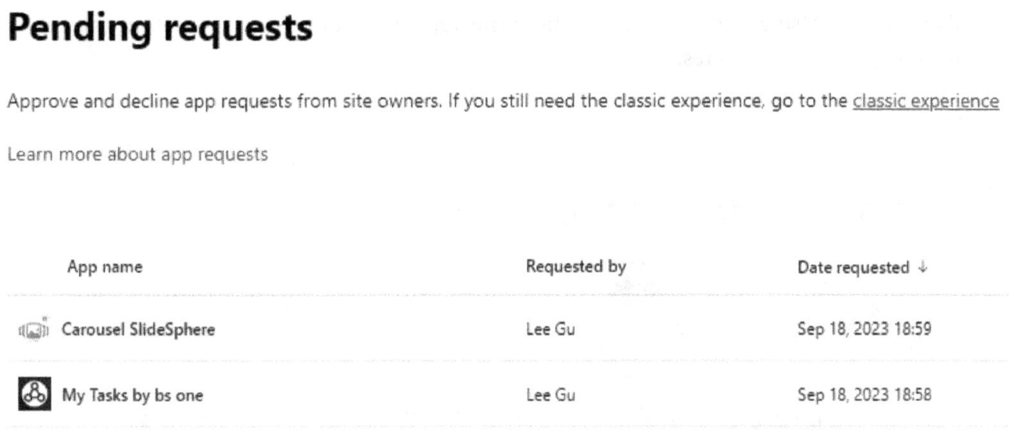

Pending requests

Approve and decline app requests from site owners. If you still need the classic experience, go to the classic experience

Learn more about app requests

App name	Requested by	Date requested ↓
Carousel SlideSphere	Lee Gu	Sep 18, 2023 18:59
My Tasks by bs one	Lee Gu	Sep 18, 2023 18:58

Figure 11.9 - Pending requests list

Administrators can approve or decline the app from the side panel, which can be opened by selecting the app from the list. This panel also displays some basic details regarding the app, ratings, and links to terms and conditions and the privacy policy:

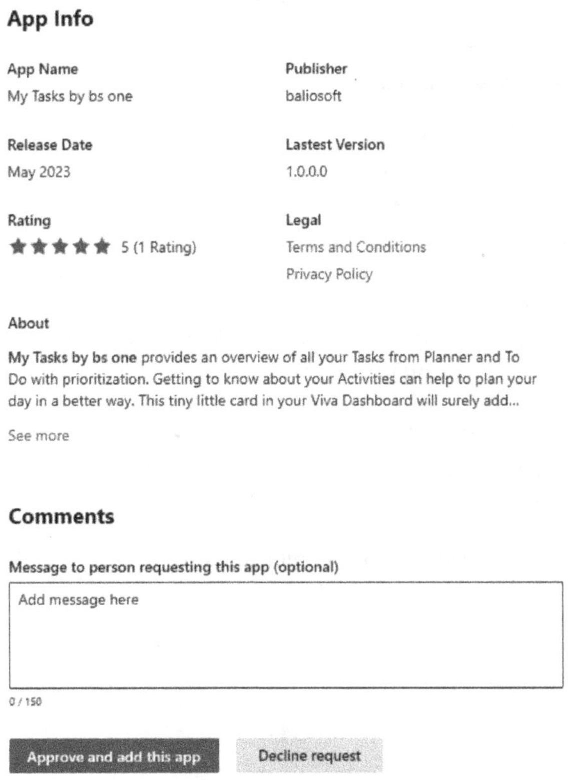

App Info

App Name
My Tasks by bs one

Publisher
baliosoft

Release Date
May 2023

Lastest Version
1.0.0.0

Rating
★★★★★ 5 (1 Rating)

Legal
Terms and Conditions
Privacy Policy

About

My Tasks by bs one provides an overview of all your Tasks from Planner and To Do with prioritization. Getting to know about your Activities can help to plan your day in a better way. This tiny little card in your Viva Dashboard will surely add...

See more

Comments

Message to person requesting this app (optional)

Add message here

0 / 150

Approve and add this app   Decline request

Figure 11.10 - The App Info panel

Administrators are also asked to confirm where the app gets data from and whether the app is automatically installed for all sites:

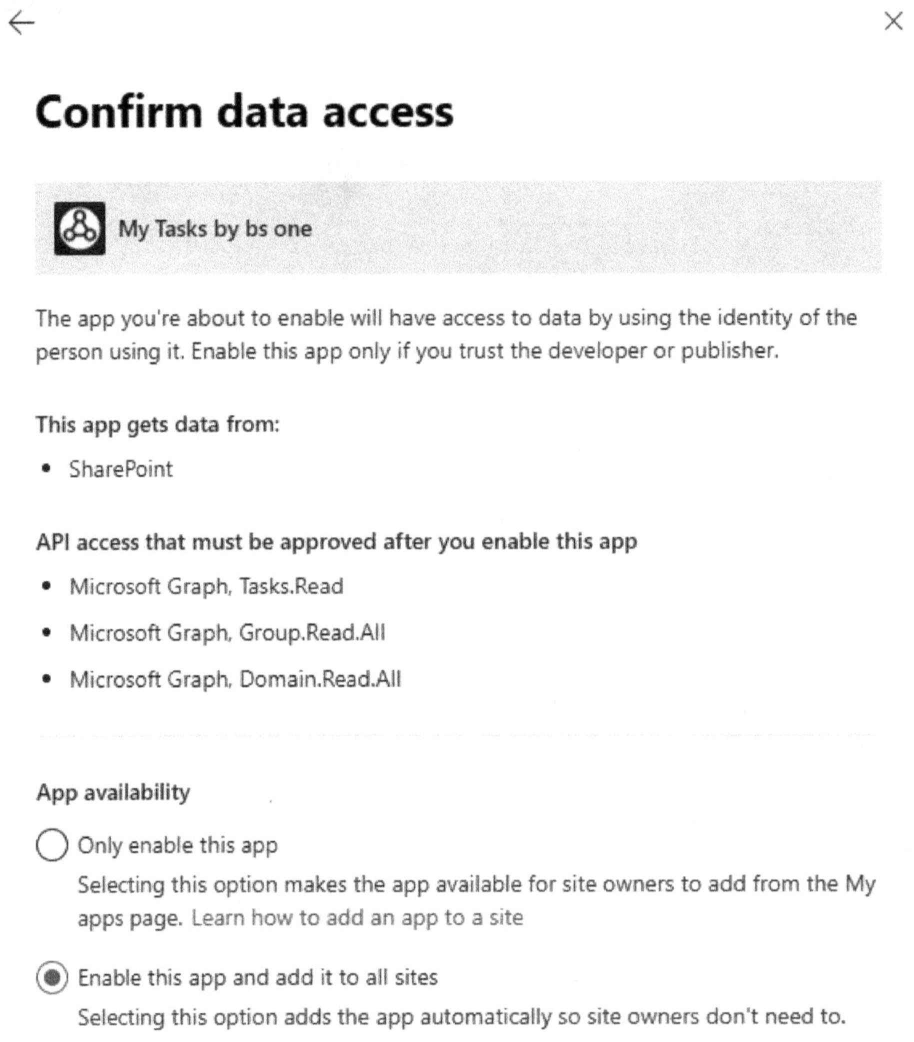

Confirm data access

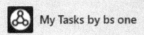 My Tasks by bs one

The app you're about to enable will have access to data by using the identity of the person using it. Enable this app only if you trust the developer or publisher.

This app gets data from:

- SharePoint

API access that must be approved after you enable this app

- Microsoft Graph, Tasks.Read

- Microsoft Graph, Group.Read.All

- Microsoft Graph, Domain.Read.All

App availability

◯ Only enable this app

   Selecting this option makes the app available for site owners to add from the My apps page. Learn how to add an app to a site

◉ Enable this app and add it to all sites

   Selecting this option adds the app automatically so site owners don't need to.

Figure 11.11 - Confirm data access

If the app requires access to a certain API, such as Microsoft Graph, those permissions are approved on the **API access** page.

When the app is approved or declined, the request is moved to the completed requests list, where administrators can see all approved or declined apps.

Before approving new apps, it's good practice to thoroughly read all terms and conditions, as well as private and data handling information. Some apps also need a license, which also needs to be considered. It's also good to check reviews and comments if there are any. Finally, visit the app vendor's website to see more detailed and licensing-related information. There needs to be a process in place for app approvals if you plan to allow third-party apps for users.

Users can check the status of their app requests from the **My request** view on the SharePoint Store. Users are also notified about app approvals and declinations.

Summary

In this chapter, we familiarized ourselves with managing custom and third-party apps in the SharePoint app catalog.

Next, we learned about app permissions and how to approve apps to access data and different APIs.

Finally, we delved into the SharePoint Store and how users can request third-party apps. The importance of the app approval process must be understood before communicating the SharePoint Store's usage to users.

In the next chapter, we will focus on creating automation for SharePoint using Microsoft Power Automate workflows.

Part 3:
Automate and Extend
SharePoint Experiences

In this part, you will learn how to automate and extend SharePoint Online using Power Platform's low-code tools, such as Power Automate and Power Apps. In addition, you will get an overview of how to use site, list, and document templates. You will also learn how to improve list experiences using view and column formatting.

This part has the following chapters:

- *Chapter 12: Automate SharePoint with Power Automate*

- *Chapter 13: Extend SharePoint with Power Apps*

- *Chapter 14: Site, List, and Document Templates*

- *Chapter 15: Improving List Experiences with View Formatting*

12

Automate SharePoint with Power Automate

Microsoft Power Automate is a powerful workflow engine that can automate repetitive tasks, build approval workflows, manage and transfer data, and build notifications and reminders. Power Automate includes triggers and actions for SharePoint Online – for example, starting a workflow when a new document is added to the document library or updating document metadata when certain criteria are met.

Power Automate belongs to the Power Platform product family, including Power Apps, Power Pages, Power BI, and Power Virtual Assistants. Power Platform is commonly stated as a low-code platform or platform for citizen developers to build solutions. Some products, such as Power Automate, Power Apps, and Power Virtual Agents, are included in Microsoft 365 user licenses with limited features and access to data.

Users can use Power Automate to build their own automation including SharePoint – for example, building a simple notification flow when an item in a list is changed. This requires data security consideration since the platform includes dozens of connectors to commonly used cloud services, potentially leading to data leakage.

In this chapter, we're going to cover the following main topics:

- Connecting to SharePoint with Power Automate
- Managing data in SharePoint
- Building approval workflows
- Using SharePoint APIs with Power Automate

Connecting to SharePoint with Power Automate

Power Automate workflows are created and managed on the Power Automate portal, which can be accessed by browsing: `https://make.powerautomate.com`.

Figure 12.1 - Power Automate portal

Creating your first flow

On Power Automate, all automations and workflows are called simply **flows** or **cloud flows**. When creating a new flow, the trigger type needs to be first selected (*Figure 12.1*). The trigger can be changed later if needed. In this book, we will use automated, instant, and scheduled flows, since they are covered in user licenses and are commonly used to manage and use data from SharePoint:

- An automated cloud flow is started on a change, such as when a new list item is added to the SharePoint list.

- An instant cloud flow is triggered manually. This type is used, for example, on SharePoint approvals, since the standard approval flow is manually triggered. This is also useful when developing or testing Power Automate features since flows can be manually started without adding any data to SharePoint.

- Scheduled cloud flows are started based on a set schedule.

Let's build our first flow, which triggers when a new item is added to a SharePoint list, so an automated cloud flow is the correct type.

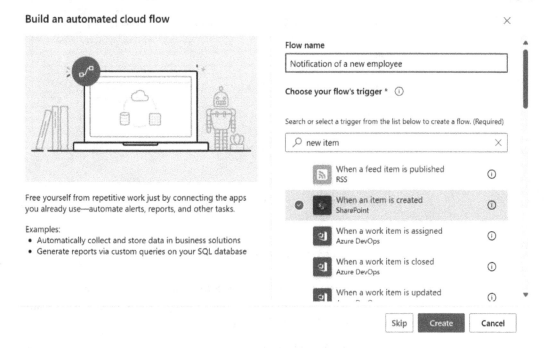

Figure 12.2 - Creating a new flow

Let's give it a descriptive name, select **When an item is created** as a trigger, and click **Create**.

When triggering a cloud flow from an action or change in SharePoint, it's good to notice that the trigger is always connected to a specific site and list; in other words, there are no global triggers when using SharePoint. When working with SharePoint, all triggers, actions, and connectors use a user identity to connect; commonly, that is the identity of the user who created the flow, and that user needs to have access to use the data in the trigger, action, or connector. In this case, the user needs to have access to the **HR Team** site and **Onboarding** list.

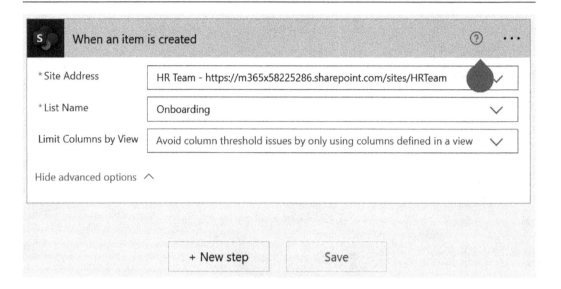

Figure 12.3 - Configuring the trigger

Power Automate offers the sites that the user has access to in the **Site Address** field, and it's also possible to add site addresses manually, especially when working with just recently created sites. When the site is selected, the list can be picked from the list of available lists.

Now the trigger is ready, the next step is to add an action or a connector. Let's add a simple Teams channel notification including the information and link to a newly created list item by selecting **New step** and searching for teams. The goal is to send a message to a channel, so **Post message in a chat or channel** is the correct action in this example case.

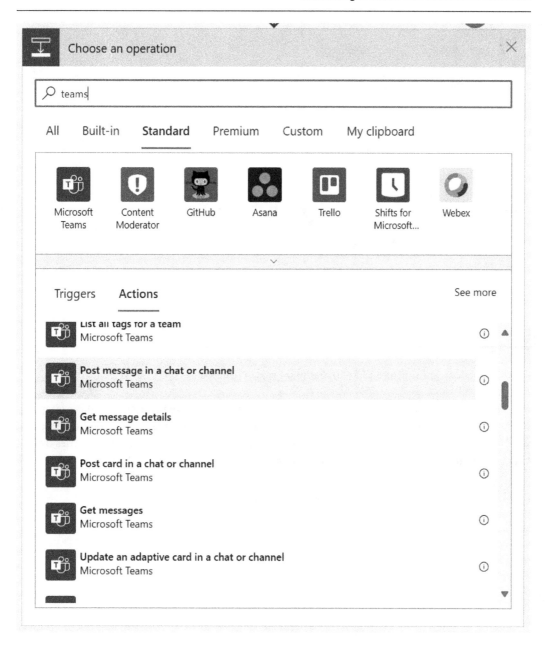

Figure 12.4 - Adding an action

For the action, the method for posting (in this case, as a flow bot) and channel are defined, as shown in *Figure 12.5*.

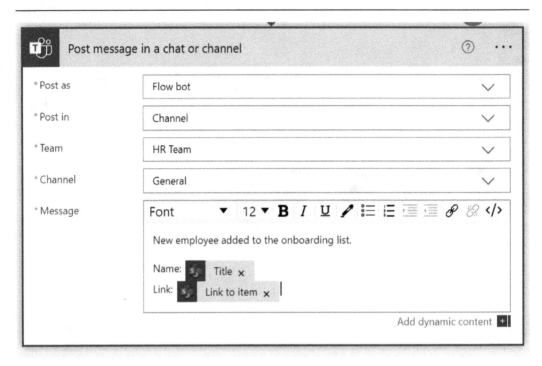

Figure 12.5 - Configuring the action for Teams post

For the **Message** part, it's possible to use data from earlier actions or from the trigger. In this example, the title of the newly created list item and the link to that list item are added as part of the message posted to the Teams channel. The Power Automate Flow editor displays all identified properties from earlier actions and triggers on the **Dynamic content** view, as shown in *Figure 12.6*.

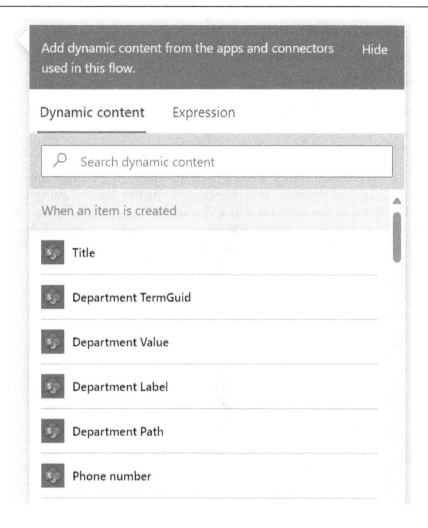

Figure 12.6 - Dynamic content view

Managing SharePoint data with cloud flows

Power Automate actions can be used to do the following:

- Create, read, update, and delete SharePoint list items, attachments, files, and list columns in list and libraries
- Manage permissions
- Manage the sharing of folders, list items, and files
- Join sites to hub sites and manage hub site join requests

- Create approval workflows
- Start Microsoft Syntex document processes
- Call SharePoint's REST APIs

Let's quickly look at how to create a list item when a form is submitted.

Creating a list item

In this example, a flow is created to create a new list item when a form is submitted. The simple form collects the name of a new employee and their phone number, starting date, and manager. Again, the process starts by creating an automated cloud flow. This time the trigger is **When a new response is submitted** on the Microsoft Forms category. When working with Forms, the trigger only returns the unique identifier of the response, so the next action needs to be **Get response details**, where **Form Id** and the dynamic value of **Response Id** are added as parameters, as shown in *Figure 12.7*.

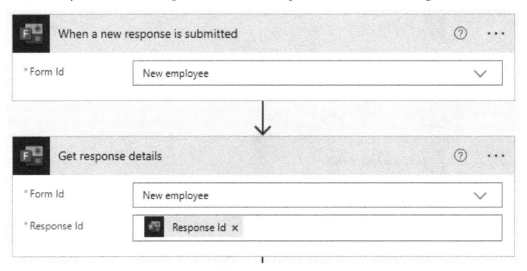

Figure 12.7 - Get response details

The next task is to add an action for creating a new list item to SharePoint; the **Create item** action is used to achieve this. When the site and list are picked, the action displays all available list columns, which can be filled. In this case, we're adding the **First and last name** field from the form to the **Title** column, the **Start date** field to the **Start date** column, and the **Phone number** field to the **Phone number** column. The **Manager Claims** column is filled with the **Responders' Email** field value, which is available on the form when the form is set to require sign-in. Now, the cloud flow can be saved.

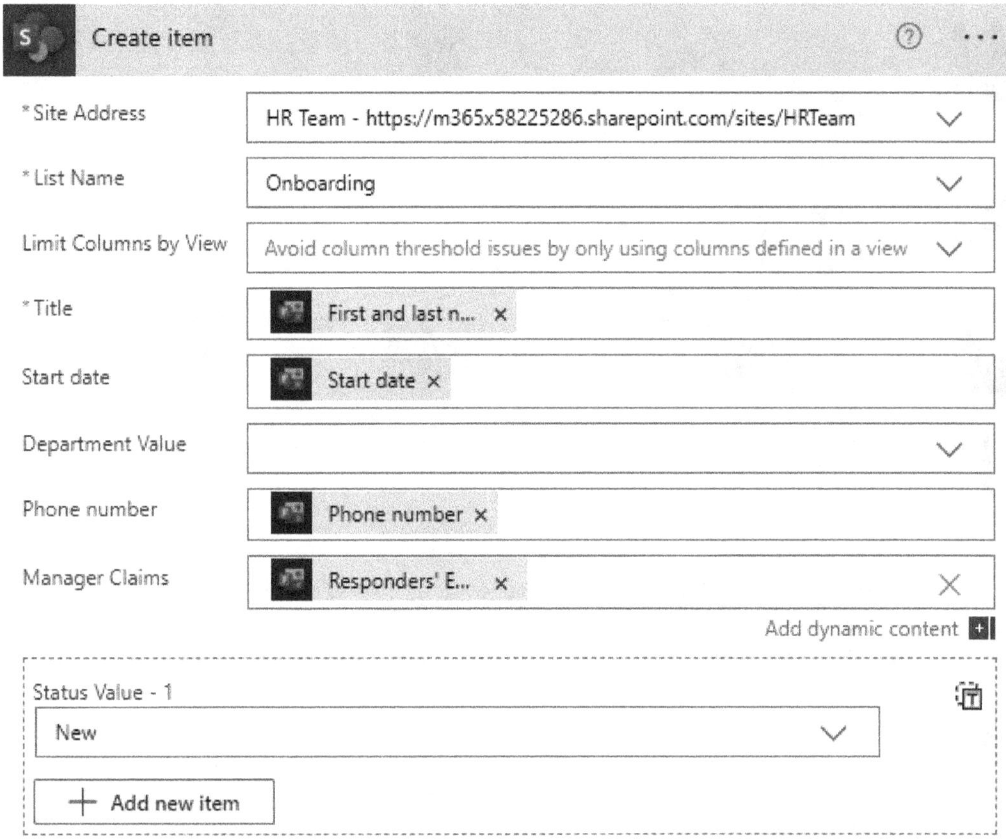

Figure 12.8 - Create item action

Let's fill in the form and see the cloud flow's run history about the progress. The run history displays all runs from the last 28 days. Each run can be opened to see what values were used and to find possible errors. We can see in *Figure 12.9* that the run was successful and the values that were saved to the list item.

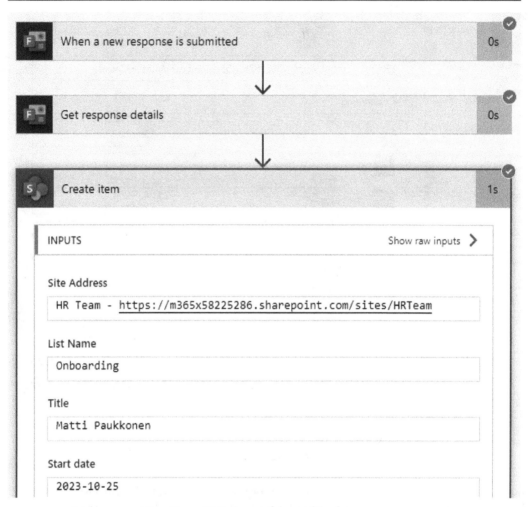

Figure 12.9 - Successful run of the flow

Optimizing data retrieval with filtering, ordering, and limiting

When working with large lists, limiting returned results to just the data needed is best. For example, returning just 10 recently created items with a **Status Value** field value of **New** is much quicker than returning and looping through 500 returned items. The filtering uses **Open Data Protocol** (**OData**) filters, a commonly used and supported mechanism when using RESTful APIs.

Filtering items

Filters can become handy when creating various kinds of review workflows – for example, checking status changes. Let's create a review workflow that checks all new employees from the **Onboarding** lists with a **Status Value** column value of **New**. The type of cloud flow is scheduled this time, and let's schedule it to run every Monday.

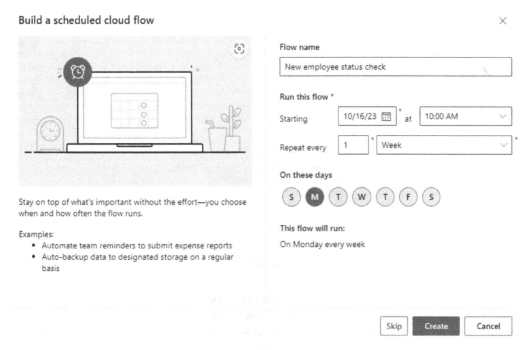

Build a scheduled cloud flow

Flow name

New employee status check

Run this flow *

Starting   10/16/23   at   10:00 AM

Repeat every   1   Week

On these days

S **M** T W T F S

This flow will run:

On Monday every week

Stay on top of what's important without the effort—you choose when and how often the flow runs.

Examples:
- Automate team reminders to submit expense reports
- Auto-backup data to designated storage on a regular basis

Skip   Create   Cancel

Figure 12.10 - Scheduled cloud flow

Let's use the **Get items** SharePoint action to retrieve items, configure the site and the list, and expand the advanced options of the action.

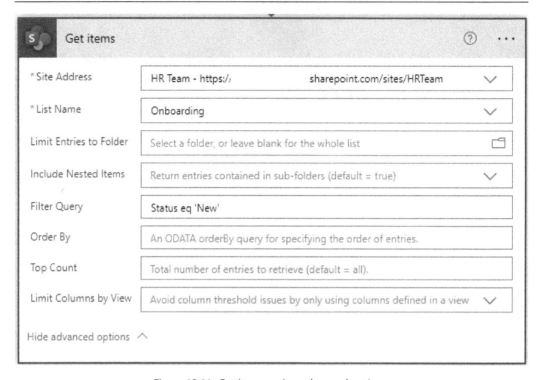

Figure 12.11- Get items action advanced options

Let's add a filter query that only returns items when the **Status Value** column is **New**. In this case, we need to use the eq operation, which compares values as exactly equal. The complete filter query formula is Status eq 'New'. Now, it's simple for all items to send notifications rather than looping all rows and comparing the **Status Value** column value with condition actions.

Let's do another example for notifying of over-week-old list items with the status of **New**. To create a correct date value, expressions are needed. It is recommended to create it using a **Compose** action because if it needs to be changed, only the date calculation part is changed, and the filter query stays intact. The **Compose** action is handy for data transformation and calculations and is more effective than variables.

Figure 12.12 - Creating a date value

To add an expression, select the **Compose** action's **Input** field, and open the **Expression** tab on the dynamic content view. To get a date from a week ago from today, two functions need to be used. The utcNow() function returns the current date and time, and the addDays function can be used to add or reduce days from a specified date and time. In this case, the number of days added needs to be negative. So, the complete expression is addDays(utcNow(),-7). Now, the date is ready and needs to be added to the filter query of the **Get items** action.

Figure 12.13 - Filter query with multiple filters

Filter queries support logical operators such and and or. In this case, we need to use the and operator since the result should be all items with the status of **New**, which were changed over a week ago. The status is filtered with Status eq 'New', as before. The change time is filtered against the **Modified** column, which contains information about when the item was last changed. The filter clause for that is Modified lt '<date>', where lt means *less than*. The date value created on the **Compose** action is added between apostrophes, such as **Outputs** in *Figure 12.13*.

Ordering items

Items can be ordered using column values in either ascending or descending order. Getting the results ordered by when they were created, in the earlier example, is done by using an **Order By** query, Created asc. Sorting items by multiple columns can be done by separating columns with a comma – for example, Status asc, Created desc.

Limiting retrieved items

The number of returned items can be defined using the **Top Count** parameter. This is important to set if more than 100 items need to be retrieved on a single call to SharePoint. The default value is **100**. Remember also that 5,000 items are the list view throttling limit, and this needs to be considered when having large lists.

Approval workflows in SharePoint

Power Automate can create approval workflows for list items, files, and pages. Approvals can be achieved using SharePoint's native content approval feature on lists and libraries or creating simple approvals just using list columns.

List item approval using content approvals

In this example, we'll extend the earlier example by adding a simple approval process by enabling the **Onboarding** list's content approvals, adding an approval action, and finally, updating the **Approval Status** list column. Content approval is enabled from the list's versioning settings, which is explained in more detail in *Chapter 4* of this book. When approvals are enabled, the list items' approval status is **Pending**.

Let's open the cloud flow created earlier in **Edit** mode and add an approval action – in this example, **Start and wait for an approval**. For the approval action, select **First to respond** as the type, add a title for the approval, an email address of the approver in **Assigned to**, and dynamic values from **Create item** action details and item link, as in *Figure 12.14*. **Assigned to** can also be fetched dynamically, for example, from previous actions, another list, or using a manager of the person set as a new employee on the list item.

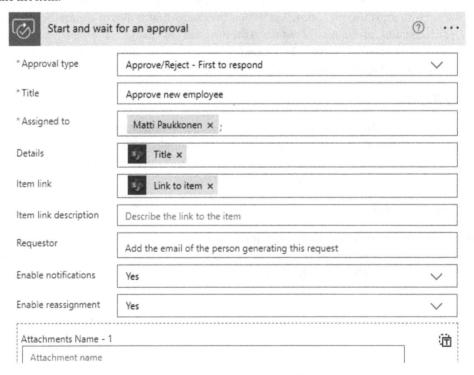

Figure 12.14 - Approval action configuration

The next step is to handle the approval's response using a **Condition** action, which checks the outcome of the approval.

Figure 12.15 - Checking the outcome of the approval

If the outcome equals **Approve**, the condition returns true and continues to the **If yes** section, where the content approval status is set as **Approve**. Notice that the site and the list need to be configured, and the list item's ID is dynamically fetched from the **Create item** action. The site address and list name could be added as variables, if needed in multiple actions.

Creating approvals for SharePoint pages

If approvals are needed for SharePoint pages – for example, in the intranet – they can be created with Power Automate. Approvals can be enabled and a predefined Power Automate cloud flow created directly from the **Site Pages** library from the **Automate** menu by selecting **Power Automate** and **Configure page approval flow**.

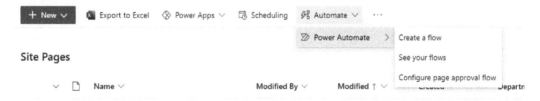

Figure 12.16 - Creating a page approval flow

The actual cloud flow is configured on the side panel. First, the required Power Automate connections need to be set up. Notice that the approval flow is run using the account of the user who created the flow.

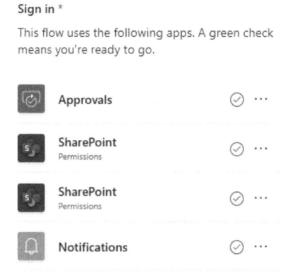

Figure 12.17 - Creating flow connectors

The next step is to give a name to the flow and assign approvers. It's recommended to use descriptive naming so it's easy to find the flow on the Power Automate portal – for example, `Page approval for the HR Team site`. Approvers should be site owners or have full control permissions to the site.

When the content editor next time edits a page, the **Publish** button is replaced by a **Submit for Approval** button.

Let's see what is included in the page approval flow. The approval flow can be edited from the Power Automate portal in the **My flows** section with the account used for approval flow creation.

The trigger of the flow is **For a selected item**. Again, the site address and list are configured with a **Message** input.

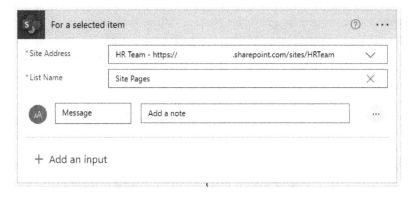

Figure 12.18 - Page approval trigger

The first action retrieves the properties of the page using the **Get file properties** action. The second action in *Figure 13.19* fetches list columns of the page using the **Get file metadata** action with the file identifier returned from the first action. Then, a page is sent for approval with the **Set content approval status** action, and finally, the approval process is started.

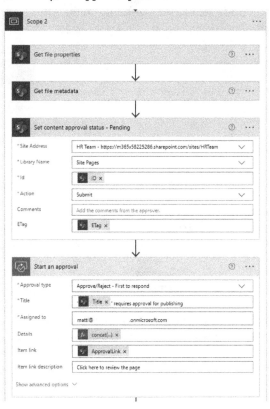

Figure 12.19 - Approval flow actions

Handling the approval status is quite a complex process with several checks of whether the page is published or scheduled and sending email notifications based on statuses. All actions are added inside of a **Scope** element, which is a container for multiple actions and can be used for error handling since it returns the error message of the failed action.

This pre-made page approval flow can be used as a template or a starting point for more complex approval processes and for learning how to handle values returned from different actions.

Working with SharePoint's REST APIs

Power Automate includes the most common function for handling content in SharePoint using pre-made and easily configurable actions, but sometimes it might be needed to automate more advanced scenarios, such as creating sites or managing site-level permissions. These can be achieved using SharePoint's REST APIs or the Microsoft Graph API, which is a unified RESTful API for accessing Microsoft 365 cloud services.

SharePoint REST APIs can be called using the **Send an HTTP request to SharePoint** action. The action takes a site address, HTTP method, and the API's URI as a parameter for making the call to the correct API. **Headers** and **Body** are needed depending on the API called. For example, creating a new modern communication site is configured as in *Figure 13.20*.

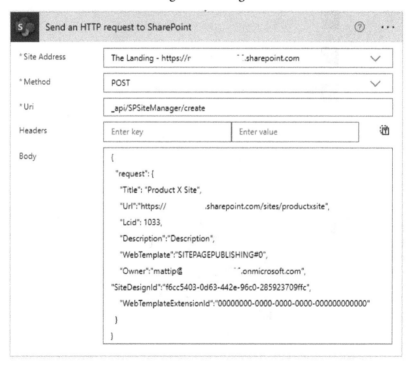

Figure 12.20 - Creating a site with an HTTP call to SharePoint

In the preceding example, the API call is made against the tenant's root site using the `SPSiteManager` API's `create` endpoint. The **Body** section includes the required properties for creating a site.

Using SharePoint REST APIs with Power Automate requires advanced knowledge of SharePoint's API capabilities and structure. When calling SharePoint REST APIs with Power Automate, user permissions need to be considered, as different operations need different permissions to complete.

New Power Automate designer

At the time of writing this book, Microsoft Power Automate designer tools have been updated. Already created automations are still using the earlier designer experience, as seen in the illustrations of this chapter.

In the new designer experience, the authoring canvas can be moved and zoomed more freely. Actions are added and configured on the left side panel.

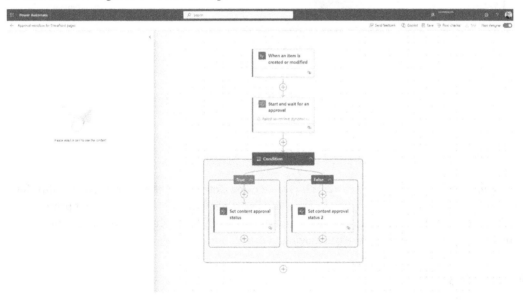

Figure 12.21 - Actions on the left side panel

The new designer also introduces Copilot, an AI assistant, which can be used to create and edit cloud flows using natural language.

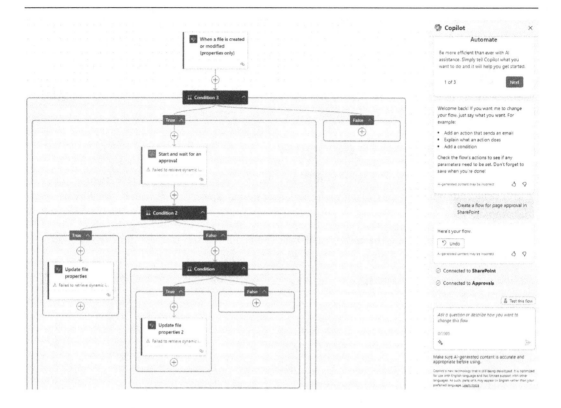

Figure 12.22 - Copilot for cloud flows

For example, the cloud flow in *Figure 12.22* is created using Copilot with the prompt **Create a flow for page approval in SharePoint**. Copilot creates a good starting point for development, but parameters might be missing, or some logic might not be working correctly, so it's always important to check the cloud flow and test it thoroughly before moving to production use.

Summary

Power Automate, as the name states, is a powerful tool to automate operations, create approval workflows for different scenarios, and manipulate SharePoint content. In this chapter, we first learned how to create a Power Automate cloud flow and connect it to SharePoint content.

Next, we were introduced to how Power Automate can manipulate SharePoint content. After that, we briefly delved into filtering, ordering, and limiting data retrieval. Finally, we looked into calling SharePoint REST APIs with Power Automate.

In the next chapter, we will learn how to extend SharePoint list forms, access SharePoint content using Power Apps, and bring Power Apps as a part of SharePoint content.

13

Extend SharePoint with Power Apps

Power Apps is a low-code application platform that allows users to create custom applications for their business requirements. Power Apps is commonly called a citizen-developer platform because of its simplicity, but it still offers various capabilities for building business solutions and accessing business data in various data storages, such as SQL databases or the Microsoft Dataverse platform. It is also a part of the Power Platform product family, which includes Power Automate, Power BI, and Power Virtual Agents.

Power Apps can also be used to extend SharePoint, connect and manage data in SharePoint lists and libraries, and create apps that can be surfaced within SharePoint content. Power Apps are one option to extend SharePoint's list of forms for creating more visual and functional form experiences. A list form created with Power Apps supports all logic operations as with canvas apps, and the editor used is the same.

Power Apps is included in Microsoft 365 licenses and can read and manage data in Microsoft 365 services. Power Apps apps that connect to Microsoft 365 data are created as canvas apps, which can be used to design and build applications just by dragging and dropping elements onto a canvas and writing the logic using Excel-like expressions or PowerFx.

In this chapter, we're going to cover the following main topics:

- Power Apps and SharePoint
- Connecting canvas apps to data in SharePoint
- Customizing list forms with Power Apps
- Limitations and delegation

Power Apps and SharePoint

Power Apps offers an effortless way to extend SharePoint's user experiences and create applications. Sometimes, the default list form functionality is not adequate; for example, it may require custom logic enabling column editing or more complex formulas for generating data that SharePoint offers. With Power Apps, a list form experience can be created as an application – for example, creating a form that allows modifying only specific list column values or filling column values automatically based on data in other Microsoft 365 services or within SharePoint. Another possibility is to create a complete application that uses SharePoint's lists or libraries as a data source but the application's business logic and behavior are built with Power Apps capabilities and formulas.

SharePoint also enables publishing Power Apps apps within modern SharePoint pages, so organizations can also offer important business applications within their intranet or other SharePoint-hosted content. Power Apps apps are added to pages using the **Microsoft PowerApps** web part (*Figure 13.1*):

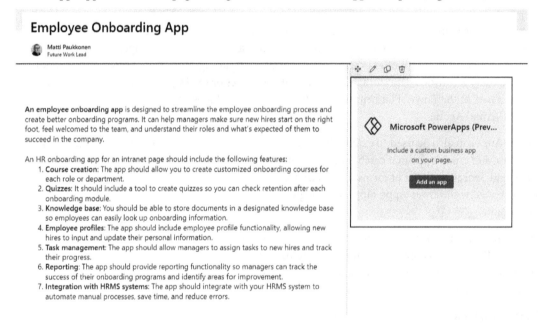

Figure 13.1 - Microsoft PowerApps web part

The application is linked to the web part using the application's web link or ID, which can be found in the Power Apps maker portal.

It's always good to remember that Power Apps connected directly to data in SharePoint are run in the user's context, which means that every operation is run using user permissions, and when something is saved (for example, to a SharePoint list), it's created by the user running the app. By using Power Automate cloud flows integrated into the app, it's possible to impersonate the user and run operations against SharePoint using the flow's permissions. These operations may require separate licenses to the Power Platform.

Connecting canvas apps to SharePoint data

Connecting a canvas app to a SharePoint list is a straightforward process. Let's first create an app in the Power Apps maker portal, which can be accessed at `https://make.powerapps.com`. In the **Create** section, let's pick **Blank app**.

Figure 13.2 - Creating a canvas app

On the next screen, let's create a blank app. The blank app name and format, which define the layout and orientation of the app, need to be picked. The **Tablet** format is a practical choice when building apps that are mainly used with a computer or a tablet and are surfaced directly on Power Apps, on a **Microsoft Teams** tab, or in wide columns in SharePoint pages. The **Phone** layout is a workable possibility when the app is used with mobile devices or, for example, narrow columns in SharePoint pages.

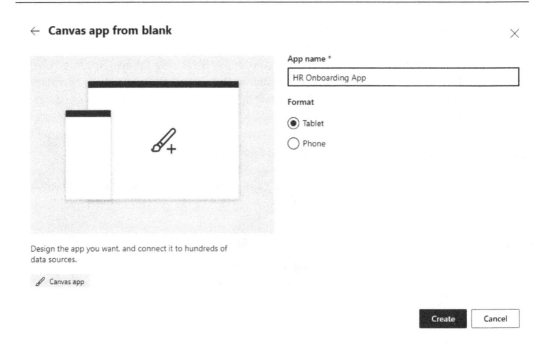

← **Canvas app from blank**   ✕

App name *

HR Onboarding App

Format

⦿ Tablet

◯ Phone

Design the app you want, and connect it to hundreds of
data sources.

🖌 Canvas app

[Create]   [Cancel]

Figure 13.3 - Canvas app layout

Once the new app is created, the Power Apps editor opens, displaying a welcome screen on which
it's possible to select whether to begin with a form or a gallery. The form layout adds a form to the
canvas, which can be connected to a data source and used to gather data. The gallery layout can be
also connected to a data source and used to visualize the data.

Welcome to Power Apps Studio

Here are a few ways to start building an app from a blank
canvas.

Create a form >

Create a gallery >

☐ Don't show me this again   [Skip]

Figure 13.4 - Power Apps Studio welcome screen

Let's skip the predefined components and start with an empty canvas.

Connection to SharePoint is created by opening the **Data** section, selecting **Add data**, and searching for the SharePoint connector (*Figure 13.5*).

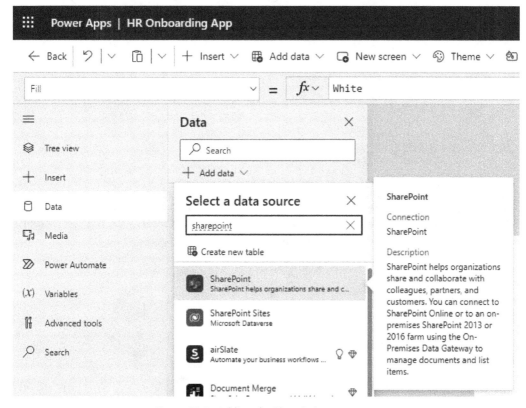

Figure 13.5 - Adding the SharePoint connector

A new connection can be made by connecting directly to cloud services or connecting to on-premises SharePoint using an on-premises data gateway – in this case, the cloud is the correct choice.

Figure 13.6 - Connection type

In the next step, a connection to the SharePoint site where the list or library lives needs to be chosen. The site can be picked by giving a URL or picking the site from the list of recent sites. The user creating the connection needs to have access to the site to be used.

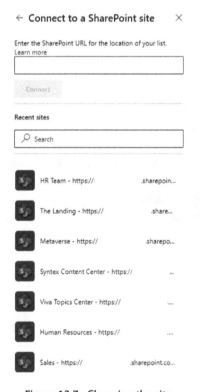

Figure 13.7 - Choosing the site

Next, the list needs to be picked from the list of available lists and libraries on the selected site.

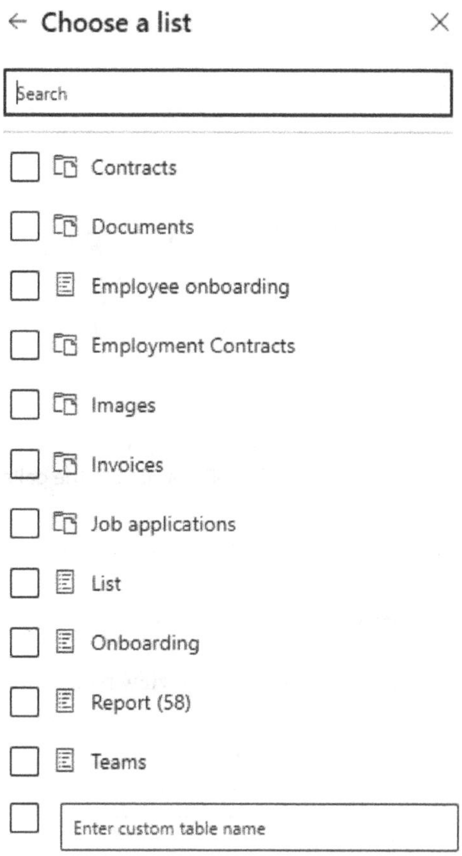

← **Choose a list** ✕

Search	

☐ ⬚ Contracts

☐ ⬚ Documents

☐ ▤ Employee onboarding

☐ ⬚ Employment Contracts

☐ ⬚ Images

☐ ⬚ Invoices

☐ ⬚ Job applications

☐ ▤ List

☐ ▤ Onboarding

☐ ▤ Report (58)

☐ ▤ Teams

☐ Enter custom table name

Figure 13.8 - Selecting the list

When the list is selected, the connection is ready. Let's insert a gallery component into the canvas and connect it to data. First, open the **Insert** section and select **Vertical gallery**. Power Apps automatically places it on the canvas and opens the data source picker with available connections.

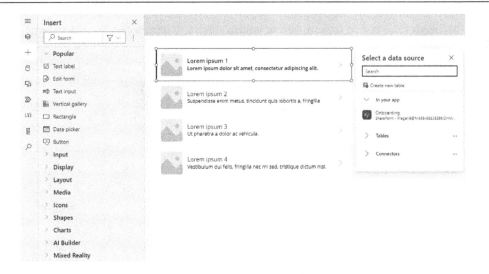

Figure 13.9 - Connecting SharePoint data to the gallery

Now, the gallery is connected and is displaying list items from the selected list.

Working with components

Components displaying the data can be seen on the **Tree view** pane.

Figure 13.10 - Tree view pane

As seen in *Figure 13.10*, some visual components, an image component, and a couple of text components are added automatically to the gallery. These components refer to a single line or element in the gallery component. Displayed content can be edited by selecting the first element in the gallery.

Let's add two text labels for department and manager information. First, select the first element of the gallery and pick the **Text** label from the **Insert** menu.

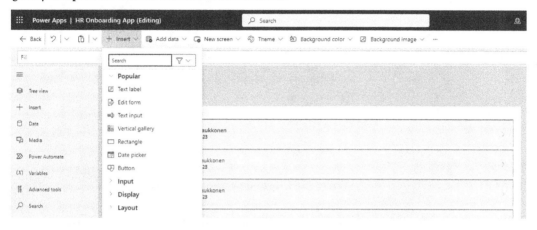

Figure 13.11 - Adding a label to the gallery

The added component appears in the gallery, and it can be dragged and dropped to the correct place and resized if needed. The added component is also linked to a column on the list and, if there is data, it's automatically displayed.

The settings of a component can be managed from the right-hand **Settings** panel when the component is selected. Let's pick the first added label and rename it first to lbl_Department. It's important to have a naming convention for different components so they are easier to find later.

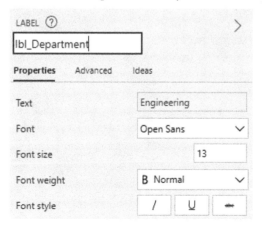

Figure 13.12 - Renaming a component

The next step is to connect it to a correct list column, which is done by updating the **Text** property on the **Advanced** tab. When linking the property to a column value of the list item, the `ThisItem` object is used as a reference. By adding a " . " sign, all available columns are listed. Let's select the **Department** column.

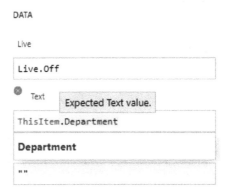

Figure 13.13 - Formula error

The formula referencing the column displays an error (*Figure 13.13*). In this case, the error means that `Department` is not text, and it's because the actual list column type is managed metadata. Let's add another dot at the end and pick the `Label` property, so the complete formula is `ThisItem.Department.Label`. Now the formula is correct, and the value is displayed in the gallery.

Let's create a second label and add information about the manager to it. This time, we want to add the text `"Manager:"` at the beginning and add the manager's name after that. Text can be appended in formulas by using an `&` sign. Since the **Manager** column is typed as the user, the `ThisItem.Manager.DisplayName` formula needs to be used to return the manager's name. So, in this case, the formula is `"Manager: "&ThisItem.Manager.DisplayName`.

Matti Paukkonen **6/22/2023**	Engineering	Manager: Megan Bowen	>
Lee GU 6/29/2023	Consulting	Manager: Megan Bowen	>
Nestor Wilke 7/13/2023	Finance	Manager: Patti Fernandez	>
Test 7/13/2023	Executive Management	Manager: U.S. Sales Members	>
Test 7/13/2023	Consulting	Manager:	>
Matti Paukkonen	IT	Manager: Megan Bowen	>

Figure 13.14 - Gallery with added columns

The design of the app is as important as the data. Each component has settings for colors, borders, fonts, transitions, and sizes. Adding company brandings such as logos, header and footer, and brand colors to the app will make it more familiar to the users and tell them that this application is our company-approved application. It's also important to take care of the accessibility of the application. Each control can also have a formula for conditional formatting.

Using formulas on components

Let's create an example of highlighting a row that doesn't include the contract-signed date. The first thing is to insert a rectangle into the gallery item and make it the same size as the gallery item. A rectangle is needed since we want to refer to an item in a gallery. The rectangle is added on top of other components; it can be sent to the background by using **Reorder** and **Send to back** from the **Tree view** pane.

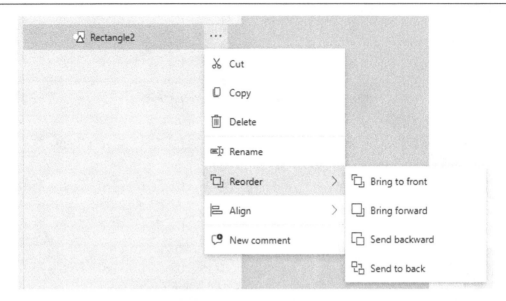

Figure 13.15 - Reordering components

To highlight a row without a contract-signed date added, the **Fill** property of the rectangle needs to include a condition. Select the added `Rectangle` component, select the **Fill** property from the formula bar, and expand the formula editor.

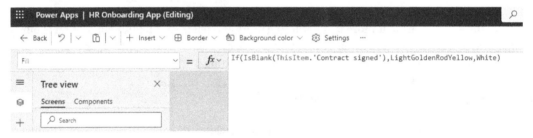

Figure 13.16 - Entering a formula in the Fill property

Enter the following formula code into the formula editor:

```
If(IsBlank(ThisItem.'Contract signed'),Color.
LightGoldenRodYellow,Color.White)
```

The code checks whether the contract-signed column of the item is empty. If it is, it sets the **Fill** color as **LightGoldenRodYellow**; otherwise, it is set as **White**.

Matti Paukkonen **6/22/2023**	Engineering	Manager: Megan Bowen	>
Lee GU 6/29/2023	Consulting	Manager: Megan Bowen	>
Nestor Wilke 7/13/2023	Finance	Manager: Patti Fernandez	>
Test 7/13/2023	Executive Management	Manager: U.S. Sales Members	>
Test 7/13/2023	Consulting	Manager:	>
Matti Paukkonen	IT		>

Figure 13.17 - Gallery with highlighted rows

Customizing SharePoint forms with Power Apps

The customization of SharePoint lists and library forms with Power Apps is a low-code method to create custom business logic and form layouts. When the Power Apps form is enabled, it is used as a default form, and SharePoint forms cannot be accessed. The form type can be controlled from the list or library form settings.

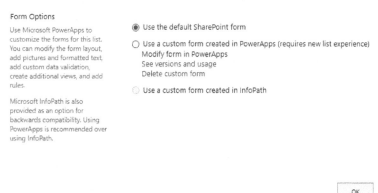

Figure 13.18 - Form Settings

Creating a custom Power Apps form for a list or library starts with the **Integrate** button on the toolbar. Clicking **Customize forms** on the **Power Apps** section opens the Power Apps maker. The created form is already connected to the list or library and includes a default form with an integration, screen, and form component with some pre-added list columns. The integration component controls the data source (which, in this case, is a connected list or library), how different views are connected to forms, and what happens when the form is submitted or canceled. By default, the same form called `SharePointForm1` is linked to all views.

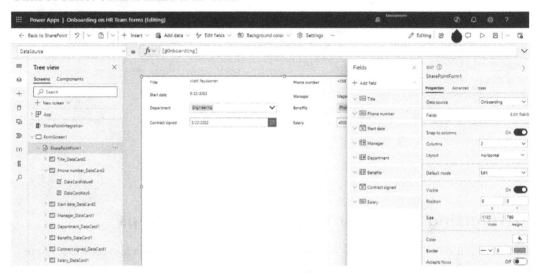

Figure 13.19 - Power Apps form

The form orientation can be chosen from either **Portrait** or **Landscape**. The size of the form can be chosen from predefined sizes or define the size manually. It's a good idea to pick the form size depending on how the list is used. For example, if the list is used mainly with mobile devices, it's a good idea to use a portrait layout and match the size to the screen sizes of used devices.

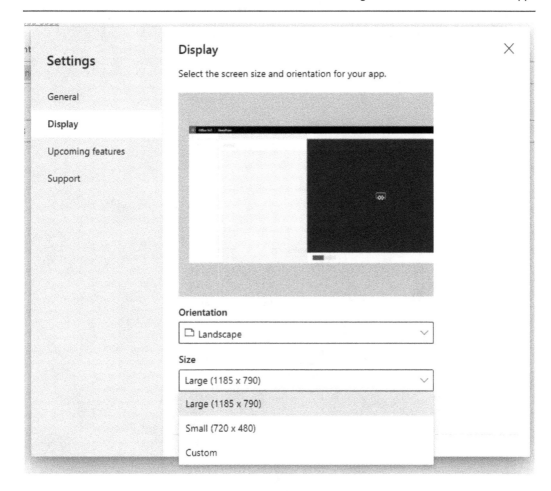

Figure 13.20 - Changing the form layout

Customizing the form

The created form can be customized with available Power Apps components, showing and hiding columns to be available on the **Form** component, adding visual elements and branding, and new form components for different views.

Columns can be added, removed, and sorted from the **Fields** panel. On the form, each column is represented as a **Card** component, which holds components for the column title, value, error message, and star icon to indicate that the column is mandatory. The content and layout of the **Card** component can also be customized. On the **Field** panel, column settings can be viewed, and you can select whether columns should behave as a **View** or **Edit** style. Depending on the column type, different options are available, as in *Figure 13.21*.

Figure 13.21 - Column view settings

Let's customize the form so that basic information such as name, phone number, start date, and manager are displayed; the department, salary, benefits, and contract-signed can be edited; and the layout is landscape.

The first thing is to change the layout from the app settings. Next, let's change the background color of the FormScreen1 component to light gray by selecting the component and changing the **Fill** property. Then, let's make the SharePointForm1 component a little lower to fit a title on top of it and change the **Fill** property to white. Add a text label component on top of the SharePointForm1 component, and add a descriptive title to the form.

The next step is to add fields. Open the field editor from the `SharePointForm1` component properties. Let's set the **Title**, **Phone number**, **Start date**, and **Manager** fields as visible, and change all of these to just **View** values. Next, let's add the **Department**, **Benefits**, **Contract signed**, and **Salary** columns. Finally, choose the layout of the columns as **Horizontal** and in two columns from the `SharePointForm1` component's properties.

> **Note**
>
> Notice that even if the **Title list** column's name was renamed on the list, it's still displayed as **Title** on Power Apps.

The form app can be previewed using the **Play** button in the top-right corner of the editor. The preview now supports testing the app in different device layouts or using custom-size screens for testing.

The app is saved using the **Save** button in the top-right corner, and this should be used when major changes are made during development. **Save** is not yet making it visible for users in SharePoint. Publishing to SharePoint is done with a separate **Publish** button.

The published form appears when an item is clicked on the list or library.

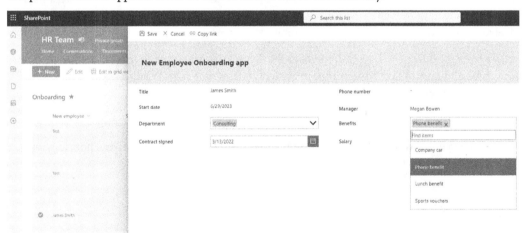

Figure 13.22 - Published custom form

Limitations and delegation

When working with SharePoint lists and libraries with Power Apps, as well as with other data sources, it's important to understand the limitations. By default, Power Apps returns the first 500 data rows from the data source. This limit can be increased to 2,000. Bringing 2,000 items from a SharePoint list to an application might not be generally a good idea. One key target to build efficient applications is to minimize the data retrieved and only bring data that is needed for the application.

For handling larger datasets, Power Apps utilizes a feature called **delegation**. Delegation moves data processing to the data source – for example, filtering the returned dataset to include rows created within two weeks or sorting rows alphabetically by title. Not all connectors and operations support delegation, and it's always important to refer to the data connector's documentation.

SharePoint also supports delegation when used as a data source. Filtering, sorting, sorting by columns, lookups, and basic logical operations are supported for delegation. As an example, let's filter the **Onboarding** list to return only items where the **Contract signed** column is empty and sort the list alphabetically by the **Title** column:

```
Sort(Filter(Onboarding,'Contract signed'=Blank()),Title)
```

Power Apps automatically uses delegation when it's supported, and the developer doesn't need to take care of it. This speeds up the usage of the application since, for example, filtering is not run on the application. Delegation should be always used when available for data retrieval.

Summary

Power Apps enables the creation of applications and extends SharePoint user experiences using simple low-code development tools. In this chapter, we first learned how Power Apps can be used with SharePoint and how Power Apps canvas applications can be surfaced within SharePoint content.

Next, we were introduced to how to connect to the SharePoint data, such as lists and libraries, from Power Apps and how to link basic components with SharePoint data. We also learned how to use formulas in components.

Next, we delved into customizing SharePoint lists and library forms with Power Apps.

In the next chapter, we will learn how to use templates to create new sites and lists and how to publish Office document templates from SharePoint.

14
Site, List, and Document Templates

Sometimes, creating consistent sites with preset settings, lists, site columns, and content types might be required, such as when you're creating sites to manage projects. SharePoint Online provides an out-of-the-box way to create reusable templates for sites. A site template consists of one or more site scripts, which are a set of instructions for creating assets (such as site columns or lists), managing site permissions, and settings (such as external access).

As we have already learned, lists are very useful in SharePoint for storing data. With list templates, these useful lists can be made reusable on different sites.

Distribution of Office document templates to be used in Office applications is possible using SharePoint's document libraries. Templates are centrally managed and they are available for users when creating a new Office document on Word, Excel, or PowerPoint.

In this chapter, we're going to cover the following main topics:

- SharePoint site templates
- What are SharePoint list templates?
- How to centrally publish document templates to users

SharePoint site templates

SharePoint Site templates (previously called **site designs**) can be used to create new sites or modify and extend existing sites with reusable configurations. SharePoint Online includes several predefined templates for communication sites and team sites, and organizations can create custom templates. Built-in site templates can be replaced with an organization's custom template, which applies the custom template during site creation automatically if the template is not chosen.

A site template consists of a title, description, web template, and one or more site scripts.

The web template property indicates which type of site the template can be applied to. The following values are supported:

- **64**: Team site template
- **1**: Team site without a link to the Microsoft 365 group
- **68**: Communication site
- **69**: Channel site

Site scripts are sets of customization actions (such as adding a list) and sub-actions (such as adding a new column to the list). A site script is represented as a JSON script that follows a predefined site script JSON schema. Site scripts are reusable, so they can be linked to multiple site templates at a time. A site script is linked to a site template using the site script's ID, which means that a site script needs to be present when creating a template.

The anatomy of a site script is as follows:

```
{ "$schema": " https://developer.microsoft.com/json-schemas/sp/site-
design-script-actions.schema.json ",
"actions": [
... <site script actions and sub actions> …
 ],
"bindata": { },
"version": 1 }
```

At the time of writing this book, the following actions are supported by on-site scripts:

- Adding content types from the content type hub
- Creating new lists
- Creating site columns
- Creating content types
- Adding and removing navigation links
- Applying a theme
- Setting a site logo
- Joining the site with a hub site
- Installing an add-in or a solution
- Registering an extension
- Activating a feature
- Configuring regional settings

- Adding users and groups to SharePoint groups

- Managing guest access

- Triggering a Power Automate flow

Working with site scripts

Let's look at a couple of examples of using site scripts to create different assets and manage settings.

Example – creating a project list

In this example, we'll create a project list to track project tasks. The list should be named `Project Tasks`, have a description, and `Title`, `Progress`, `Assigned To`, and `Deadline` as list columns:

```
{
    "$schema": "schema.json",
    "actions": [
        {
            "verb": "createSPList",
            "listName": "Project Tasks",
            "templateType": 100,
            "subactions": [
                {
                    "verb": "setDescription",
                    "description": "Project tasks lists."
                },
                {
                    "verb":"addSPField",
                    "fieldType":"User","displayName":"Assigned To","is
Required":false,"id":"10222670-850a-4f97-a888-b98f4601f31b","addToDefa
ultView":true            },
                {
                    "verb":"addSPField","fieldType":"DateTime","displ
ayName":"Deadline","isRequired":false,"id":"b7bf94a1-5f00-489b-87b6-
0710423ca00f","addToDefaultView":true            },
                {

                    "verb": "addSPFieldXml",
                    "schemaXml": "<Field ID=\"{f069d42e-bce3-
4dda-9cbe-91f8529df162}\" Type=\"Choice\" DisplayName=\"Progress\"
Required=\"FALSE\" Format=\"Dropdown\" StaticName=\"Progress\"
Name=\"Progress\"><Default>Not started</Default><CHOICES><CHOICE>Not
started</CHOICE><CHOICE>In progress</CHOICE><CHOICE>Done</CHOICE></
CHOICES></Field>"
                } ]
```

```
        }
    ],
    "bindata": { },
    "version": 1
}
```

In this example, the first action is to create the list with the `createSPList` action. The description for the list is set by the `setDescription` sub-action. The `Assigned To` and `Deadline` columns were added using the `addSPField` sub-action, but the `Progress` column, which is typed as a `Choice` value, was added with the `addSPFieldXml` sub-action. That's because the `addSPField` action only supports creating Text, Note, Number, Boolean, User, or DateTime typed columns. The `addSPFieldXml` action uses **Collaborative Application Markup Language** (**CAML**), which is an XML-based language that's used in SharePoint to define different assets, such as site columns and list views.

> **Note**
>
> It's important to generate the ID to column definitions as this helps you avoid creating duplicate columns if the site script is run multiple times.

In this example, columns are added as list columns and can only be used on the created list. Another way is to create them as site columns and then add them to the list. A site column can be created with an action, like so:

```
{ "verb": "createSiteColumn", "fieldType": "User", "internalName":
"Assigned To", "displayName": "Assigned To", "isRequired": false,
"id": "10222670-850a-4f97-a888-b98f4601f31b " }
```

This can also be done by using a CAML definition:

```
{    "verb": "addSPFieldXml",
    "schemaXml": "<Field ID=\"{f069d42e-bce3-4dda-9cbe-
91f8529df162}\" Type=\"Choice\" DisplayName=\"Progress\"
Required=\"FALSE\" Format=\"Dropdown\" StaticName=\"Progress\"
Name=\"Progress\"><Default>Not started</Default><CHOICES><CHOICE>Not
started</CHOICE><CHOICE>In progress</CHOICE><CHOICE>Done</CHOICE></
CHOICES></Field>" }
```

A site column is referenced with its internal name when it's added to the list:

```
{ "verb": "addSiteColumn", "internalName": "AssignedTo",
"addToDefaultView": true }
```

Example – a collaboration site with external access enabled

In this example, we'll create a collaboration site with external access enabled, a specific Microsoft 365 group as an owner, and navigation links to the project tasks list and partner portal, at which point we'll join a hub site:

```
{
    "$schema": "schema.json",
    "actions": [
            { "verb": "addPrincipalToSPGroup",
              "principal": pmo-team@tenant.onmicrosoft.com,
"group": "Owners"
},
{ "verb": "setSiteExternalSharingCapability",
"capability": "ExistingExternalUserSharingOnly" },
{"verb": "addNavLink",
"url": "/Project Tasks",
"displayName": "Project Tasks",
"isWebRelative": true },
{
"verb": "addNavLink",
"url": https://tenant.sharepoint.com/sites/PartnerPortal,
"displayName": "Partner Portal",
"isWebRelative": false
},
{"verb": "joinHubSite",
"hubSiteId": "2cde617a-bbda-4111-b0b2-35a71e838a3d"}'
],
"bindata": { },
"version": 1
}
```

The addPrincipalToSPGroup action adds a Microsoft 365 group, whose identity is pmo-team@tenant.onmicrosoft.com, to the Owners SharePoint group. The setExternalSharingCapability action enables external access for existing guest users in the Microsoft Entra ID. The possible choices are as follows:

- **Disabled**: External access is disabled

- **ExistingExternalUserSharingOnly**: Guest access is allowed for accounts that have already been invited to Microsoft Entra ID

- **ExternalUserSharingOnly**: New and existing guest accounts

- **ExternalUserAndGuestSharing**: New and existing guest accounts, and support for sharing with anonymous links

`AddNavLink` actions add two navigation links to the site's navigation. The first link uses the web's relative address, as indicated by the `isWebRelative` parameter. The second link is a full URL to a SharePoint site. Here, the `isWebRelative` parameter is set to `false`. The `addNavLink` action can be used to add navigation links to the hub site's navigation. This can be done by setting the `navComponent` parameter to `hub` and the footer of the site's `navComponent` parameter to `Footer`. If the URL parameter is empty, a header is created for navigation. Sub-links can be created in the same way, except you must add a `parentDisplayName` parameter.

Finally, the `joinHubSite` action links the site to a hub site using the hub site's ID.

Creating site scripts

Site scripts can be created using SharePoint Online Management Shell. It's also possible to create and manage site scripts using PnP PowerShell, a community-driven solution for managing Microsoft 365.

A site script can be created using the `Add-SPOSiteScript` cmdlet of SharePoint Online Management Shell. Script JSON can be added as inline code when calling the cmdlet, but it's better to read the JSON from a file to a variable, as shown here:

```
$sitescript = Get-Content 'script.json' -Raw –Encoding UTF8
Add-SPOSiteScript -Title "Project Tasks List" -Description "Create a
Project Tasks List" -Content $sitescript
```

Running this command returns the details of the created site script, including the ID needed to link the script to a site template:

```
RunspaceId          : 5c776e57-fafa-45a9-b14d-4ce27563555a
Id                  : a72d68a1-b0e4-4bf5-b188-a1d5ef599d72
Title               : Project Tasks List
Description         : Project Tasks List
Content             :
Version             : 0
IsSiteScriptPackage : False
```

Figure 14.1 - Creating a site script object

Let's create a site script for the partner site configuration:

```
Add-SPOSiteScript –Title "Partner Site" -Description "Partner Site
Settings" –Content $sitescript
```

Already created site scripts can be listed – for example, to retrieve IDs for site template linking – using the `Get-SPOSiteScript` cmdlet:

```
PS C:\> Get-SPOSiteScript

RunspaceId          : 5c776e57-fafa-45a9-b14d-4ce27563555a
Id                  : a72d68a1-b0e4-4bf5-b188-a1d5ef599d72
Title               : Project Tasks List
Description         : Project Tasks List
Content             :
Version             : 1
IsSiteScriptPackage : False

RunspaceId          : 5c776e57-fafa-45a9-b14d-4ce27563555a
Id                  : 59d6bb7d-71ff-4e2b-9737-501321fa7653
Title               : Partner Site
Description         : Partner Site Settings
Content             :
Version             : 1
IsSiteScriptPackage : False
```

Figure 14.2 - Listing the available site scripts

Site scripts can be removed using the `Remove-SPOSiteScript` cmdlet using the script's ID as the `Identity` parameter:

```
Remove-SPOSiteScript –Identity a72d68a1-b0e4-4bf5-b188-a1d5ef599d72
```

Triggering Power Automate cloud flows from a site script

As we learned in *Chapter 12*, Power Automate cloud flows are a powerful way to modify SharePoint, but also create notification workflows and gather information.

> **Note**
>
> Triggering a flow from a site script is done by calling Power Automate's HTTP trigger, which is a premium trigger and requires a premium Power Automate or Power App license for running the cloud flow.

The Power Automate cloud flow needs to be created first using the HTTP trigger. When the trigger is created, it will provide a trigger URL, which is then added to the `triggerFlow` action:

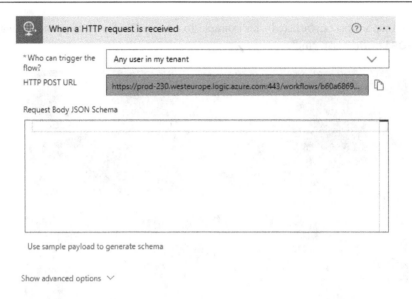

Figure 14.3 - Power Automate request trigger

```
{ "verb": "triggerFlow",
"url": "[https://prod-230.westeurope.logic.azure.com:443/
workflows...",
"name": "Create a partner site", "parameters": { "event": "site
creation", "product": "SharePoint Online" } }
```

The site script can include parameters to the call of the cloud flow, and included parameters can used within the flow. For example, when applying the site template to a site and continuing the configuration of the site using the cloud flow, the site's URL can be passed to the flow. It's also possible to include the name and email of the person who created the site, as well as the time when the site was created.

Creating a site template from the existing site

A site script can be created from an existing site using the Get-SPOSiteScriptFromWeb cmdlet:

```
$extractedTemplate = get-SPOSiteScriptFromWeb -WebUrl https://tenant.
sharepoint.com/sites/templatesite -IncludeBranding -IncludeTheme
-IncludeRegionalSettings -IncludeSiteExternalSharingCapability
-IncludeLinksToExportedItems -IncludedLists ("Shared%20Documents",
"Lists/Project%20Tasks")
```

Optional parameters can be used to define which assets and settings are included in the exported template. The cmdlet returns a JSON script that can be used as content when creating a new site script.

This method is useful when you're creating complex site templates, especially when complex lists such as site or list columns, content types, and views are included. It's also a good way to create the first site script template to start from.

Creating and applying site templates

Now that we have created two site scripts to add a project list and manage the settings of a partner site, we can create a site template:

```
Add-SPOSiteDesign -Title "Partner Project Site" -Description
"Partner Project Site Template" -SiteScripts a72d68a1-b0e4-4bf5-b188-
a1d5ef599d72,59d6bb7d-71ff-4e2b-9737-501321fa7653 -WebTemplate 64 -
ThumbnailUrl https://tenant.sharepoint.com/siteassets/site.jpg
```

Site scripts are linked to the template with the `SiteScripts` parameter using site script IDs separated by a comma. `WebTemplate` is `64`, which means that a team site with a Microsoft 365 group is created. `ThumbnailUrl` refers to an image that is displayed on the site creation dialog.

When the template is created, it's visible on the **From your organization** tab on the site creation dialog after the template is selected:

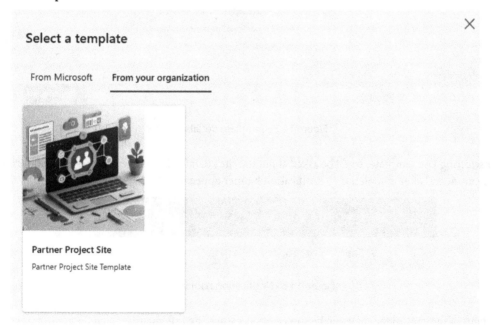

Figure 14.4 - Custom template on site creation

When the template is chosen, it displays a list of actions that are executed during site creation:

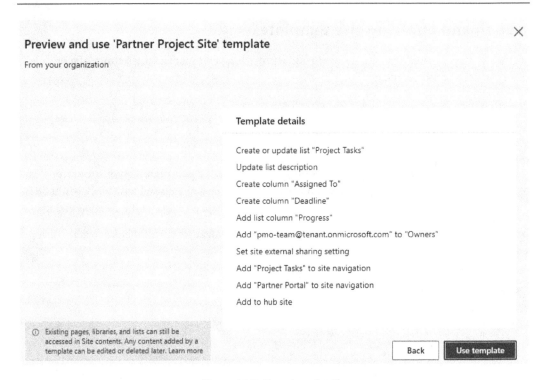

Figure 14.5 - Template details

After selecting **Use template**, you'll be asked about the site's details. The site template is applied during site creation, and after completion, a notification banner appears at the top of the site:

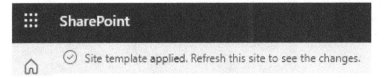

Figure 14.6 - Notification banner

The status of the applied template can be shown by accessing **Site information** from the settings menu, selecting **View template history**, and choosing the applied template from the list:

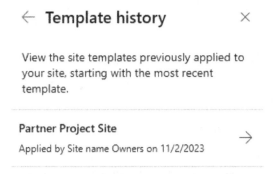

Figure 14.7 - History of applied templates

Selecting the applied template shows the status of all applied actions. As *Figure 14.8.* shows, there will be some errors during the run:

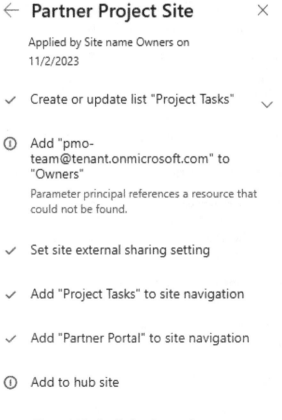

Figure 14.8 - Applied actions and statuses

It's a good idea to do test runs before publishing your templates. Site scripts are checked against the site script schema during creation, but actual values such as IDs might be wrong. In this case, fixing the template requires changing the mistaken site script, which can be updated using the `Set-SPOSiteScript` cmdlet, and updating the JSON script using the `Content` parameter, as shown here:

```
Set-SPOSiteScript -Identity 59d6bb7d-71ff-4e2b-9737-501321fa7653 -
Content $updatedScript
```

With this method, the site script is updated to all linked site templates.

You can apply a site template to an existing site by clicking the **Apply a template** link in the **Site Settings** menu; this displays the same template picker dialog that's displayed during site creation. A site template can also be applied multiple times, such as when site scripts are changed. It's also possible to apply multiple templates to the same site but keep in mind that the latest will always overrun the assets and settings of previously applied templates.

Changing the default site template

A custom site template can be changed to the default site template that's offered when a site is created. This can be done when a site template is created by adding the `IsDefault` parameter to the script:

```
Add-SPOSiteDesign -Title "Partner Project Site" -Description
"Partner Project Site Template" -SiteScripts a72d68a1-b0e4-4bf5-
b188-a1d5ef599d72,59d6bb7d-71ff-4e2b-9737-501321fa7653 -WebTemplate
68 -ThumbnailUrl https://tenant.sharepoint.com/siteassets/site.jpg
-IsDefault
```

Be aware that the original default site template can only be restored by removing the custom template.

Scoping custom site templates

The visibility of site designs can be scoped to a set of users or a group. The scoped template will only be available for specified users and groups. The scope is defined using the `Grant-SPOSiteDesignRights` cmdlet, where `Identity` is the ID of the site design, `Principals` is the target users and groups separated by a comma, and `Rights` is always set to `View`:

```
Grant-SPOSiteDesignRights -Identity 0cadb35a-df27-41cd-9fa3-
adf5dd6e8263 -Principals pmo-team@tenant.onmicrosoft.com -Rights View
```

Limiting the visibility of site templates might come in handy when the creation of externally shared sites needs to be controlled or subsidiary-themed sites are created using templates, for example.

Managing built-in templates

Built-in site templates can be hidden from users using SharePoint Online Management Shell. Hiding built-in templates comes in handy when an organization wants to use specific custom site templates or an organization's customized default template for new sites. This setting also hides templates from the site's **Apply a site template** view.

Hiding a specific built-in template can be done with `Set-SPOBuiltInSiteTemplateSettings` command. The template is a reference that specifies the template's ID and can be found in Microsoft's documentation:

```
Set-SPOBuiltInSiteTemplateSettings -Identity "73495f08-0140-499b-8927-
dd26a546f26a" -IsHidden $true
```

To hide all built-in templates, use the following code:

```
Set-SPOBuiltInSiteTemplateSettings -Identity "00000000-0000-0000-0000-
000000000000" -IsHidden $true
```

Built-in site template settings can be checked using the following command:

```
Get-SPOBuiltInSiteTemplateSettings
```

What are SharePoint list templates?

List templates are a way to create consistent lists for unique needs. Microsoft provides several ready-made list templates for most common use cases and can be used when you're creating lists on SharePoint sites, Teams channels, or the Microsoft Lists app:

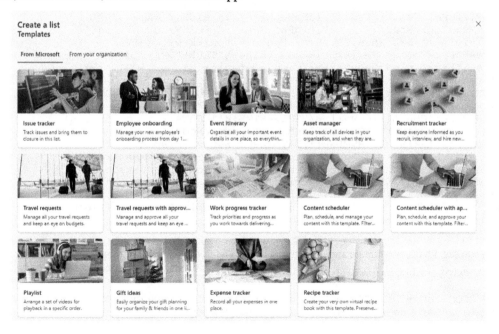

Figure 14.9 - Microsoft-provided list templates

Organizations can also create and publish their own list templates. The basic idea of list templates is the same as in site templates. List columns, content types, views, and so on are defined in a similar JSON script and schema as site scripts. For a list template, only one script is linked since it holds the whole list definition.

Creating a list template

Creating a list template starts by creating and configuring a list, which is then used as a template. The next step is to extract the script from the created list using the `Get-SPOSiteScriptFromList` cmdlet:

```
$extractedList = Get-SPOSiteScriptFromList -ListUrl https://tenant.
sharepoint.com/sites/HRTeam/Lists/Project%20Task%20Tracker
```

At the time of writing, this is the recommended way to create a list template. The script that is exported can be close to 100 lines of code, even when creating a fairly simple list with just a few list columns. All columns and column settings are defined using XML schema, which is fairly complicated to create from scratch. Here's an example of how to create a choice column:

```
{ "verb": "addSPFieldXml",
"schemaXml": "<Field ID=\"{82642ec8-ef9b-478f-acf9-31f7d45fbc31}\"
DisplayName=\"Title\" Description=\"\" Name=\"LinkTitle\"
SourceID=\"http://schemas.microsoft.com/sharepoint/v3\"
StaticName=\"LinkTitle\" Type=\"Computed\" ReadOnly=\"TRUE\"
FromBaseType=\"TRUE\" Width=\"150\" DisplayNameSrcField=\"Title\"
Sealed=\"FALSE\"><FieldRefs><FieldRef Name=\"Title\"
/><FieldRef Name=\"LinkTitleNoMenu\" /><FieldRef Name=\"_
EditMenuTableStart2\" /><FieldRef Name=\"_EditMenuTableEnd\"
/></FieldRefs><DisplayPattern><FieldSwitch><Expr><GetVar
Name=\"FreeForm\" /></Expr><Case Value=\"TRUE\"><Field
Name=\"LinkTitleNoMenu\" /></Case><Default><HTML><![CDATA[<div
class=\"ms-vb itx\" onmouseover=\"OnItem(this)\"
CTXName=\"ctx\"]]></HTML><Field Name=\"_EditMenuTableStart2\"
/><HTML><![CDATA[\">]]></HTML><Field Name=\"LinkTitleNoMenu\"
/><HTML><![CDATA[</div>]]></HTML><HTML><![CDATA[<div class=\"s4-
ctx\" onmouseover=\"OnChildItem(this.parentNode); return
false;\">]]></HTML><HTML><![CDATA[<span> </span>]]></
HTML><HTML><![CDATA[<a onfocus=\"OnChildItem(this.parentNode.
parentNode); return false;\" onclick=\"PopMenuFromChevron(event);
return false;\" href=\"javascript:;\" title=\"Open Menu\"></a>]]></
HTML><HTML><![CDATA[<span> </span>]]></HTML><HTML><![CDATA[</
div>]]></HTML></Default></FieldSwitch></DisplayPattern></Field>"
        }
```

As you can see, it's faster to create and configure a list and fetch the script from that. Once the script has been extracted, the first step is to create a site script, similar to what we created for the site templates:

```
Add-SPOSiteScript -TItle "Project Tracker List" -Description "List
template for project tracker" -Content $extractedList
```

After the list script has been added, the list template can be created:

```
Add-SPOListDesign -Title "Project Tracker List" -Description "List
for tracking project tasks" -SiteScripts <script id> -ListColor
Red -ListIcon CubeShape -Thumbnail https://tenant.sharepoint.
com/siteassets/list.jpg -TemplateFeatures "Project tasks","Task
status","Deadline"
```

At the time of writing, the `ListColor` parameter supports `DarkRed`, `Red`, `Orange`, `Green`, `DarkGreen`, `Teal`, `Blue`, `NavyBlue`, `BluePurple`, `DarkBlue`, `Lavender`, and `Pink` as color values.

`ListIcon` also supports the `Bug`, `Calendar`, `BullseyeTarget`, `ClipboardList`, `Airplane`, `Rocket`, `Color`, `Insights`, `CubeShape`, `TestBeakerSolid`, `Robot`, and `Savings` icons.

`TemplateFeatures` can used to describe the functionality of the list. The list is displayed as a bulleted list on the list preview dialog.

> **Note**
> List templates cannot be updated after creation. The only way to do this is to remove the template and recreate it.

The **Create a list** template is visible on the list creation dialog on the **From your organization** tab:

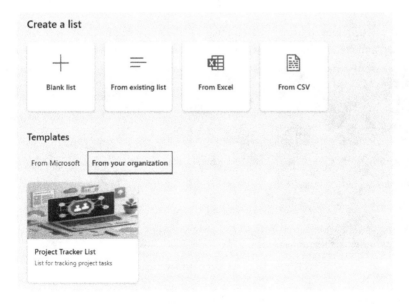

Figure 14.10 - List template

The set color, icon, and template can be found in the list preview dialog:

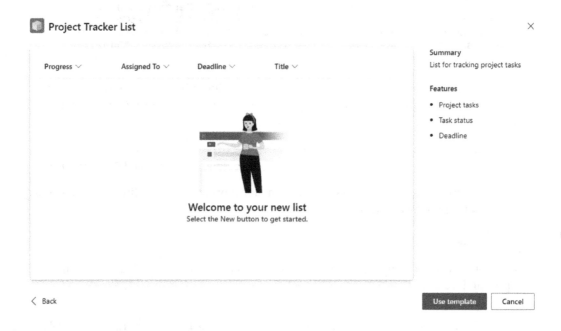

Figure 14.11 - Preview of the custom list

The list template can be removed using the Remove-SPOListDesign cmdlet with the list template ID specified as a parameter. All list templates can be listed using the Get-SPOListDesign cmdlet:

```
PS C:\> Get-SPOListDesign

RunspaceId       : 25530251-c9aa-48a4-b6bd-5681f761e398
Id               : 26f1b912-c977-4bf1-851d-605779568da8
Title            : Project Tracker List
SiteScriptIds    : {54c02f20-c7b3-4038-a3e5-74d18c8ac742}
Description      : List for tracking project tasks
ThumbnailUrl     : https://m365x58225286.sharepoint.com/siteassets/site.jpg
TemplateFeatures : {Project tasks, Task status, Deadline}
Version          : 1
ListColor        : Red
ListIcon         : CubeShape
```

Figure 14.12 – Listing list templates

List templates can also be scoped like site templates so that they can be made available for a set of users or groups. Scoping works the same as with site templates – that is, by using the same Grant-SPOSiteDesignRights cmdlet.

Publishing document templates from SharePoint to Office applications

When users are making documents, presentations, and spreadsheets with templates, they need to have access to the latest versions of those templates. Otherwise, they may end up using outdated ones or copying from previous documents. SharePoint organization asset libraries allow you to distribute document templates from one place to all users.

At the time of writing this book, the client applications that support this feature are Word, Excel, and PowerPoint desktop applications, and PowerPoint Online applications.

When planning the usage of organization asset libraries, it's important to note that there can only be 30 asset libraries in total and all of them reside within a single SharePoint site collection. This is commonly the root site of the tenant or other site set as the SharePoint home site for all users. Libraries can have different permissions – for example, for sharing different templates for different countries or divisions. Organization asset libraries can have folders, and it's a clever idea to use folders when there are a lot of templates available.

Templates must be in Office template format (`.dotx`, `.potx`, `.xltx`); otherwise, they won't be visible on client applications. Different types of templates can live in the same library; applications just show templates that can be used.

Setting up an asset library

To set up an asset library, a document library needs to be created for the chosen site:

```
Add-SPOOrgAssetsLibrary -LibraryUrl https://tenant.sharepoint.com/
Templates -ThumbnailUrl https://tenant.sharepoint.com/siteassets/
asset.jpg -OrgAssetType OfficeTemplateLibrary -CdnType Private
```

The `OrgAssetType` parameter sets the library for Office templates with the `OfficeTemplateLibrary` value. Another choice is to set the library as `ImageDocumentLibrary`, which enables the library to host images used in SharePoint and adds your organization's choice to the image picker on modern SharePoint sites.

A **content delivery network** (**CDN**) is also needed for asset libraries. Fortunately, this is enabled during setup. The CDN's type can be public or private. A public CDN can be used for hosting web assets, such as Java scripts, CSS stylesheets, fonts, and non-proprietary images, and can be anonymously accessed. On the other hand, a private CDN always requires you to call the content from SharePoint; users need to have access to the origin – in this case, the document library. A private CDN is the correct choice for hosting document template libraries:

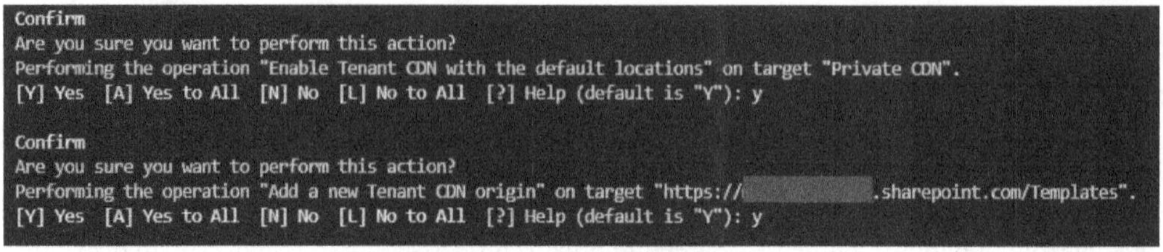

```
Confirm
Are you sure you want to perform this action?
Performing the operation "Enable Tenant CDN with the default locations" on target "Private CDN".
[Y] Yes  [A] Yes to All  [N] No  [L] No to All  [?] Help (default is "Y"): y

Confirm
Are you sure you want to perform this action?
Performing the operation "Add a new Tenant CDN origin" on target "https://          .sharepoint.com/Templates".
[Y] Yes  [A] Yes to All  [N] No  [L] No to All  [?] Help (default is "Y"): y
```

Figure 14.13 - Enabling the usage of CDNs

If the CDN is not enabled on the tenant, it will be enabled and set up when you run the `Add-SPOOrgAssetLibrary` cmdlet.

> **Note**
> It may take up to 24 hours for users to see the asset library on their applications.

Managing asset libraries

All configured asset libraries can be listed using the `Get-SPOOrgAssetLibrary` cmdlet:

```
PS C:\> Get-SPOOrgAssetsLibrary

Location of organization asset libraries
/

RunspaceId    : f3c35ec3-0bda-45f0-87f6-3de1f9239ccd
DisplayName   : RestrictedTemplates
LibraryUrl    : /RestrictedTemplates
ListId        : 0f697f00-3243-466f-a58f-ca7431874405
OrgAssetType  : OfficeTemplateLibrary
ThumbnailUrl  : SiteAssets/site.jpg

RunspaceId    : f3c35ec3-0bda-45f0-87f6-3de1f9239ccd
DisplayName   : Templates
LibraryUrl    : /Templates
ListId        : d4dbbdcb-cc75-43d7-9c25-9f9c45903920
OrgAssetType  : OfficeTemplateLibrary
ThumbnailUrl  : SiteAssets/site.jpg
```

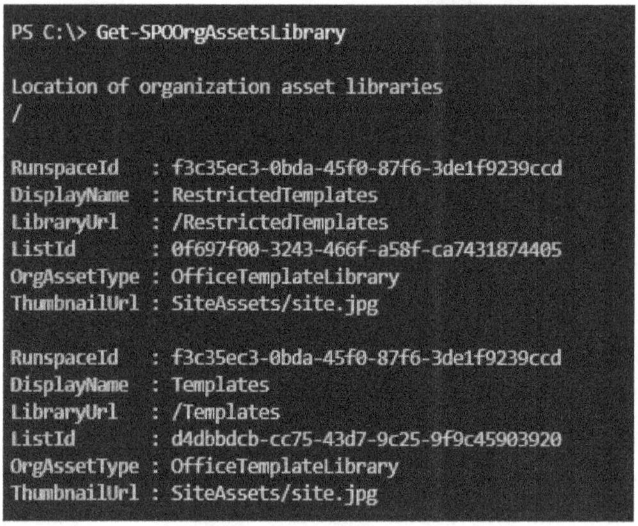

Figure 14.14 - Listing all asset libraries

When removing an asset library, it's referenced by the library URL or list's ID. Let's look at an example of this by removing the `RestrictedTemplates` library from *Figure 14.14*:

```
Remove-SPOOrgAssetLibrary –LibraryUrl /RestrictedTemplates
```

The Remove command doesn't remove the CDN's origin. This needs to be done separately:

```
Remove-SPOTenantCDNOrigin -OriginUrl RestrictedTemplates -CdnType
Private
```

The asset library's thumbnail image can be set using the following command:

```
Set-SPOOrgAssetLibrary -LibraryUrl /RestrictedTemplates -ThumbnailUrl
https://tenant.sharepoint.com/siteassets/library.jpg
```

Experience for users

On Office desktop applications, users see published asset libraries as a tab on the **New** view. Users can pin templates, and recently used templates are available on the top.

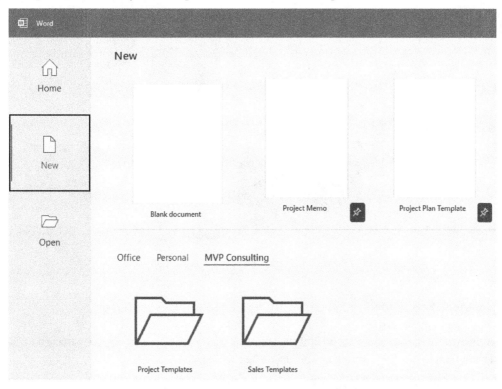

Figure 14.15 - Document templates on Word

On PowerPoint Online, templates are available when creating new content via the Microsoft 365 portal (https://www.microsoft365.com/):

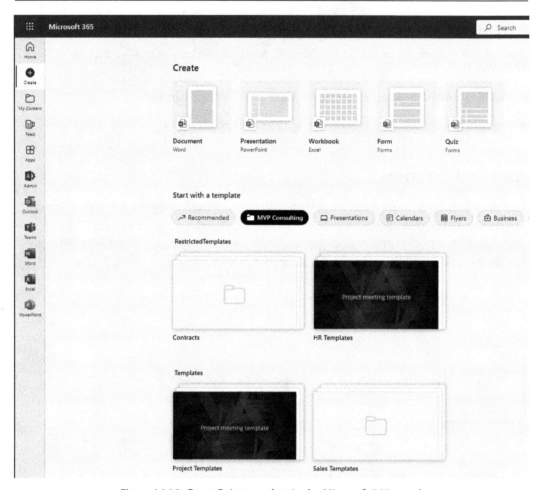

Figure 14.16 - PowerPoint template in the Microsoft 365 portal

Summary

In this chapter, we learned about SharePoint site templates and site scripts, and how to manage built-in and default templates when creating new or updating existing sites.

Next, we were introduced to list templates, which enable the creation of consistent lists for specific purposes on the SharePoint site and the Microsoft Lists app.

Finally, we learned how to publish Office document templates from SharePoint to Office applications and PowerPoint Online applications.

In the next chapter, we will delve into customizing and creating SharePoint list experiences using view formatting capabilities.

15

Improving List Experiences with View Formatting

As we already learned in *Chapter 4*, the lists and libraries are key elements for hosting content in SharePoint. In the same chapter, we also looked at how the user experience of lists and libraries can be customized using views, different view styles, and view and column formattings by changing fonts, colors, and border settings. Simple rules for conditional formatting are also possible.

With advanced column and view formattings, it's possible to customize the HTML structure and CSS styles of lists and libraries for more flexible customization options. Advanced formatting also supports adding links, launching Power Automate cloud flows, and customizing click actions.

Advanced column and view formattings are done using JSON with a specified schema. Column or view JSON formatting is applied using an editor, which opens for advanced formattings. I recommend using an editor, such as Visual Studio Code, which supports JSON formatting and validation to make the changes, and then copying them to an advanced formatting editor. The editor validates the JSON, and in debug mode errors are visible on the used browser's console. But when creating more advanced formattings where JSON get more complex, it's recommended to use an editor, for example, Visual Studio Code, which supports syntax highlighting, automatic formatting, and validation.

In this chapter, we're going to cover the following main topics:

- Advanced Column Formatting
- Formatting Column Values
- Advanced View Formatting
- Creating actionable links using formattings

Advanced Column formatting

Advanced column formatting allows customizing how a specific list column is displayed. Customization can be done using predefined HTML elements and CSS styles. Conditional formatting based on the column value or value ranges.

Column formatting is a quick and effortless way to extend user experience since it can be done using a browser and changes are instantly visible. Formatting capabilities are available for users who give permission to manage list and library views.

Advanced column formatting is opened from the **Format columns** tab, which can be opened by double-clicking the list column or opening view formatting from the view selector and switching to the **Format columns** tab, and selecting **Advanced mode** from the bottom.

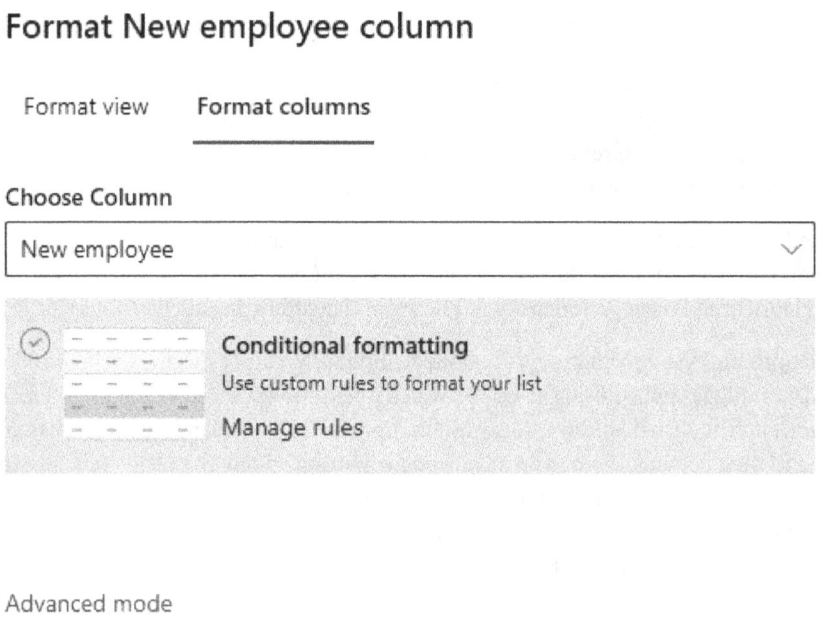

Figure 15.1 - Column formatting

The JSON editor is opened with a default formatting JSON.

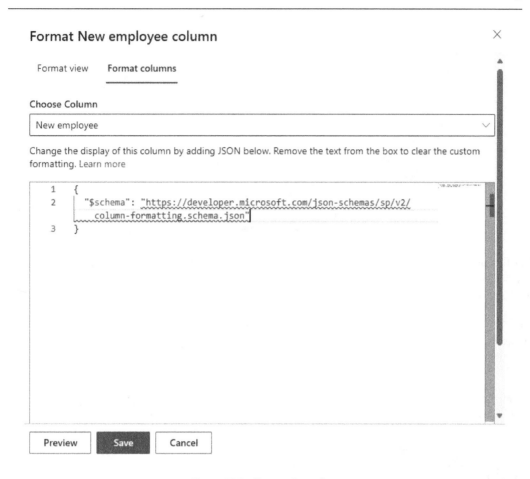

Figure 15.2 - Formatting editor

Let's make the first column formatting by adding a phone icon next to the phone number on a text column. There are two ways of adding the icon: using the Fluent UI Icons (the first example) or simply using an emoji keyboard to add the icon (the second example). Both examples create a HTML div element using two span elements inside of it. In the first example, an icon is displayed using **iconName** attribute of the first span element. The actual column value is displayed on the second span, and it can be referenced using **@currentField** token.

```
{"$schema": https://developer.microsoft.com/json-schemas/sp/v2/column-
formatting.schema.json,
"elmType": "div",
"children": [
    {
        "elmType": "span",
        "attributes":{"iconName":"Phone"}
```

```
    },{
        "elmType": "span",
        "txtContent":"@currentField"
    }
]}
```

Phone number ∨

           ☏+358 555 555 5555

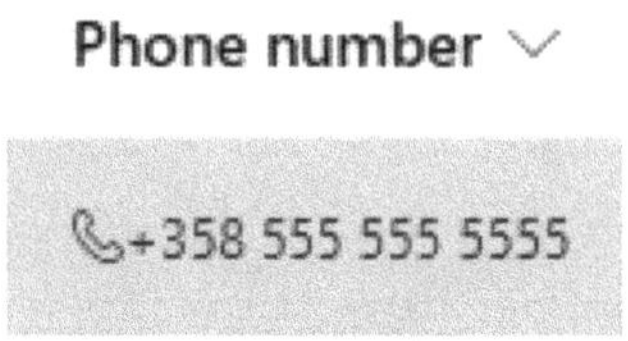

Figure 15.3 - First example

The first phone number example can be viewed and downloaded from: `https://github.com/ PacktPublishing/Customizing-and-Extending-SharePoint-Online/blob/ main/ch15/phone-number-example-1.json`

In the second example, icon is added as an emoji directly to the first span's **txtContent** attribute and resized to 24px using styles.

```
{"$schema": "https://developer.microsoft.com/json-schemas/sp/v2/
column-formatting.schema.json",
"elmType": "div",
"children": [
{
    "elmType": "span", "style":{"font-size":"24px"},
    "txtContent":"☎"
},{
    "elmType": "span", "txtContent":"@currentField"
}]}
```

Phone number ∨

Figure 15.4 - The layout in the second example

The second phone number example can be viewed and downloaded from: `https://github. com/PacktPublishing/Customizing-and-Extending-SharePoint-Online/ blob/main/ch15/phone-number-example-2.json`

Using Fluent UI icons is a safer choice for compatibility, but emoji enable more flexibility and options.

Conditional formatting

Conditional formatting can be used to apply styles, CSS classes, icons and content to columns based on column values.

As a first example, let's format a Status list column, which is typed as choice, and use icons and colors to show different statuses.

```
{ "$schema": https://developer.microsoft.com/json-schemas/sp/v2/
column-formatting.schema.json,
"elmType": "div",
"attributes": {
    "class": "=if(@currentField == 'Done', 'sp-field-        severity-
-good',if(@currentField == 'In Progress','sp-    field-severity--
warning', if(@currentField ==              'New','sp-field-severity--
severeWarning',''))"
},
"children": [
{
    "elmType": "span",
    "style": {
        "display": "inline-block",
        "padding": "0 4px"
    },
    "attributes": {
        "iconName": "=if(@currentField ==
'Done',           'CheckMark', if(@currentField == 'In
Progress',     'ProgressRingDots', if(@currentField == 'New',
'Info',     '')))"
    }
    },
    {
    "elmType": "span",
    "txtContent": "@currentField"
}
]}
```

In the example above, first column background color is set based on the column value using predefined CSS classes. The structure of the basic condition is:

```
=if(@currentField == Value,when true,when false)
```

Full example formatting can be downloaded here: https://github.com/PacktPublishing/ Customizing-and-Extending-SharePoint-Online/blob/main/ch15/conditional- formatting-example.json

Conditions can be chained like in the example by adding new if-condition to the false value. Remember to set the false value at least as an empty string, otherwise the condition will not work correctly.

The icon is set to the span elements using iconName attribute with Fluent UI icons using the similar conditions.

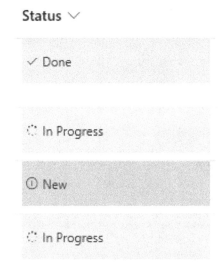

Figure 15.5 - Status column with conditional formatting applied

Working with dates and date ranges

When formatting columns based on date and time, it's possible to use values from the formatted columns or other columns on the list and compare against current date and time or predefined date and time, for example, adding a month to the current date. Date and time are compared as milliseconds, which means that if you want to add a month to a specific data, it's calculated as follows:

```
30*24*60*60*1000= 2 592 000 000 milliseconds
```

As an example, let's add an exclamation mark to columns if the **Status** column is In Progress and items haven't been updated within a week.

```
{"$schema": https://developer.microsoft.com/json-schemas/sp/v2/column-
formatting.schema.json,
"elmType":"div",
"children": [
{
    "elmType": "span","txtContent":"@currentField" },
    {
    "elmType": "span",
    "attributes":{
        "iconName":"=if([$Status] == 'In
Progress',        if([$Modified] < @
now+604800000,                    'Warning',''),'')"
},"style":{"font-size":"18px","color":"red"}
} ]
}
```

And the end result is as follows:

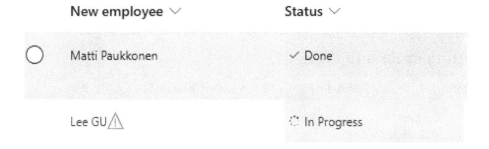

Figure 15.6 - Formatting based on date comparison

As seen in the previous example, other columns of the list or library can be referred using [$column display name] format, like [$Modified]. It's also possible to refer using the column's internal by replacing the dollar sign with exclamation mark, like this [!Modified].

The current date and time are referred using the @now expression, which is the date and time when the user has loaded the view. Some other special expressions are:

- @me, which returns the current user object
- @currentWeb, which returns the URL of the current site
- @rowIndex, index of the items row in the view

- `@isSelected`, return true when list item is selected
- `@lcid`, current culture id

For example, highlighting a user column where current user is added:

```
{ "$schema": https://developer.microsoft.com/json-schemas/sp/v2/
column-formatting.schema.json,
"elmType":"div",
"attributes":{
    "class":"=if(@currentField.email == @me,'sp-field-    severity--
good','')"
}
,"txtContent":"@currentField"
}
```

When a column is typed as user, the `@currentField` is an object which contains properties related to the user. `@me` is the user's email address and it's compared against `@currentField.email` value.

Formatting column values

Column formatting enables dozens of operators to manipulate column values. In this section, I'll present the most common use cases.

Formatting dates and times

Column formatting includes several formulas for formatting dates and times.

- `"txtContent":"=Date(@currentField)"` returns date and time formatted like 11/23/2023, 01:15:00 AM.
- `"txtContent":"=toDateString(@currentField)"` returns only the date formatted like `Thu Nov 23 2023`. This presentation does not vary based on user's locale.
- `ToLocaleDateString` returns the date formatted like `11/23/2023`. And `toLocaleTimeString` return the time formatted like `1:15:00 AM`. These values are localized based on user's locale. For example, for Finnish user, these values are displayed as.

Sometimes returning just a day, month, or year is required, and these can be achieved using `getDate`, `getMonth`, or `getYear` operators. For example, showing a year on a date field can be done like in the example below:

```
"txtContent":"=getYear(@currentField)"
```

Date and time operators can also be used to format current date and time using `@now` operator.

Showing user images

Users' profile images can be shown in different sizes using the getUserImage operator, which returns the URL to the profile image. The operator can return small, medium, or large images. For example, displaying a large user profile image on a user-typed column with the user's name can be done with the example code below:

```
{"$schema": https://developer.microsoft.com/json-schemas/sp/v2/column-
formatting.schema.json,
"elmType": "div","children": [ {
"elmType": "img","attributes":{
"src":"=getUserImage(@currentField.email,'small')"
},
"style":{"border-radius": "50%", "width":"50px","padding":"5px"}}, {
elmType":"span","txtContent":"@currentField.title}]
}
```

Formatting returns a square image, which is then styled as a circle using border-radius css style. If a user doesn't have a profile image added, the default grey user shape is returned, also in this example, the shape is returned if the user is linked to the column.

Figure 15.7 - Custom user field

Displaying image field thumbnails

By default, image column is displayed as a small square on the list. Formatting the image in the column, can be achieved using getThumbnailImage operator. For example, showing new employee's photo as an ellipsis in the image column can be done like example below:

```
{ "$schema": https://developer.microsoft.com/json-schemas/sp/v2/
column-formatting.schema.json,
"elmType": "img",
"
attributes": {
    "
```

```
src": "=getThumbnailImage(@currentField,100,100)",
"
alt": @currentField.fileName
},
"style": {"width": "120px","object-fit": "cover","height":
"120px","border-radius": "50%" }
}
```

And the result looks like this:

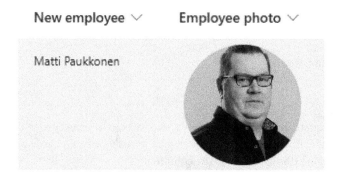

Figure 15.8 - Formatted image column

More options for column formatting and available operators can be found on Microsoft's SharePoint column formatting documentation (https://learn.microsoft.com/en-us/sharepoint/dev/declarative-customization/formatting-syntax-reference).

Advanced view formatting

List view formatting is used to customize how list or library items are displayed. With advanced formatting, it's possible to change the layout and style of items using HTML and CSS. Advanced view formatting uses similar JSON patterns as advanced column formatting. View formatting supports list, gallery, board and calendar layouts and customization of item groupings.

Formatting list layouts

Highlighting rows based on a condition using predefined SharePoint Online styles can be achieved using `additionalRowClass` attribute, for example highlighting rows based on **Status** column can be done like example below:

```
{ "$schemahttps://developer.microsoft.com/json-schemas/sp/v2/row-
formatting.schema.json", "additionalRowClass": "": "=if([$Status]
== 'New','sp-field-severity—severeWarning', if([$Status] == 'In
```

```
Progress','sp-field-severity—warning', if([$Status] == 'Done','sp-
field-severity—good','')))"}
```

The example uses predefined classes based on the **Status** column's value. The result of the formatting looks like this.

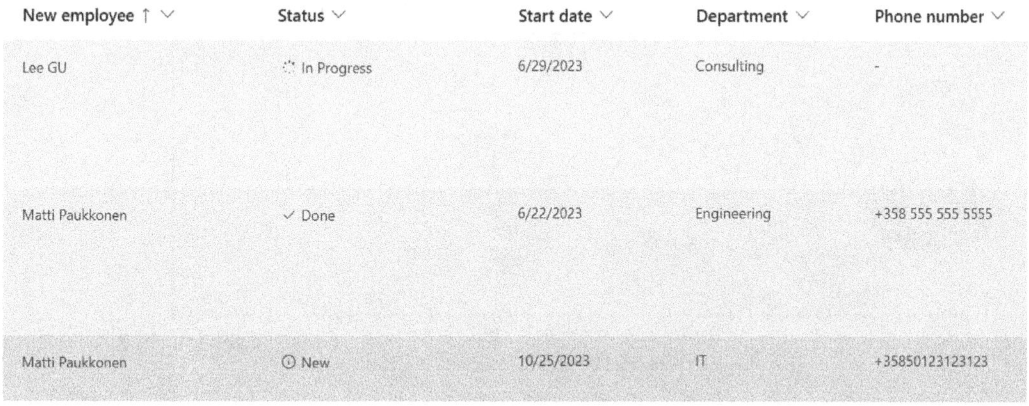

New employee ↑ ∨	Status ∨	Start date ∨	Department ∨	Phone number ∨
Lee GU	⠿ In Progress	6/29/2023	Consulting	-
Matti Paukkonen	✓ Done	6/22/2023	Engineering	+358 555 555 5555
Matti Paukkonen	ⓘ New	10/25/2023	IT	+35850123123123

Figure 15.9 - Additional row styles

For another example, let's display list items as a custom contact card including a photo from the image column, name, department and phone number.

Full example JSON formatting can be viewed and downloaded from: `https://github.com/ PacktPublishing/Customizing-and-Extending-SharePoint-Online/blob/ main/ch15/custom-contact-card-formatter.json`

The first step is to hide column header from the view by setting `hideColumnHeader` to true, also in this example items cannot be selected and `hideSelection` is also set to true.

The custom formatting is called `rowFormatter` operator, which holds the custom HTML and CSS styles of the row. Photo is retrieved using `getThumbnailImage` operator referencing to `EmployeePhoto` column. Other shown information is referenced to `txtContent` operator using column internal names. Notice that all referenced columns need to be set as visible on the view settings.

Onboarding ★

Figure 15.10 - Custom Contact Card

As seen in the example above, with HTML and CSS it's possible to create a customized layout, which can be used for example to use the list or library as an app or display it on a modern SharePoint page.

Formatting gallery and board layouts

Gallery and board layout formatting allows creation of custom cards with custom layout and columns.

```
{ "$schema": https://developer.microsoft.com/json-schemas/sp/v2/tile-
formatting.schema.json,
"height": "300",
"width": "200",
"formatter": {
<custom column formatting>
```

The gallery formatting starts by setting the height and the width of the card. The custom formatting is implemented using formatter operator. Notice that when using custom formatting for gallery layout, the card layout also needs to be taken care of on the formatting.

Onboarding ★

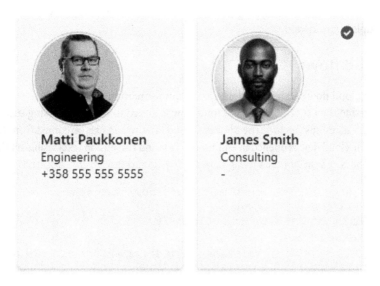

Figure 15.11 - Custom gallery layout

Full example JSON formatter can be viewed and downloaded from here: `https://github.com/PacktPublishing/Customizing-and-Extending-SharePoint-Online/blob/main/ch15/people-gallery-formatting.json`

On board view, the width of the card is predefined, and the height depends on added columns. The formatting is added inside of the formatter operator like in gallery layouts.

Figure 15.12 - Custom board layout

Creating actionable links using formatting

Custom row actions can be used to start Power Automate cloud flows, add actions to custom layouts and update multiple column values.

Starting cloud flows

A button to start a cloud flow can be added using column formatting. The cloud flow to be used needs to be first connected to the list or library. The cloud flow is linked to the button using `executeFlow` action. `ActionParams` must include the id of the cloud flow, which can be copied from the browser's address line when the cloud flow is opened in edit mode. Title and run button texts visible on the flow panel can be defined in the `actionParams` using `headerText` and `runFlowButtonText` properties.

```
{ "$schema": https://developer.microsoft.com/json-schemas/sp/v2/
column-formatting.schema.json,
"elmType": "button", "customRowAction": {
"action": "executeFlow",
"actionParams": "{\"id\": \"510e9047-a72d-423b-b10d-cb21eac42e1d\",
\"headerText\":\"Start approval\",\"runFlowButtonText\":\"Start\"}"
}, "style": {
"border": "1px solid lightgrey",
"border-radius": "5px",
"background-color": "transparent",
"cursor": "pointer"
},
"children": [
{
"elmType": "span",
"attributes": {
"iconName": "Process" },
"style": {"padding-right": "6px"}
},
{ "elmType": "span", "txtContent": "Start Approval" }
] }
```

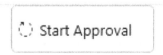

Figure 15.13 - Start approval button

Adding click action

Click actions can be added either on column or view formatting using button HTML element. Click actions support:

- **defaultClick**, which does the same action as clicking the item on uncustomized view
- **Share**, which opens a share dialog
- **Delete**, opens the delete confirmation dialog
- **EditProps**, open the edit properties view of the item
- **OpenContextMenu**, opens the context menu

In the example below, button is using the share action, and opens sharing of the selected item on the board layout.

```
{"elmType": "button",
"txtContent": "Share this item",
"customRowAction":
{ "action": "share"
},
"attributes": {
"class": "sp-card-displayColumnContainer"
}
}
```

The example code is added as the last element on the custom view formatting JSON.

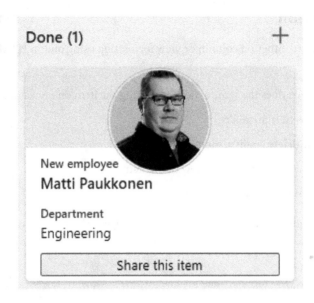

Figure 15.14 - Custom share button on the board layout

Updating columns values on click

With `setValue` custom row action it's possible to update multiple column values by clicking an element on the item. For example, adding a current user as manager and setting the **Status** column as done can be achieved using code below.

```
customRowAction": {
    "action": "setValue",
    "actionInput": {
        "Manager": "@me",
        "Status": "Done"
        }
}
```

Example uses @me operator to update the current user to **Manager** column.

Summary

Column and view formatting offers flexible customization options for extending list and library views. In this chapter, we first learned the key concepts of the column formatting and how to use formattings to highlight and modify list and library columns.

Next, we delved into view formatting and we're introduced how to customized different layouts, highlight important items and how to make custom layouts for different purposes.

Finally, we're introduced how to create actionable links using formattings and how to start Power Automate cloud flows using actions.

In the next chapter, we are introduced to SharePoint Framework, which is a developer platform and tooling for building custom solutions to SharePoint and other Microsoft 365 services, such as Teams and Outlook.

Part 4:
Create Your Own Customization using SharePoint Framework and Microsoft Graph

In this part, you will get an overview of the SharePoint Framework application development model, learn how to install the required tools, and deploy customization. You will also get an overview of Microsoft Graph API and its resources. In addition, you will also learn different customization options in SharePoint Framework to not only extend its experiences but also to use the tools within Microsoft Teams and extend Viva Connections. You will also be introduced to community-driven solutions supplied by Microsoft 365 and the Power Platform community.

This part has the following chapters:

16
Introduction to SharePoint Framework

SharePoint Framework, commonly known as **SPFx**, was first introduced in May 2016 alongside the modern SharePoint Online. SharePoint Framework is a modern, client-side web development platform for developing applications and extending SharePoint Online, but also Microsoft Teams, Microsoft Viva, Outlook, and Microsoft 365 apps (Office). On-premises versions of SharePoint are also supported, but not covered in this book. Applications and extensions developed with SPFx are run on the browser and can have access to different REST APIs, such as SharePoint REST API or Microsoft Graph, which is a unified REST API for accessing Microsoft Cloud.

SharePoint Framework supports modern development tools and JavaScript development frameworks, such as React, Handlebars, and Vue.js. Developer tools are based on open-source client-side development tools such as NPM (Node Package Manager), TypeScript, and Yeoman. The development environment doesn't require a local installation of SharePoint; everything can be tested and debugged against SharePoint Online. Developers can choose their preferred development tools, and the development tools are not tied to any operating system.

In this chapter, we're going to cover the following main topics:

- SharePoint Framework – modern application development model
- Setting up the development environment
- Creating your first SharePoint Framework project
- Packaging and deploying custom solutions to SharePoint

SharePoint Framework – modern application development model

SharePoint Framework (**SPFx**) is a modern client-side development model for customizing and extending SharePoint Online and also Microsoft Teams, Microsoft Viva, Outlook, and Office applications. SPFX is supported on both SharePoint Online and SharePoint on-premises, beginning with SharePoint Server 2016. Developers can use development tools and JavaScript frameworks of their choice, and the development toolchain is built on top of open-source development tools, such as NPM, Gulp, and Yeoman.

A Local installation of SharePoint is not needed, and development and debugging can be done against the local workbench, which is run on Node.js, or against a workbench running on the cloud. The best part is that the development of SPFx customization can be run on any platform, such as Windows, Mac, or Linux, which supports modern client-side development tools.

SharePoint Framework supplies simple mechanisms for accessing data on SharePoint Online, such as lists or libraries and other Microsoft 365 services via Microsoft Graph API, which is a unified API for Microsoft cloud services. Microsoft Graph API is introduced in *Chapter 17*.

SharePoint Framework customizations are either installed from **SharePoint Store** or deployed using **SharePoint App Catalog**. Depending on a solution, customizations can be scoped for specific sites or all sites in the tenant. Site collection app catalogs are also supported for deploying SharePoint Framework solutions.

SharePoint Framework components

SharePoint Framework supports customizations based on web parts, extensions, adaptive card extensions, and library components.

Web parts are building blocks that content authors can add to pages. Most commonly, web parts are used to visualize certain information, integrate data from external systems, or create visual elements.

Extensions can be used to extend SharePoint user experience. There are several types of extensions:

- **Application customizers**: This can load scripts and render content to well-known HTML placeholders.
- **Field customizers**: This can be used to extend views of columns in a list or library.
- **Command sets**: This can be used to add new actions to different SharePoint menus, command bars, and views.
- **Form customizers**: This can be used to override and customize list and library forms.
- **Adaptive card extensions** (**ACE**): These are used to extend Microsoft Viva Connections with custom cards and functionality. ACEs can be shown on the Viva Connections dashboard, which is visible on Viva Connections Home or in SharePoint using the Viva Dashboard web part.

Library components enable the creation of shared code libraries, which can be used inside of customizations and are deployed in a similar manner as other SharePoint customizations in App Catalog.

Introduction to client-side development tooling

As mentioned, SharePoint Framework is built using open source client-side development tools.

Node.js

Node.js is an open source, cross-platform JavaScript runtime that supplies the environment for tools and libraries. Node.js is only needed in the developer's environment, and it's not connected to SharePoint. It's good to keep in mind that the Node.js version updates when SharePoint Framework version upgrades, so it is quite common that developers must use multiple versions of Node.JS when working with multiple customizations.

NPM (Node Package Manager)

NPM is a package manager for JavaScript programming language, and it's the default package manager on Node.js. NPM is used to install and manage code packages, which are ready-made code made available by other developers. NPM also handles the versioning and dependencies of code packages since a package can have a dependency on another package and needs to be installed.

Gulp

Gulp is an open source and JavaScript-based task runner service that is used in SharePoint Framework development to run repetitive tasks, such as building, bundling, and packaging the developed solution.

Yeoman

Yeoman, commonly known as **yo**, is a modern scaffolding tool web application. In SharePoint Framework development, Yeoman is used to create the project structure and manage dependencies.

Visual Studio Code

The developer can choose their own code editor, but I'm recommending **Visual Studio Code**. Visual Studio Code supports a wide range of different programming languages and a variety of extensions and has a terminal supporting PowerShell scripting, which might be needed when debugging and deploying SPFx customizations. Visual Studio Code also has support for GitHub Copilot, which is an AI code assistant and can help developers improve code quality, automate repetitive code patterns, and decrease development time.

It's also possible to use different tools to build the development environment, such as replacing Gulp with a different task runner or NPM with a different package manager, but at the time of authoring this book, the tools listed in this section are Microsoft-recommended tools for the development environment.

Postman

Postman is a useful tool when developing solutions that retrieve data from different APIs. Postman can be used to create parametrized HTTP calls and receive responses to see how data is formatted. It's also useful when debugging solutions.

Fiddler

Since SharePoint Framework solutions are run on the user's browser, sometimes it's a requirement to see what traffic is handled between the browser and SharePoint. Fiddler is a particularly useful tool for debugging APIs.

GitHub or other code repository

It's always a clever idea to have a code repository to store development solutions and manage changes and versioning. GitHub is one preferred choice, but the developer can choose the code repository they are familiar with and which suits their needs best.

NVM

NVM is a node version manager that allows a user to install and use different Node.JS versions on the same computer simultaneously. This is especially useful when developing several customizations using different Node.JS versions. Sometimes, it's not meaningful to update to the latest version of SharePoint Framework, especially when working with community-supplied templates and examples.

Setting up the development environment

Setting up the development environment starts by installing the client-side development tooling:

1. The first step is to install Node.js. The installation package can be downloaded from the Node.js website (`https://nodejs.org`) or installed using common package managers, such as Winget on Windows or with Homebrew on macOS.

Important note

Always refer to Microsoft's documentation about the SharePoint Framework development environment to see which Node.js version is supported by SharePoint Framework. Sometimes, the latest long-term support (LTS) version is not yet supported by it.

Also, if you are continuing the development of a solution created earlier or using an example provided by the developer community, refer to the documentation to see which Node.js version is supported with the solution's SPFx version.

---

2. The next step is to install **Gulp** and **Yeoman** using the terminal of your choice:

```
npm install gulp-cli --global
npm install yo --global
```

3. The last step is to install **Yeoman SharePoint generator**, which includes project structures for different SharePoint solutions:

```
npm install @microsoft/generator-sharepoint –global
```

The –global attribute makes the installation globally available, without the parameter packages being installed locally in the project's node_modules folder, and is only available in the folder.

4. Now, you can install the code editor of your choice if you haven't done so yet.

It's also a good idea to have a Microsoft 365 development tenant available for debugging and testing before deploying the solution in the production tenant. Microsoft has an offer for a Microsoft 365 developer tenant, which is a free and fully functional Microsoft 365 environment that includes 25 licenses. To retrieve the free tenant, the developer needs to sign up for Microsoft 365 Developer Program.

> **Important note**
> Microsoft 365 developer tenants are activated for a period of 90 days at a time. The tenant stays activated when it's actively used for development purposes during the 90-day period.

Creating your first SharePoint Framework project

Creating a first SharePoint Framework project starts by creating a folder location for the project. The next step is to create and scaffold the project using Yeoman:

```
yo @microsoft/sharepoint
```

Figure 16.1 – Project creation using Yeoman generator

If you don't remember the exact name of the generator, you can just type yo, and Yeoman will list all the added generators. The yo command can also be used to update the generator to the latest version:

```
C:\code\SPFx\test-project>yo
? 'Allo! What would you like to do? (Use arrow keys)
  Run a generator
> @microsoft/sharepoint
  ──────────────────────────
  Update your generators
  Install a generator
  Find some help
  Get me out of here!
(Move up and down to reveal more choices)
```

Figure 16.2 – Listing all installed Yeoman generators

Yeoman will guide through the project creation and ask for details about the project. For this first example, let's choose **web parts** as the component type and **React** as the JavaScript framework to be used. After that, the project scaffolding phase starts, and it may take a few minutes to complete, depending on the network capacity. During project creation, some warnings may appear on the console; this is normal behavior and happens because of package dependencies:

```
      _=+#####!
   ###########|
   ###/   (##|(@)      ┌────────────────────────────────────────────┐
   ###  ######|    \   |           Congratulations!                  |
   ###/  /###|   (@) | | Solution important-weeks-web-part is created.|
   ####### ##|   /    '└────────────────────────────────────────────┘'
   ###    /##|(@)
   ###########|
     **=+####!

PS C:\code\SPFx>
```

Figure 16.3 – Complete project generation

Now we have the first project created, let's explore the project structure:

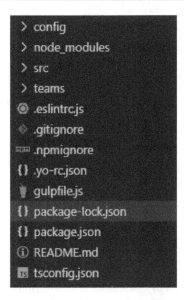

Figure 16.4 – Project structure

The project has several folders:

- `config`: This includes configurations for the web part settings and linked resources, the packaging of the solution, debugging, and deployment.
- `node_modules`: This includes all needed modules for deployment. These are handled by NPM. This folder may contain tens of thousands of files, which is normal behavior because of the module and code package dependencies.
- `src`: This contains the source code of the web part.
- `teams`: In a web part project, this contains icons, which are required for deploying the web part to Teams.

And several configuration files:

- `.npmignore`: This lists the files and folders to be excluded when the code package is published to NPM.
- `.gitignore`: This acts to exclude the files and folders that should be pushed to the Git code repository.
- `yo-rc.json`: This contains a configuration of the Yeoman generator.
- `gulpfile.js`: This defines the task runner configuration for Gulp.

- `package-lock.json`: This is an automatically generated file that holds an exact version of each package the project depends on.

- `package.json`: This is an important configuration that contains project metadata, such as name and version and dependencies on the libraries and scripts that are used in the project. This is an important file since the needed dependencies and development dependencies are installed based on this file.

- `README.md`: This is for the documentation of the generated project.

- `Tsconfig.json`: This is related to **TypeScript**, which is a statically typed superset of JavaScript that adds types and compiles to plain JavaScript; it identifies the root folder of the project and the options for the compiler.

Running and debugging the code

1. Now, the code is ready for testing, but the first environment needs to have a trust-to-development certificate set up, which is used by SharePoint Framework to communicate using HTTPS. It's done by running a gulp command in the root folder of the project and needs to be done once in the development environment:

   ```
   gulp trust-dev-cert
   ```

2. Now, debugging can be started using the following:

   ```
   gulp serve
   ```

3. During the first time, the command gives a warning about the tenant domain, which is not set to the configuration:

```
[18:52:12] Starting gulp
[18:52:12] Starting subtask 'spfx-serve'...
[18:52:12] [spfx-serve] To load your scripts, use this query string: ?debug=true&noredir=t
rue&debugManifestsFile=https://ltps://localtps://localhost:4321/temp/manifests.js
[18:52:12] Warning - [spfx-serve] Placeholder {tenantDomain} was found in server.json but
OS variable SPFX_SERVE_TENANT_DOMAIN is not set. Either set the environment variable or up
date the serve.json initial page url.
```

Figure 16.5 – Gulp warning about tenant domain setting

4. The tenant domain can be set up by using the `serve.json` configuration file found in the config folder. Add your tenant URL address to the `initialPage` parameter, and run `gulp serve` again:

```
spfx-first-web-part > config > {} serve.json > ...
  1   {
  2       "$schema": "https://developer.microsoft.com/json-schemas/spfx-build/spfx-serve.schema.json",
  3       "port": 4321,
  4       "https": true,
  5       "initialPage": "https://tenant.sharepoint.com/_layouts/workbench.aspx"
  6   }
  7
```

Figure 16.6 – Tenant configuration for debugging

5. Another way is to open a SharePoint site on the development tenant and add the workbench URL with query string parameters to the site address:

```
/_layouts/workbench.
aspx?debug=true&noredir=true&debugManifestsFile=https://
localhost:4321/temp/manifests.js
```

6. When loading the workbench, the first user is asked to accept the loading of debug scripts:

Allow debug scripts?

WARNING: This page contains unsafe scripts that, if loaded, could potentially harm your computer. Do not proceed unless you trust the developer and understand the risks.

If you are unsure, click Don't load debug scripts.

Load debug scripts   Don't load debug scripts

Figure 16.7 – Confirmation of debug scripts

7. Now, the web part can be tested on the workbench by clicking the add icon and finding the web part by the name defined during project creation:

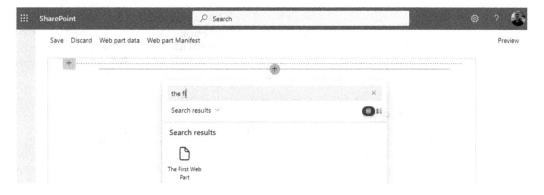

Figure 16.8 – Adding a web part to workbench

8. The workbench allows the web part settings to be changed, and this is displayed on different column layouts. The changes made to the source code can be tested without stopping the debugging session by reloading the page on the browser.

9. Let's add some code to see the change in real time. First, let's open the TheFirstWebPart. tsx file from the src/webparts/thefirstwebpart/components folder, as in *Figure 16.9*:

Figure 16.9 – React component

10. This file is the React component, which is rendered when the web part is loaded. The next step is to replace the return method's content in the render function:

```
public render(): React.ReactElement<ITheFirstWebPartProps>
{       return (
          <section className={`${styles.theFirstWebPart} `}>
     <div className={styles['book-intro']}>
               <div className={styles['book-cover']}>
                    <img src={require("../assets/book-cover.jpg")}
alt="Book Cover" />
               </div>
               <div className={styles['book-details']}>
                    <h1 className={styles['book-
title']}>Customizing and Extending SharePoint Online: Design
tailor-made solutions using modern SharePoint features to meet
your organization's unique needs 1st Edition, Kindle Edition</
h1>
                    <p className={styles['book-author']}>Author:
<b>Matti Paukkonen</b></p>
                    <a href="https://www.amazon.com/Customizing-
Extending-SharePoint-Online-organizations-ebook/dp/B0CBS6G1Z5"
className={styles['book-link']}>Read More</a>
               </div>
          </div>
        </section>
      );
    }
```

11. Add style definitions to the `TheFirstWebPart.module.scss` file, which stores styles as CSS modules. CSS modules help to apply styles to a specific SPFx component, in this case, the web part, and avoid conflict between different components:

```scss
.book-intro {
  display: flex;
  justify-content: space-between;
  padding: 20px;
  .book-cover {
      flex: 1;
      img {
              max-width: 100%;
              height: auto;
      }
  }
  .book-details {
      flex: 2;
      padding-left: 20px;
      .book-title {
              font-size: 18px;
              font-weight: bold;
      }
      .book-author {
              font-size: 16px;
              color: #666;
      }
      .book-link {
              display: inline-block;
              margin-top: 10px;
              padding: 10px 15px;
              background-color: #f4f4f4;
              color: #333;
              text-decoration: none;
      }
  }
}
```

After the component file and the CSS Module file are saved and the page reloads, the web part will be rendered, as in *Figure 16.10*:

Figure 16.10 – Web part on the workbench

Packaging and deploying custom solutions to SharePoint

Once testing and debugging are done, and the solution is ready, it's time to deploy the custom solutions to SharePoint. The deployment requires the creation of a production-optimized solution package, which can then be uploaded to SharePoint App Catalog and deployed to sites:

1. The first step is to create an optimized code bundle for production use by running the following:

    ```
    gulp bundle --ship
    ```

    The bundle task generates minified assets that need to be uploaded to the **content delivery network (CDN)**. The optimized bundles are created in the temp/deploy folder in the project.

2. The next step is to package the project code to a SharePoint Framework solution package by running the following:

    ```
    gulp package-solution --ship
    ```

    The package solution task creates a solution package file to the /sharepoint/ solution folder. The solution package, which is named by default according to the project's name and file extension, is .sppkg.

The solution can be deployed to SharePoint using the tenant's app catalog or site collection app catalog by uploading the .sppkg file to the **Apps for SharePoint** library.

Use cases for SharePoint Framework

SharePoint Framework web parts enable organizations to bring data to SharePoint pages from external systems. An example might be retrieving an organization's public news from their website using RSS feeds or connecting the web part to an HR system and displaying a personal dashboard to users based on their identity, such as available holidays, employment details, and actions. Web parts are also useful when a page structure needs to be customized, such as creating tab content or creating a table of contents for the page.

List View Command Set Extensions could be used to extend document management capabilities in SharePoint document libraries, such as creating a custom archiving solution or calling an organization's custom AI model to analyze the content of the document.

Adaptive card extension enables the customization of Viva Connection Home Experience. It can be used to create custom dashboard cards for frontline users, which display important safety information, actionable task views, or warnings from external line-of-business apps.

Summary

In this chapter, we first learned about the basics of SharePoint Framework, different component types, and development tooling.

Next, we delved into setting up the development environment for SharePoint Framework development using Microsoft's preferred tooling. After that, we learned how to create a first web part project using SharePoint Framework and how to run and debug code on the cloud.

Finally, we learned how to package the solution for deployment using the Gulp task manager. In the next chapter, we will be delving into **Microsoft Graph API**, which is a unified API for accessing Microsoft 365.

17

Access SharePoint Data using Microsoft Graph

Microsoft Graph is a unified RESTful API providing access to different resources and data available on Microsoft Cloud services. It offers a single endpoint to different cloud services, such as SharePoint, Teams, and Entra ID. Access and authorizations to the Graph API's resources are controlled in Entra ID using OAuth access tokens. The Graph API can be accessed by the signed-in user (which is called **delegated access**) or with the application's own identity (which is called **app-only access**).

The SharePoint API in Microsoft Graph provides access to assets on SharePoint sites, such as lists, list items, document libraries, tenant-level settings, and managed metadata taxonomies. There are separate APIs for accessing files, folders, and OneNote notebooks. All these APIs work under the same Microsoft API umbrella and access can be managed to all of those APIs using Entra ID.

Graph API access has been available in the SharePoint Framework since version 1.4.1. The SharePoint Framework uses MSGraphClient to work as a signed-in user. The user does not need to worry about authentication and permissions when they use SharePoint Online. The API access page on the SharePoint admin center or SharePoint Online Management Shell can control the SharePoint Framework's Graph API permission.

In this chapter, we're going to cover the following main topics:

- Microsoft Graph – an API for Microsoft Cloud service resources
- How to use Graph Explorer to call the API
- How to use the Microsoft Graph PowerShell SDK with the Graph API
- Access SharePoint data with the Graph API and the SharePoint Framework

Microsoft Graph: an API for Microsoft Cloud service resources

Microsoft Graph supplies a unified model for accessing data within Microsoft 365 services (such as SharePoint, Teams, and Mail), Enterprise Mobility + Security services (such as Microsoft Entra ID and Microsoft Intune), and Windows services (such as device and notifications, and Dynamics 365 Business Central). Microsoft Graph's API is constantly updating, supplying new capabilities and services regularly.

Microsoft Graph can be used to build experiences around user context – for example, by supplying insights about recently updated documents, new colleagues, or upcoming events. When working in a user's context, using so-called delegated access, the access to data and insights is based on the user's permissions set on different services.

An application can also use its own identity to access data and insights, called app-only access. The application can just have read access to certain services, or have full access to create, update, and delete assets and data.

Microsoft Entra ID (previously known as Azure Active Directory) governs access and authorization, needing each application interfacing with Microsoft Graph to be registered with Entra ID. The application can either be registered to the tenant where the user lives or it can function as a multi-tenant application. If the latter, the application is registered to a home tenant and granted authorization to other tenants via service principals. In the multi-tenant application model, application permissions are set on the home tenant and consent is granted to other tenants by their respective global administrators.

An application needs to conduct an authentication process to receive an authorization token as the Microsoft Graph API endpoint cannot be called directly using a browser. There are several good tools such as Postman to try out and investigate the API during development. Microsoft also supplies a tool called Graph Explorer, which can be used directly from the browser and is introduced in the next section of this book.

The Microsoft Graph API includes two publicly available versions:

- **Version 1.0** is commonly referenced as v1.0, which is a production version of the API.
- **Beta** includes endpoints, which are in the preview phase. Beta endpoints can be used for experimenting with new and upcoming capabilities, but they might change without any notice during the preview phase or when moved to the v1.0 version.

> **Note**
>
> Also, there might be differences in permissions between these versions. Most commonly, app-only permissions are not supported on the beta version.

The API structure

Most of the Microsoft Graph API's resources, methods, and enumerations are defined in the `microsoft.graph` OData namespace in Microsoft Graph's metadata.

The API can be called using standard HTTP methods:

- **GET**: Reading data from a resource
- **POST**: Creating new resources or performing actions
- **PATCH**: Updating resources with new values
- **PUT**: Replacing a resource with another one
- **DELETE**: Removing a resource

A call to the API is structured as follows:

```
<HTTP method> https://graph.microsoft.com/<version>/<resource>?<query
parameters>
```

For example, the code for retrieving all SharePoint lists from a specified site would be as follows:

```
GET https://graph.microsoft.com/v1.0/sites/ tenant.sharepoint.
com,28e328a9-00f4-4b6e-b850-abf67531ec21,f3d3bc0d-216a-4b27-a2bd-
278bba0c9e1a/lists?$select=displayName,webUrl
```

The previous example calls lists resource using a site ID, which consists of a tenant hostname (`tenant. sharepoint.com`) and two **Globally Unique Identier (GUIDs)**. The call also includes an OData select query at the end to return just the `displayName` and `webUrl` properties of each list.

The response returns an array of lists within the site:

```
{      "@odata.context": "https://graph.microsoft.com/
v1.0/$metadata#sites(tenant.sharepoint.com%2C28e328a9-00f4-
4b6e-b850-abf67531ec21%2Cf3d3bc0d-216a-4b27-a2bd-278bba0c9e1a')/
lists(displayName,webUrl)",
    "value": [{
    "@odata.etag": "\"f3f52ef9-a202-456b-95e3-ae230c3642a,223\"",
    "webUrl": https://tenant.sharepoint.com/sites/HRTeam/Lists/HR%20
Onboarding,
                "displayName": "Onboarding"
    },
```

```
    {
        "@odata.etag": "\"e9a36fa1-d1b9-4de1-8a6a-    2e38fd0dd0c9,0\"",
        "webUrl":              https://tenant.sharepoint.com/sites/HRTeam/
    Lists/ComponentManifests,
    "displayName": "Client Side Component Manifests"
    }
```

For all the previous examples, the tenant URL is masked as `tenant.sharepoint.com`.

Redefining the query with OData parameters

Depending on the resource, OData query parameters can be used to filter, sort, or expand related resources, or limit the returned dataset. It's a good practice to retrieve just the items and properties needed in the application making the call for better performance and faster API calls. OData queries are only supported in HTTP GET operations. Each resource supports a diverse set of OData query parameters, referring to the resource's Optional query parameters on Microsoft Graph API reference (`https://learn.microsoft.com/en-us/graph/api/overview`) for a list of supported parameters.

As an example of using OData query parameters, let's search for a site related to HR using search parameters, order the results by when the site was created, and return the `displayName` and `createdDateTime` properties. The API call is as follows:

```
https://graph.microsoft.com/v1.0/sites?$search="HR"&$orderBy=created-
DateTime&$select=displayName,name,createdDateTime
```

The result is an array of sites:

```
{"@odata.context": "https://graph.microsoft.com/v1.0/$metadata-
#sites(displayName,name,createdDateTime)",
"value": [{
        "createdDateTime": "2022-08-25T06:11:08Z",
        "name": "Human Resources",
        "displayName": "Contoso Works"
},
{
        "createdDateTime": "2023-02-05T17:22:05Z",
        "name": "HRTeam",
        "displayName": "HR Team"
    }
]}
```

Paging

Some Microsoft Graph resources may page results, especially when a substantial number of items or data is returned. This kind of paging happens automatically on the API's end. It's also possible to call the API using paging with the `$top` OData parameter. When a response requires more than one call to retrieve all results, the `@odata.nextLink` property is returned as part of the response. The next set of results can be retrieved by calling the URL value of the `@odata.nextLink` property. The property is returned in the result until all result pages are retrieved.

For example, let's call the users resource on Graph API and return just two objects with `displayName`:

```
HTTP GET https://graph.microsoft.com/v1.0/
users?$top=2&$select=displayName
```

And the response begins as follows:

```
{"@odata.context": "https://graph.microsoft.com/v1.0/$metadata#us-
ers(displayName)","@odata.nextLink": https://graph.microsoft.com/v1.0/
users?$top=2&$select=displayName&$skiptoken=RFNwdAIAAQAAACU6QWRlbG-
VWQE0zNjV4NTgyMjUyODYuT25NaWNyb3NvZnQuY29tKVVzZXJfYzk5MmJkM2ItODk5NS-
00MGNkLWFjMTEtOTZkODM2NTUxYWM2uQAAAAAAAAAAAAA
```

As in the previous example, `@odata.nextLink` includes the original call with `$skiptoken` added. `$skiptoken` will tell the API which page to return. This token is only usable on this specified query and shouldn't be used on other queries.

Paging needs to be considered when building Microsoft Graph-enabled applications, especially when applications are returning substantial amounts of objects or data. It's also a good practice to include paging in the application when it uses just one part of the data at a time and returns more when the user requests more data.

Throttling

Throttling is a mechanism that maintains the reliability of Microsoft Graph and limits the number of concurrent calls to the API. When an API call is throttled, the API returns an `HTTP 429` status code, which means too many requests, and the original request will fail. On the response's headers, there is a `Retry-After` parameter included, which gives the number of seconds after the call can be retried. `Retry-After` delay is not a guarantee that the call will succeed when retried.

Throttling can be avoided by reducing the number of operations per single request and reducing the frequency of API calls. Error handling for throttling is important to be included in the application design.

Metered APIs

Some Microsoft Graph APIs, such as exporting Teams chats and channel conversations or assigning sensitivity labels on SharePoint or OneDrive, require a separate payment of usage. The usage of metered APIs is billed with an Azure subscription.

Teams-related APIs are priced with two different pricing models regarding the usage of the application:

- **Model A**, which is targeted to applications for security and compliance purposes. Usage of this model requires a Microsoft Communications DLP plan for users, which is included in Microsoft 365 A5/E5/G5, Office 365 A5/E5/G5, and security and compliance add-ons. This model includes a license-based quota of calls. Calls exceeding the calculated quota are billed per operation.

- **Model B**, which is for other types of apps. All calls are billed per operation.

> **Note**
> Sensitivity label operations are always billed per operation.

An application using these metered APIs needs to be connected to an active Azure subscription. The solution needs to use application registration in Microsoft Entra ID, which is then linked to a `Microsoft.GraphService/account` type Azure resource in the subscription. Currently, resource linking can be done by using Azure Cloud Shell on the Azure portal or by using a locally installed Azure **command-line interface (CLI)** using the following:

```
az resource create --resource-group rg-GraphBilling --name
graphAppBilling --resource-type Microsoft.GraphServices/accounts
--properties  "{`"appId`": `"5a641a23-2b87-42b5-83d9-a2cb1e9c0a98`"}"
--location Global --subscription 5a641a23-2b87-42b5-83d9-a2cb1e9c0a10
```

In the previous example, `appId` in the properties is the application ID of the Entra ID-registered application.

How to use Microsoft Graph Explorer to call the API

Microsoft Graph Explorer is a browser-based tool that can be used to call Graph API resources. Explorer is extremely useful when developing solutions calling the Graph API, testing API queries, exploring how the Microsoft Graph API works, and also doing real-life changes and configuration. The tool itself can be found at `https://developer.microsoft.com/en-us/graph/graph-explorer`.

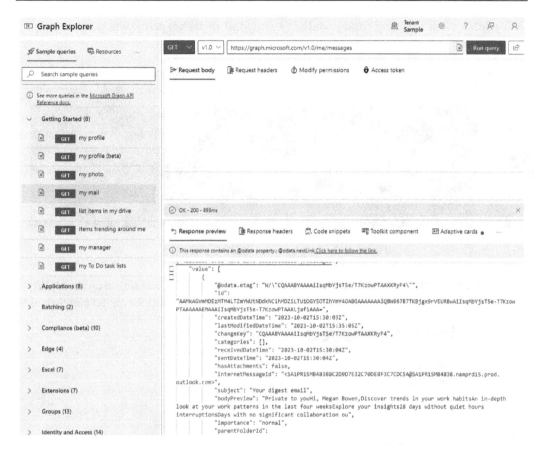

Figure 17.1 - Graph Explorer

Graph Explorer can be used to investigate imaginary demo data, which includes a small set of calls, but the real value of the tool comes when connected to the real Microsoft 365 environment. When testing, the free Microsoft 365 development environment, which can be created by joining the Microsoft 365 Developer Program (https://developer.microsoft.com/en-us/microsoft-365/dev-program), comes in very handy. It's also possible to sign in and connect to the production-grade environment. Almost all API calls that are not linked to the current user require Graph API permissions to be granted consent by the underlying application in Microsoft Entra ID, and in that case, the Global Administrator role.

All API calls are made in the logged-in user's context – in other words, as delegated. So, when something is changed using the API, the current user is marked responsible for changing the object. Users cannot change objects or perform actions they do not have access to.

One example where Graph Explorer might become useful is managing Entra ID directory settings, which is, at the time of authoring this book, available in the beta endpoint. These settings are commonly managed using the AzureADPreview PowerShell module.

Let's disable Microsoft 365 group creation and add a group that always has permission to create groups at the same time:

1. The first thing is to consent the needed permissions for Graph Explorer from the **Modify permissions** tab. Updating this setting requires the `Directory.ReadWrite.All` permission:

Figure 17.2 - Permission for Graph Explorer

2. When calling different resources, different permissions are needed and shown on the **Modify permissions** tab. Always refer to the Graph API documentation to select the correct permissions.

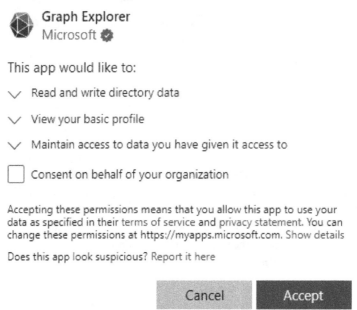

Figure 17.3 - Permission consent screen

3. The consent screen displays permissions that are granted consent for Graph Explorer.

4. The next step is to get the ID of the `Group.Unified` directory setting by calling the `directorySettings` resource:

    ```
    HTTP GET https://graph.microsoft.com/beta/
    settings?$select=displayName,Id
    ```

> **Note**
>
> Notice that the previous call lists all directory settings since the `directorySettings` resource doesn't support OData filtering.

The response displays `displayName` and ID of the directory settings:

```
"@odata.context": "https://graph.microsoft.com/beta/$metadata#settings(displayName,id)",
"value": [
    {
        "displayName": "Group.Unified",
        "id": "7d633f99-c3c2-492a-a7ae-00a71d5a4d79"
    }
]
```

Figure 17.4 - Response of the directory settings from Entra ID

Currently, only the `Group.Unified` directory setting is created on Entra ID, and the ID is needed for the next call.

5. For updating group creation settings, an updated call is needed, and when something is updated, it's always an `HTTP PATCH` call:

    ```
    HTTP PATCH https://graph.microsoft.com/beta/settings/7d633f99-
    c3c2-492a-a7ae-00a71d5a4d79
    ```

A request body is also required since values are updated. The request body content is a simple JSON representation of name-value pairs:

```
{       "values": [
        {
                "name": "EnableGroupCreation",
                "value": "false"
        },
        {

                "name": "GroupCreationAllowedGroupId",
                "value": "eeb3035b-82dd-4f17-9515-daa9d21d32e3"

        }

    ]

}
```

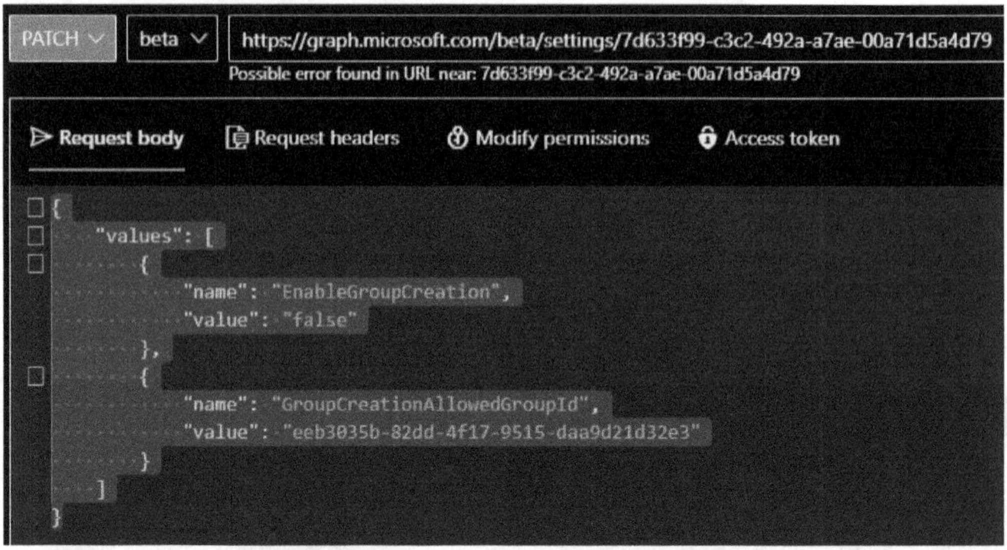

Figure 17.5 - Using Graph Explorer to update directory settings

The Microsoft Graph PowerShell SDK

Another great tool for building solutions, especially automation, on top of the Microsoft Graph API is the Microsoft Graph PowerShell SDK, which is a set of PowerShell cmdlets representing the Graph API's resources.

The Graph PowerShell SDK module can be installed from the PowerShell Gallery, which is a public, centralized repository for sharing PowerShell scripts, modules, and code. The SDK is supported on Windows PowerShell and PowerShell 7, which is the recommended version to be used. Installing the SDK can be done using the following:

```
Install-Module Microsoft.Graph -Scope CurrentUser
```

The Scope parameter's `CurrentUser` value will install the module for the current user only and doesn't require administrator permissions on the computer. With the `AllUsers` value, the module is installed for all users.

If the beta version of the SDK is required, it's included in a separate module and is installed with the following:

```
Install-Module Microsoft.Graph.Beta -Scope CurrentUser
```

The SDK structure is divided into the `Microsoft.Graph` and `Microsoft.Graph.Beta` main modules and 38 submodules, which are installed when the main modules are installed. Sometimes, only a few of these modules are required, and it's good practice to install the submodules needed, per the following example:

```
Install-Module Microsoft.Graph.Sites -Scope CurrentUser
Install-Module Microsoft.Graph.Files -Scope CurrentUser
```

The authentication submodule is installed automatically. To see which Graph SDK modules are already installed, use the following:

```
Get-InstalledModule Microsoft.Graph*
```

```
● PS C:\code> get-installedmodule Microsoft.Graph*

Version     Name                                   Repository   Description
-------     ----                                   ----------   -----------
2.8.0       Microsoft.Graph                        PSGallery    Microsoft Graph PowerShell module
2.8.0       Microsoft.Graph.Applications           PSGallery    Microsoft Graph PowerShell Cmdlets
2.8.0       Microsoft.Graph.Authentication         PSGallery    Microsoft Graph PowerShell Authentication Module.
2.8.0       Microsoft.Graph.Bookings               PSGallery    Microsoft Graph PowerShell Cmdlets
2.8.0       Microsoft.Graph.Calendar               PSGallery    Microsoft Graph PowerShell Cmdlets
2.8.0       Microsoft.Graph.ChangeNotifications     PSGallery    Microsoft Graph PowerShell Cmdlets
2.8.0       Microsoft.Graph.CloudCommunications     PSGallery    Microsoft Graph PowerShell Cmdlets
2.8.0       Microsoft.Graph.Compliance             PSGallery    Microsoft Graph PowerShell Cmdlets
2.8.0       Microsoft.Graph.CrossDeviceExperie…     PSGallery    Microsoft Graph PowerShell Cmdlets
```

Figure 17.6 - List installed Graph modules

Connecting to Microsoft Graph with the PowerShell SDK

The Graph PowerShell SDK can connect to the Microsoft Graph API using delegated authentication, when accessed by the user, or app-only authentication using the Entra ID-registered application.

For **delegated authentication**, there are three methods to be used:

- The first method is to connect directly using user credentials:

  ```
  Connect-MgGraph -Scopes "Sites.Read.All","Files.ReadWrite.All"
  ```

  The previous example uses interactive user authentication, which opens a Microsoft 365 login screen for a username, password, and possible strong authentication method. The `Scopes` parameter defines the access to the Graph API. In the example, `Sites.Read.All` allows access to read all sites in the target environment and `Files.ReadWrite.All` allows access to read and write all files. These permission scopes are documented per resource in the Microsoft Graph API's documentation.

- The second method is to connect using device authentication:

  ```
  Connect-MgGraph -Scopes "Sites.Read.All","Files.ReadWrite.All"
  -UseDeviceAuthentication
  ```

In the previous example, the `UseDeviceAuthentication` parameter enables device-code flow, which enables authentication using a different device. This is useful, for example, when using Azure Cloud Shell or logging against a specific tenant.

- The third method to connect is using an access token already acquired:

```
Connect-MgGraph -AccessToken $accessToken
```

For app-only access, the connection is made using client credentials with a certificate. For the connection, the ID of the Entra ID-registered application and the Microsoft 365 tenant ID are needed:

```
Connect-MgGraph -ClientId e8fdb70e-ec91-46ce-94c3-84126070b295 -
TenantId 86f285e8-0af4-46ee-9835-72f659c3fa35 -CertificateThumbprint
86f285e80af446ee983572f659c3fa35
```

Permissions for app-only access are set and controlled on the Entra ID-registered application's API permissions. App-only access is especially needed when building automations that are running independently without user interaction.

Using the SDK

The SDK uses standard PowerShell verbs and naming conventions for cmdlets. Each resource is represented as a cmdlet – for example, listing all SharePoint sites is achieved using `Get-MgAllSite`, or `New-MgSiteList` can be used to create a new list to a site.

Each cmdlet has a distinct set of properties, so it is important to read the cmdlet documentation.

As an example, let's find a Human Resources site and list all lists on the site:

1. First, the connection needs to be made with permission to access all sites:

```
Connect-MgGraph -Scopes "Sites.Manage.All" -UseDeviceCode
```

2. The next step is to search for a site since we don't have the site's ID, and as OData filtering is not available, search needs to be used:

```
Get-MgSite -Search "HR"
```

Figure 17.7 - Searching for sites

3. For the next call, the site's ID is needed, and it's highlighted in *Figure 17.7*:

```
Get-MgSiteList -SiteId 28e328a9-00f4-4b6e-b850-abf67531ec21
```

```
● PS C:\code> Get-MgSiteList -SiteId 28e328a9-00f4-4b6e-b850-abf67531ec21

DisplayName                              Id                                        Name
-----------                              --                                        ----
Onboarding                               f3f52ef9-a202-456b-95e3-2ae230c3642a      HR Onboarding
Client Side Component Manifests          e9a36fa1-d1b9-4de1-8a6a-2e38fd0dd0c9      ComponentManifests
Project Task Tracker                     023cd1f4-6204-424b-b586-317622eb1403      Project Task Tracker
Employee onboarding                      b7a83ce5-8b00-43c4-9722-57cc32b2ddbd      Employee onboarding
Documents                                4b8ba269-116e-4137-b79e-591c6ec63d94      Shared Documents
Invoices                                 7579532d-9386-4f58-8ced-6d03c46c757c      Invoices
Client Side Assets                       58ad3c14-219a-4658-b8ae-7458165abfa8      ClientSideAssets
Teams                                    f8b98791-2f25-4215-b7b5-7887c6637c4b      Teams
Project Tracker List                     733e93a1-6426-4799-aa53-85715e6ee8b5      Project Tracker List
Apps for SharePoint                      becc7551-a2a0-4014-b322-9e603284f319      AppCatalog
```

Figure 17.8 - List on the site

The Graph PowerShell SDK supplies a couple of helpful tools to find the correct cmdlets and get the list of permissions details.

With Find-MgGraphCommand, it's possible to search for cmdlets using wildcards, resource URIs, or command names. For example, commands to access document libraries using Drives resources can be looked for using a URI:

```
Find-MgGraphCommand -URI "/drives/{id}"
```

```
● PS C:\code> Find-MgGraphCommand -URI "/drives/{id}"

    APIVersion: v1.0

Command          Module Method URI                   OutputType          Permissions
-------          ------ ------ ---                   ----------          -----------
Get-MgDrive      Files  GET    /drives/{drive-id}    IMicrosoftGraphDrive {Files.Read, Files.Read.All, Files.ReadWrite, Files.ReadWrite.All…}
Remove-MgDrive   Files  DELETE /drives/{drive-id}                         {}
Update-MgDrive   Files  PATCH  /drives/{drive-id}    IMicrosoftGraphDrive {}
```

Figure 17.9 - Using Find-MgGraphCommand

The response lists all commands for managing a drive. It also shows needed permissions.

The Find-MgGraphPermissions command can be used to discover which permissions to use with a specific cmdlet. For example, discovering which permissions are needed to read all sites can be achieved using the following:

```
Find-MgGraphPermissions sites
```

```
● PS C:\code> Find-MgGraphPermission sites

    PermissionType: Delegated

Id                                     Consent Name                Description
--                                     ------- ----                -----------
5a54b8b3-347c-476d-8f8e-42d5c2424d29   Admin   Sites.FullControl.All  Allows the application to have full control of all site collections on behalf of the signed-in user.
65e50fdc-43b7-4915-933e-0d138f11f40a   User    Sites.Manage.All       Allow the application to create or delete document libraries and lists in all site collections on your behalf.
205e70e5-aba6-4c52-a976-6d2d46c48043   User    Sites.Read.All         Allow the application to read documents and list items in all site collections on your behalf
89f6ba52-be36-487e-b7d8-d061c450a026   User    Sites.ReadWrite.All    Allow the application to edit or delete documents and list items in all site collections on your behalf.

    PermissionType: Application

Id                                     Consent Name                Description
--                                     ------- ----                -----------
a82116e5-55eb-4c41-a434-62fe8a61c773   Admin   Sites.FullControl.All  Allows the app to have full control of all site collections without a signed in user.
0c0bf378-bf22-4483-8f81-9e09a9b490ba   Admin   Sites.Manage.All       Allows the app to create or delete document libraries and lists in all site collections without a signed in user.
332a536c-c7ef-4017-ab91-33897092d4f0   Admin   Sites.Read.All         Allows the app to read documents and list items in all site collections without a signed in user.
9492366f-7d69-46a4-8d15-edfa20070fff   Admin   Sites.ReadWrite.All    Allows the app to create, read, update, and delete documents and list items in all site collections without a sig
883ea228-0bf2-4a8f-9f9d-92c9162a727d   Admin   Sites.Selected         Allow the application to access a subset of site collections without a signed in user.  The specific site collecti
```

Figure 17.10 - List permissions

The response lists all permissions for accessing the Sites resource with descriptions. Consent columns show that admin consent for that specific permission is needed. For example, if the Graph API is connected using the `Sites.FullControl.All` permission scope as a user, admin consent is required for accessing the underlying API.

Accessing SharePoint data with the Graph API and the SharePoint Framework

The Microsoft Graph API's resources can also be accessed within the SharePoint Framework for creating solutions to consume, update, and create new data for Microsoft Cloud services. The SharePoint Framework supplies a ready-made HTTP client, which handles user authentication and permissions automatically, to access the Graph API's resources. Calling Graph from the SharePoint Framework is simple; just use an import clause to introduce the MSGraphClientV3 client to the solution:

```
import {MSGraphClientV3} from '@microsoft/sp-http';
```

And then it can be used to call the Graph API:

```
this.context.msGraphClientFactory.getClient("3").
then((client:MSGraphClientV3): void=>{client.api("/me").get((error,
response:any, rawResponse?:any)=>{
        this.userProf.displayName = response.displayName;
        this.userProf.mail = response.mail;
        this.userProf.jobtitle = response.jobTitle;
    });
  });
```

The previous example first loads the client and then calls the Graph API's /me resource, which returns the basic profile information of the currently signed-in user. The user's `displayName`, `mail`, and `jobTitle` are then added from the response to the named `userProf` object for later handling.

> **Note**
> The most recent MSGraphClientV3 version is available for solutions built with the SharePoint Framework version 1.15.0 or later.

Calls for the Graph API are made in the user's context using permission scopes introduced in the SharePoint Framework solution's `package-solution.json` configuration file. By default, calling Graph will return an authentication token with the `user_impersonation` permission scope, which doesn't allow reading any data. Requesting a Graph API permission is done by adding a `webApiPermissionRequests` object to `package-solution.json`:

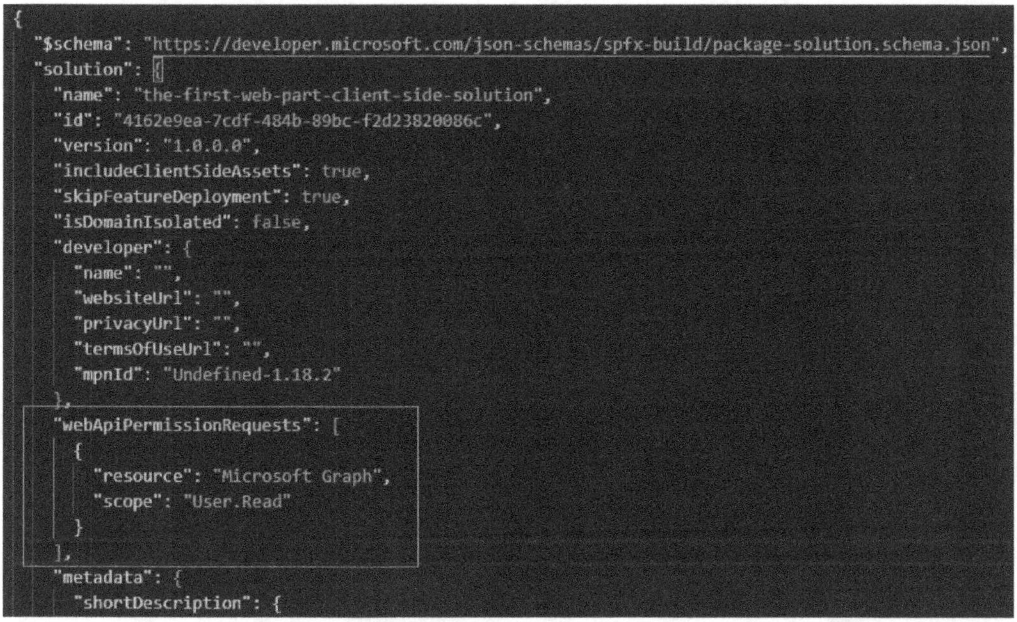

```json
{
  "$schema": "https://developer.microsoft.com/json-schemas/spfx-build/package-solution.schema.json",
  "solution": {
    "name": "the-first-web-part-client-side-solution",
    "id": "4162e9ea-7cdf-484b-89bc-f2d23820086c",
    "version": "1.0.0.0",
    "includeClientSideAssets": true,
    "skipFeatureDeployment": true,
    "isDomainIsolated": false,
    "developer": {
      "name": "",
      "websiteUrl": "",
      "privacyUrl": "",
      "termsOfUseUrl": "",
      "mpnId": "Undefined-1.18.2"
    },
    "webApiPermissionRequests": [
      {
        "resource": "Microsoft Graph",
        "scope": "User.Read"
      }
    ],
    "metadata": {
      "shortDescription": {
```

Figure 17.11 - WebApiPermissions configuration

In *Figure 17.11*, the User.Read permission is requested for the Microsoft Graph API. Once the solution is deployed to the SharePoint App Catalog, administrators can approve requested permissions on the API access management page in the SharePoint admin center:

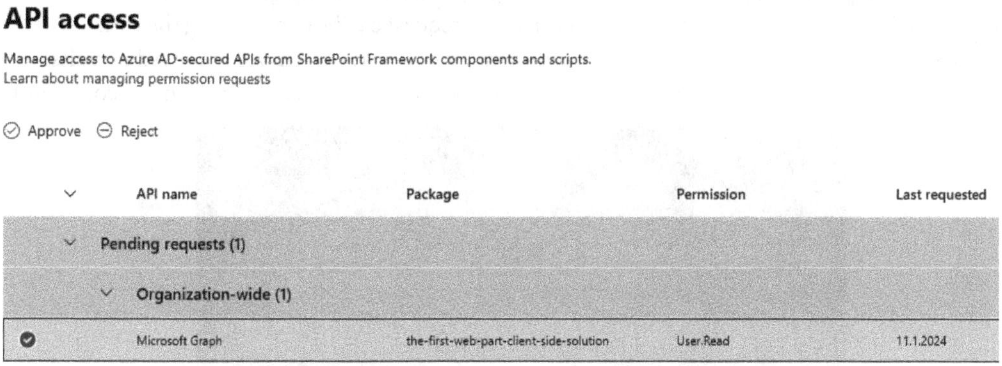

API access

Manage access to Azure AD-secured APIs from SharePoint Framework components and scripts.
Learn about managing permission requests

⊘ Approve   ⊖ Reject

	API name	Package	Permission	Last requested
∨ **Pending requests (1)**				
∨ **Organization-wide (1)**				
●	Microsoft Graph	the-first-web-part-client-side-solution	User.Read	11.1.2024

Figure 17.12 - Permission approval

> **Note**
> Granted permissions are available for all web parts consuming the Graph API.

Permission requests can also be managed and approved using the SharePoint Online Management Shell.

With `Get-SPOTenantServicePrincipalPermissionsRequest`, it's possible to list all requests that haven't been approved:

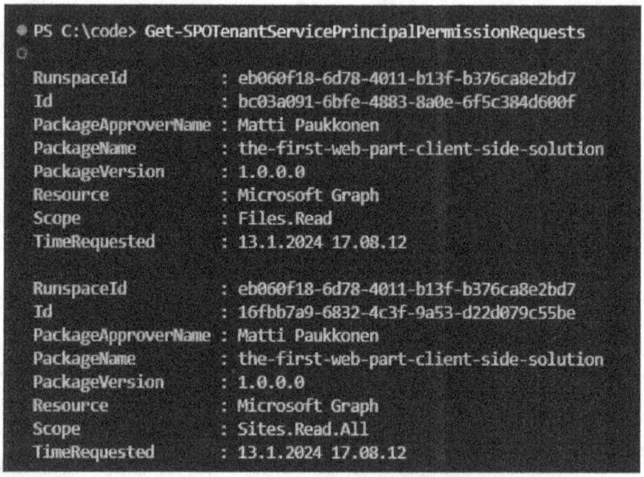

```
PS C:\code> Get-SPOTenantServicePrincipalPermissionRequests

RunspaceId           : eb060f18-6d78-4011-b13f-b376ca8e2bd7
Id                   : bc03a091-6bfe-4883-8a0e-6f5c384d600f
PackageApproverName  : Matti Paukkonen
PackageName          : the-first-web-part-client-side-solution
PackageVersion       : 1.0.0.0
Resource             : Microsoft Graph
Scope                : Files.Read
TimeRequested        : 13.1.2024 17.08.12

RunspaceId           : eb060f18-6d78-4011-b13f-b376ca8e2bd7
Id                   : 16fbb7a9-6832-4c3f-9a53-d22d079c55be
PackageApproverName  : Matti Paukkonen
PackageName          : the-first-web-part-client-side-solution
PackageVersion       : 1.0.0.0
Resource             : Microsoft Graph
Scope                : Sites.Read.All
TimeRequested        : 13.1.2024 17.08.12
```

Figure 17.13 - Permission requests

Requested permissions can be approved using the following:

```
Approve-SPOTenantServicePermissionsRequest -RequestId bc03a091-6bfe-
4883-8a0e-6f5c384d600f
```

The previous example code approved the `Files.Read` permission shown in *Figure 17.13*. The `RequestId` parameter is the ID value of the request. The permissions request can be denied using the `Deny-SPOT enantServicePermissionsRequest` command with `RequestId`. All approved permissions can be listed with the `Get-SPOTenantServicePrincipalPermissionGrants` command:

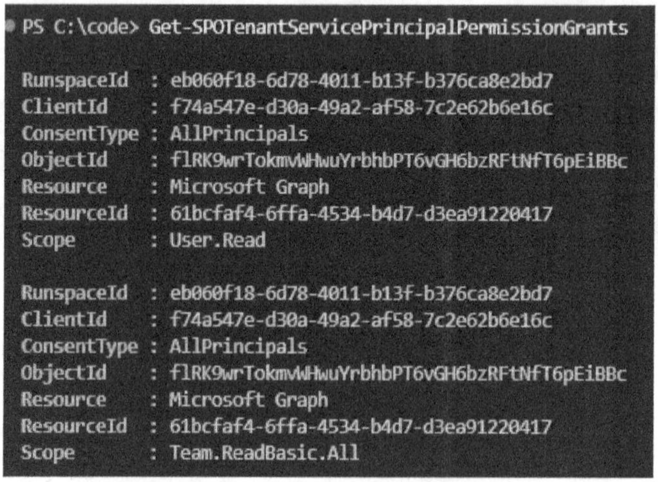

```
PS C:\code> Get-SPOTenantServicePrincipalPermissionGrants

RunspaceId  : eb060f18-6d78-4011-b13f-b376ca8e2bd7
ClientId    : f74a547e-d30a-49a2-af58-7c2e62b6e16c
ConsentType : AllPrincipals
ObjectId    : flRK9wrTokmvWHwuYrbhbPT6vGH6bzRFtNfT6pEiBBc
Resource    : Microsoft Graph
ResourceId  : 61bcfaf4-6ffa-4534-b4d7-d3ea91220417
Scope       : User.Read

RunspaceId  : eb060f18-6d78-4011-b13f-b376ca8e2bd7
ClientId    : f74a547e-d30a-49a2-af58-7c2e62b6e16c
ConsentType : AllPrincipals
ObjectId    : flRK9wrTokmvWHwuYrbhbPT6vGH6bzRFtNfT6pEiBBc
Resource    : Microsoft Graph
ResourceId  : 61bcfaf4-6ffa-4534-b4d7-d3ea91220417
Scope       : Team.ReadBasic.All
```

Figure 17.14 - All approved permissions

Summary

In this chapter, we were first introduced to the Microsoft Graph API, including the API structure and the usage of the API. We also learned how to use OData queries to filter, order, and define API calls.

Next, we delved into using Microsoft Graph Explorer with the Graph API, and learned how it can be used to discover the API and test API calls, but also used for small configurations.

Next, we learned how to use the Microsoft Graph PowerShell SDK to access Microsoft Graph.

Finally, we were introduced to how the Graph API can be accessed within the SharePoint Framework, and how the SharePoint Framework's Graph API permissions are managed.

In the next chapter, we will delve into SharePoint Framework web parts.

18

Web Parts and App Part Pages

One of the key features of SharePoint is the ability to customize the look and functionality of pages with web parts. A web part is a reusable component that can display content or information from various sources, such as lists and libraries, or external sources such as the Microsoft Graph API. The web part can also act as a user interface and create and update data.

An app part is a special representation of a web part. When the web part can be added like a component to a page, the app part is the whole page, such as a **single-page application** (**SPA**). A single web part can either be a component on a page or act like an SPA with the same code base. The behavior is controlled with a SharePoint Framework solution setting.

Web parts can also be used inside Microsoft Teams, where they can be added as an application. A web part can be hosted as a tab in Microsoft Teams channels, or as a personal application, which is targeted to a user and located in the left rail menu on Teams.

In this chapter, we're going to cover the following main topics:

- SharePoint Framework web parts
- SPAs with web parts
- Extending Teams tabs and personal apps with web parts

SharePoint Framework web parts

A web part is the most common way to customize modern SharePoint Online. It's a reusable component that can be added to pages, and it can show data from SharePoint or external sources using APIs. It can also be a user interface for a list in SharePoint Online or it can manage data living in an external system. Web parts developed using the SharePoint Framework support both modern and classic SharePoint pages.

A web part's code is a client-side JavaScript code, which is executed within the user's browser. Development can be made using plain JavaScript or by using common web frameworks such as React, Angular, or Vue.js.

Creating and deploying a web part

Let's create a SharePoint Framework web part project for managing the Human Resources onboarding list on SharePoint. The web part should display assigned items from the list and use Microsoft's Employee Onboarding list as a template and data storage.

An environment for SharePoint Framework development needs to be set up before creating a new project. This is explained in more detail in *Chapter 16*.

First, let's create a new project with the following:

```
yo @microsoft/sharepoint
```

In **Settings**, pick **WebPart** as the component, give the solutions a name, and select **React** as the template. Once the project is completely created, let's open Visual Studio Code or another preferred development tool, and see the web part's source code structure:

Figure 18.1 - Web part source code structure

The project consists of several folders and files (these are created automatically when the project is created):

- **Assets folder**: For assets that are used in the web part, such as images and icons

- **Components folder**: Includes a class for the web part's properties, style definitions, and a React component, which is used for rendering the view

- **Loc folder**: Files for localization of the web part

- **OnboardingTasksWebPart.manifest.json file**: Includes specific web part settings

- **OnboardingTasksWebPart.ts file**: The web part class file that acts as a main entry point
- **Index.ts file**: Required just for the TypeScript compiler

Let's first open the web part class, which, in this example, is the `OnboardingTasksWebPart.ts` file, and go through the basic elements.

In the **Imports** section, all required external classes and modules are imported to the web part. When new modules are needed, imports also need to be updated:

```typescript
1   import * as React from 'react';
2   import * as ReactDom from 'react-dom';
3   import { Version } from '@microsoft/sp-core-library';
4   import {
5     type IPropertyPaneConfiguration,
6     PropertyPaneTextField
7   } from '@microsoft/sp-property-pane';
8   import { BaseClientSideWebPart } from '@microsoft/sp-webpart-base';
9   import { IReadonlyTheme } from '@microsoft/sp-component-base';
10
11  import * as strings from 'OnboardingTasksWebPartStrings';
12  import OnboardingTasks from './components/OnboardingTasks';
13  import { IOnboardingTasksProps } from './components/IOnboardingTasksProps';
```

Figure 18.2 - Importing external modules and classes

The `render()` method controls what is rendered when the web part is loaded. Since this example is using React, a new React element is created with specified web part properties, which are defined in the `IOnBoardingTasksProps` interface:

```typescript
public render(): void {
  const element: React.ReactElement<IOnboardingTasksProps> = React.createElement(
    OnboardingTasks,
    {
      description: this.properties.description,
      isDarkTheme: this._isDarkTheme,
      environmentMessage: this._environmentMessage,
      hasTeamsContext: !!this.context.sdks.microsoftTeams,
      userDisplayName: this.context.pageContext.user.displayName
    }
  );
```

Figure 18.3 - Web part's render method

Access to the SharePoint list data

The first step is to create a data model for the list data. For this example, we need the **ID** of the list item, **Title**, **Description**, **Completed**, and **Completed On**. These can be defined in an interface, in this example, called IOnboardingTask:

```
export interface IOnboardingTask{
    ListItemId: number;
    Title: string;
    Description: string;
    Complete: boolean;
    CompletedOn: Date;
}
```

The interface can also be defined in the web part class file, but for clarity, it's better to create a separate file called IOnBoardingTask.ts and put it in a separate folder for typing and interfaces.

After that, we can create a service class for accessing data on the SharePoint list, again in a separate file and folder for clarity. Let's call it ListService. The service class implements a constructor, which has the site URL and list's name as parameters, and the getItems method, which is used to do the actual HTTP call to the SharePoint list:

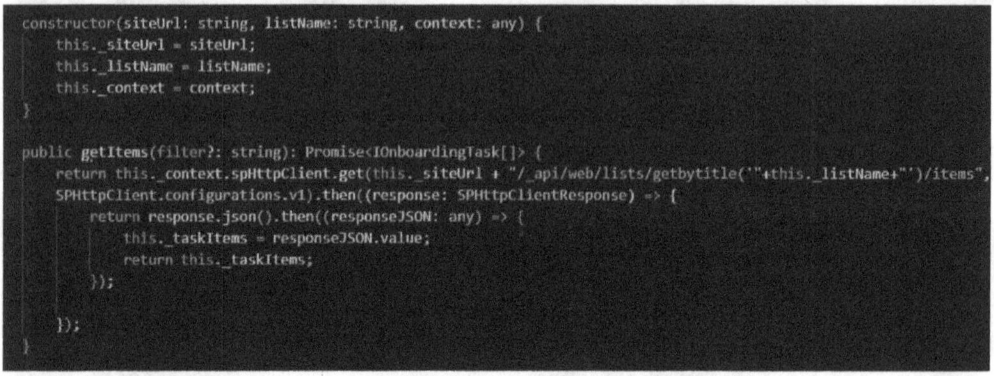

```
constructor(siteUrl: string, listName: string, context: any) {
    this._siteUrl = siteUrl;
    this._listName = listName;
    this._context = context;
}

public getItems(filter?: string): Promise<IOnboardingTask[]> {
    return this._context.spHttpClient.get(this._siteUrl + "/_api/web/lists/getbytitle('"+this._listName+"')/items",
SPHttpClient.configurations.v1).then((response: SPHttpClientResponse) => {
        return response.json().then((responseJSON: any) => {
            this._taskItems = responseJSON.value;
            return this._taskItems;
        });
    });
}
```

Figure 18.4 - The ListService class

Implementing the service class to the web part is to initialize a new instance of it in the onInit method of the web part class and to pass it to the React element of the render method using the web part properties:

```
private _isDarkTheme: boolean = false;
private _environmentMessage: string = '';
private _listService: ListService;

protected async onInit(): Promise<void> {
  super.onInit();
  this._listService = new ListService(this.context.pageContext.web.absoluteUrl, "Employee onboarding tasks", this.context);

  return this._getEnvironmentMessage().then(message => {
    this._environmentMessage = message;
  });
}
public render(): void {
  const element: React.ReactElement<IOnboardingTasksProps> = React.createElement(
    OnboardingTasks,
    {
      description: this.properties.description,
      isDarkTheme: this._isDarkTheme,
      environmentMessage: this._environmentMessage,
      hasTeamsContext: !!this.context.sdks.microsoftTeams,
      userDisplayName: this.context.pageContext.user.displayName,
      context: this.context,
      listService: this._listService
    }
  );

  ReactDom.render(element, this.domElement);
}
```

Figure 18.5 - Implementing the service class

Finally, implement the call to the `getItems` method in the React element called `OnboardingTasks.tsx`. Since this is a React solution, the management of the state is important to render the response of the `getItems` call.

For handling the component's state, an interface describing the data included in the state needs to be implemented. For this example, simply including an array of `IOnboardingTask` is enough, like in the following code:

```
export interface IOnboardingTasksState {
    items: IOnboardingTask[];
}
```

Next, the `getItems` call is made in the React component's `componentDidMount` method, and the response is set to the state of the component:

```
public async componentDidMount() {
    this._spListService.getItems("").then((response) => {    this.
setState({ items: response });
  });
}
```

Here, we're rendering the content of the state as a list:

```
<ul className={styles.links}>                          {this.state.items.
map((item, index) => (
```

```
    <li key={index} className={styles.taskListItem}>
    <div className={styles.task}>
    <h4>{item.Title}</h4>
    <p>{item.Description}</p>
    <p>Completed: {item.Complete ? 'Yes' : 'No'}</p>
    {item.Complete && <p>When Completed:        {item.
Completedon}            </p>}
    </div>
    </li>
    ))}
</ul>
```

The pattern presented in this example is just one choice of SharePoint Framework development patterns. It always depends on which JavaScript framework is used and how data is accessed and displayed to users.

Web part properties and the property pane

Web part properties can be gathered from users using the web part's property pane. The **Property** pane can hold a property or have multiple pages, with multiple property groups and properties. The **Property** pane supports these field types:

- Button
- Checkbox
- Choice group
- Dropdown
- Link
- Slider
- Textbox and multi-line textbox
- Toggle

It's also possible to create custom property fields.

Let's extend the earlier example by adding the name of the list as a configurable property. The property pane contents are controlled on the `getPropertyPaneConfiguration` method on the web part class:

```
protected getPropertyPaneConfiguration(): IPropertyPaneConfiguration {
    return {
        pages: [
            {
```

```
        groups: [
            {
                groupName: "Configuration",
                groupFields: [
                    PropertyPaneTextField('listName', {
                        label: "List name"
                    })
                ]
            }
        ]
    };
}
```

The example holds just one property pane page, a group named Configuration, and a text field property called listName.

The property needs to exist in the web part's property interface, which is defined in the web part class file:

```
export interface IOnboardingTasksWebPartProps {
    listName: string;
}
```

After that, the property can be used in the code, like in the example, as a parameter for the ListService class constructor:

```
this._listService = new ListService(this.context.pageContext.web.
absoluteUrl, this.properties.listName, this.context);
```

The web part's **Property** pane looks like *Figure 18.6*:

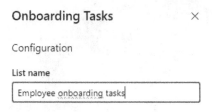

Figure 18.6 - Web part's Property pane

The web part's properties can be predefined in the preconfiguredEntries section in the web part's manifest. In the following example, the listName property is set as Employee onboarding tasks:

```
"preconfiguredEntries": [{
    "groupId": "5c03119e-3074-46fd-976b-c60198311f70", // Advanced
```

```
      "group": { "default": "Advanced" },
      "title": { "default": "Onboarding Tasks" },
      "description": { "default": "Onboarding Tasks description" },
      "officeFabricIconFontName": "Page",
      "properties": {
         "listName": "Employee onboarding tasks"
      }
   }]
```

Localization

The SharePoint Framework supports localization natively. Localization support is automatically included in the project during project creation. Each localized language is created as a separate file for translations, typically on the `loc` folder in the project. The file itself holds a key-value pair of localized texts. The file needs to be named using the country and language code combination, such as `en-us.js` for United States English or `fi-fi.js` for Finnish.

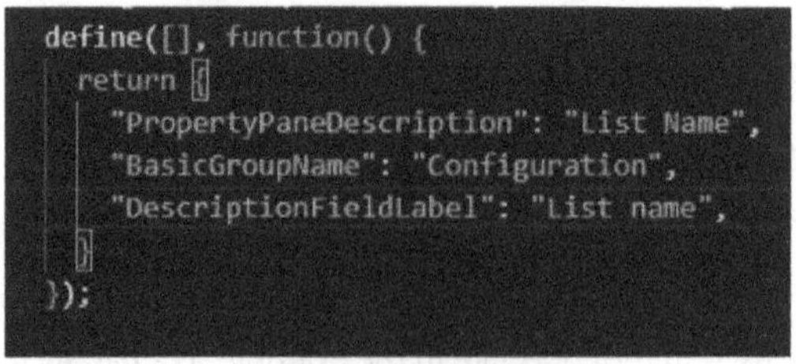

```
define([], function() {
   return {
      "PropertyPaneDescription": "List Name",
      "BasicGroupName": "Configuration",
      "DescriptionFieldLabel": "List name",
   }
});
```

Figure 18.7 - Language file

All keys need to be defined in an interface, which is exported as a module. This file is typically found in the same folder as the translation files. In the earlier example, this file is named `mystring.d.ts`.

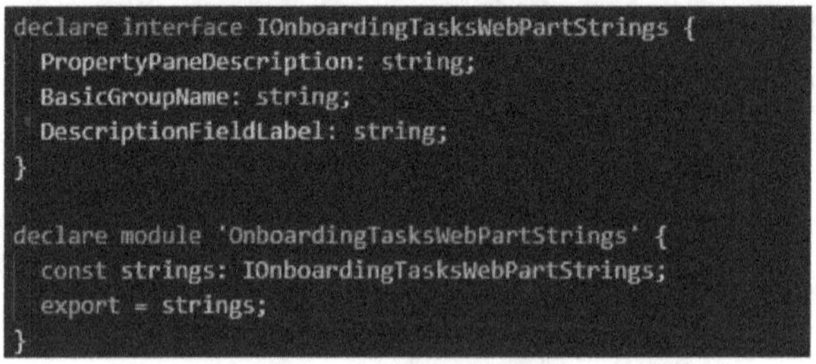

```
declare interface IOnboardingTasksWebPartStrings {
   PropertyPaneDescription: string;
   BasicGroupName: string;
   DescriptionFieldLabel: string;
}

declare module 'OnboardingTasksWebPartStrings' {
   const strings: IOnboardingTasksWebPartStrings;
   export = strings;
}
```

Figure 18.8 - Module for localization

And finally, the module is imported into the web part class:

```
import * as strings from 'OnboardingTasksWebPartStrings';
```

The localized text can be called in the code using `strings.<key>` – for example, `strings.BasicGroupName`.

Creating SPAs with web parts

A SharePoint Framework web part can be displayed inside of a single app part page like an SPA. The web part controls the whole canvas. The app part page itself cannot be edited or configured. The web part's settings and the name of the page can be changed in the **Property** pane. The page doesn't have a header section like article pages or news pages do, so the header needs to be handled within the web part's code.

The support for app part pages is enabled in the web part's manifest by adding `SharePointFullPage` to the `supportedHosts` property. This is automatically set during project creation. The `supportedHosts` property controls how the web part can be used in SharePoint and Microsoft Teams:

```
"supportedHosts": ["SharePointWebPart", "TeamsPersonalApp",
"TeamsTab", "SharePointFullPage"]
```

After the property is set, the web part needs to be deployed before it can be used. The Workbench doesn't support testing the web part in single app part page mode, which means that the web part needs to be deployed for testing the layout in the single app part page mode. The packaging and deployment of a SharePoint Framework solution are explained in more detail in *Chapter 16*.

Once the web part is deployed and available on the site, the new app part page can be created. The app part page is created in a similar way to a modern SharePoint article page. The **Page templates** dialog displays an **Apps** tab when web parts supporting app part pages are deployed to the site.

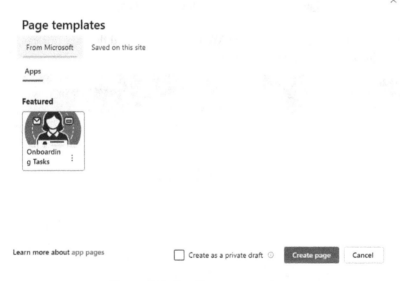

Figure 18.9 - Creating an app part page

After the page is created, the **Property** pane opens. The pane displays a text field for the page title, which needs to be set the first time the pane is opened, and a setting for displaying the page in the site's navigation. Underneath these settings are settings for the web part itself:

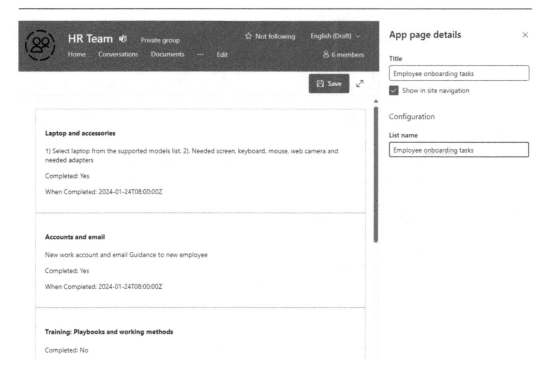

Figure 18.10 - Configuring the app part page

After saving, the web part is displayed as a page. Web part settings and the page title can be changed by clicking **Edit**, which opens the **Property** pane:

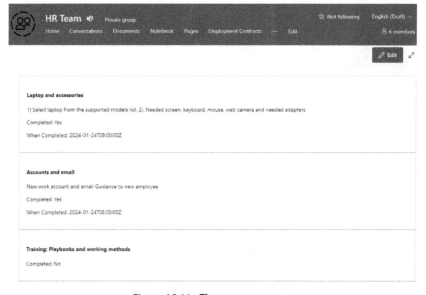

Figure 18.11 - The app part page

When using web parts within app part pages, the layout of the web part needs to be considered. The web part uses the whole width of the page canvas, so it's important to consider how content is displayed to avoid too much white space on wide screens. Also, the page header section is not visible on app part pages, so it needs to be considered and rendered inside of the web part.

Single app part pages are useful for displaying large dashboards – for example, gathering information from the Microsoft Graph API, creating more complex dialogs, or creating user interfaces for external systems.

Extending Teams tabs and personal apps with web parts

Web parts can also be used to extend Microsoft Teams functionality by either adding them as tabs on Teams channels or using them as personal apps that are accessed from Teams' left rail menu. SharePoint supplies the hosting platform for the application, so there is no need for any external hosting platform for running the application. Deployment is also simple; the application is first deployed to the SharePoint App Catalog and can be deployed at the same time or later as an organization app to Microsoft Teams.

Enabling a web part on Teams is done in a similar way to single app part pages. The support is defined in the web part's manifest using the `supportedHosts` property. Support for the Teams tab is enabled using the `TeamsTab` parameter and for personal apps using the `TeamsPersonalApp` parameter. Both settings are enabled when the project is created:

```
"supportedHosts": ["SharePointWebPart", "TeamsPersonalApp",
"TeamsTab", "SharePointFullPage"]
```

Icons, which are shown in Teams, are found in the `teams` folder of the solution. Icon filenames include the web part's ID and `_outline` for small icons and `_color` for large icons – for example, `073cef49-efce-43c1-ad9e-ec518e20fd61_outline.png`. Both icons need to be in the PNG file format. Specifications for small icons are 32 x 32 pixels (with white outline and transparent background), and for large icons are 192 x 192 pixels (which can also include colors).

When using web parts in Microsoft Teams, it's important to take care of different themes that users can select. The SharePoint Framework web part class holds predefined methods for identifying that the web part is run inside Microsoft Teams and identifying when the theme is changed. By default, colors are inverted, but it's possible to extend for more convenient theme support.

Deploying a web part to Microsoft Teams

When the web part is uploaded to the SharePoint App Catalog (`https://tenant.sharepoint.com/sites/appcatalog/_layouts/15/tenantAppCatalog.aspx/manageApps`), the **Enable app** pane is opened. The web part needs to be deployed to all sites, and enabling the **Add to Teams** checkbox deploys the web part to Teams at the same time:

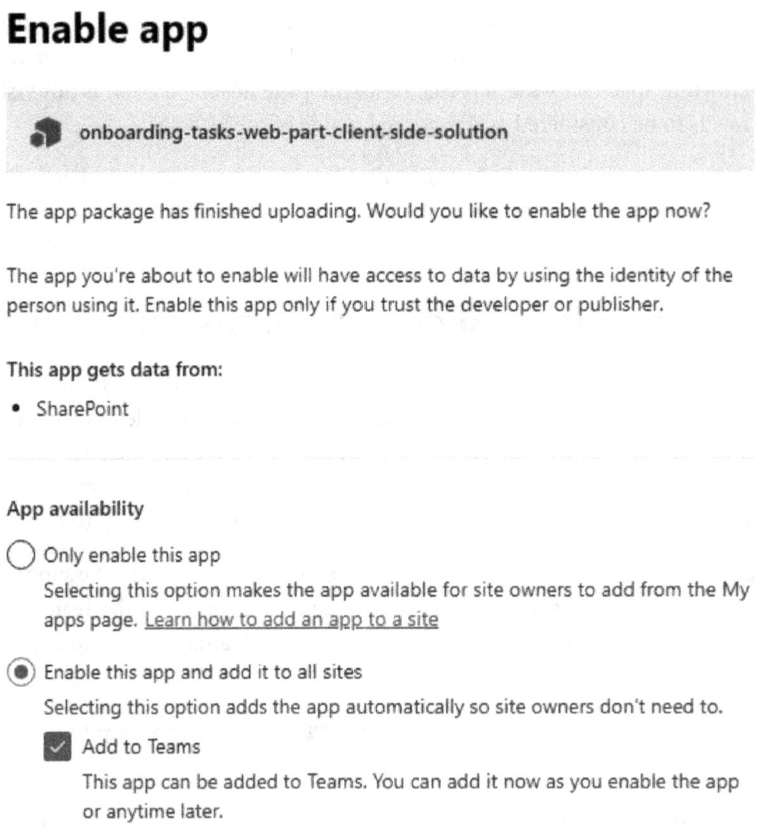

Enable app

 onboarding-tasks-web-part-client-side-solution

The app package has finished uploading. Would you like to enable the app now?

The app you're about to enable will have access to data by using the identity of the person using it. Enable this app only if you trust the developer or publisher.

This app gets data from:

• SharePoint

App availability

○ Only enable this app

Selecting this option makes the app available for site owners to add from the My apps page. Learn how to add an app to a site

◉ Enable this app and add it to all sites

Selecting this option adds the app automatically so site owners don't need to.

☑ Add to Teams

This app can be added to Teams. You can add it now as you enable the app or anytime later.

Figure 18.12 - Deploying the web part to Teams

Another way is to select the web part in the SharePoint App Catalog and select **Add to Teams** from the toolbar.

Adding a web part to a tab

Adding the web part to a **Teams** tab is done by clicking the + sign from the Teams channel's tab bar, searching for the web part, and selecting the web part:

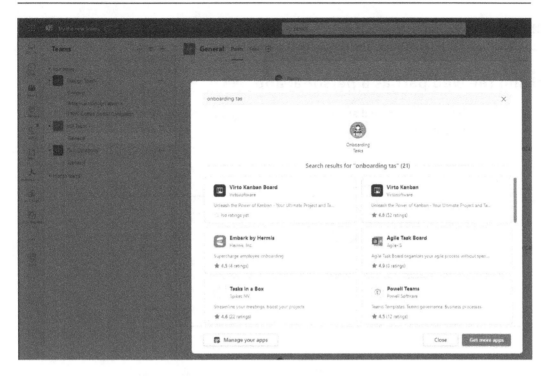

Figure 18.13 - Adding the web part to a tab

The first time the **Property** pane is opened, the necessary configuration for the web part can be done:

Figure 18.14 - First-time experience on a tab

The **Property** pane can be accessed later by opening the menu using the small arrow icon beside the tab name and selecting **Settings**. The tab can be removed from the same menu.

Using the web part as a personal app

Adding the web part as a personal app is done by selecting Teams' left rail menu's three dots and searching for the web part:

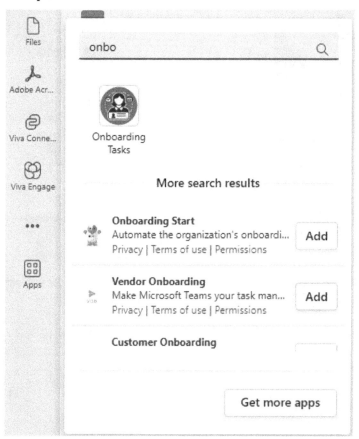

Figure 18.15 - Web part as a personal app

The web part opens in full-screen mode inside Teams. Personal apps do not support configuration of the web part, so it's important either to use predefined configuration or include all necessary configuration to the code. For example, personal apps do not have the context of a team or a site and cannot use the site's URL from the context.

Summary

In this chapter, we were first introduced to the structure of the SharePoint Framework web part project and common parts of the web part classes.

Next, we learned how to access the contents of a list on SharePoint Online and how to render the list's content on a web part. We also learned how to manage a web part's properties and localize the web part.

Then, we learned how web parts can be used like a single-page app using SharePoint single app part pages.

Finally, we learned how to deploy and use web parts on Microsoft Teams tabs and personal apps.

In the next chapter, we will be focusing on SharePoint Framework extensions and how they can be used to extend SharePoint capabilities.

Extending User Experiences with SharePoint Framework Extensions

SharePoint Framework Extensions can customize different surfaces on modern SharePoint Online. It enables a supported way to load scripts and add customized elements on defined placeholders on a page, create custom views for columns in lists and libraries, add custom commands to toolbars and context menus, and customize list and library forms. As with SharePoint Framework web parts, a developer can choose their favorite JavaScript frameworks, such as React, Angular, or Vue.js, or use plain JavaScript for development.

Adaptive Card Extensions are a mechanism for creating custom cards to Viva Connections dashboard. The card is a simple entry point, which can be extended using Quick View. Quick View is opened as a dialog and created using Adaptive Cards technology. Adaptive Card Extensions also support location and media capabilities and can be connected to SharePoint or other backend systems as well.

In this chapter, we're going to cover the following main topics:

- Bring custom elements to pages with application customizers
- Customize fields with SharePoint Framework
- Extend SharePoint commands
- Create Custom SharePoint Forms
- Extending Viva Connections with Adaptive Card Extensions

Technical requirements

For testing examples of this chapter SharePoint Framework v1.18 must be installed. The installation of SharePoint Framework is explained in *Chapter 16*.

A Microsoft 365 tenant, where SharePoint Framework solutions can be tested and deployed is needed.

All examples of this chapter can be found at: `https://github.com/PacktPublishing/Customizing-and-Extending-SharePoint-Online/tree/main/ch19`

Bringing custom elements and scripts to pages with application customizers

Application customizers offer a mechanism to load and run custom scripts and add custom HTML elements and content to two defined placeholders on the SharePoint page's HTML DOM (**Document Object Model**). Placeholders for custom HTML are found at the top and bottom of the page (*Figure 19.1*):

Figure 19.1 - Top and bottom placeholders

The layout and styles of these placeholders can include custom styles, layouts, and even fonts, but it's a good practice to refer to SharePoint Framework's documentation and utilize Office UI Fabric, which is a premade set of controls and styles, when possible.

> **Note**
>
> Using Application Customizers to modify SharePoint's HTML DOM is not a supported method for customizing modern SharePoint. Changes made to the page HTML DOM may cause issues with the customization.

Building an application customizer

You can create a project for an Application Customizer with Yeoman in the project folder using:

```
Yo @microsoft/sharepoint
```

`Extension` is the type of the client-side component, and `Application Customizer` is the type of client-side extension.

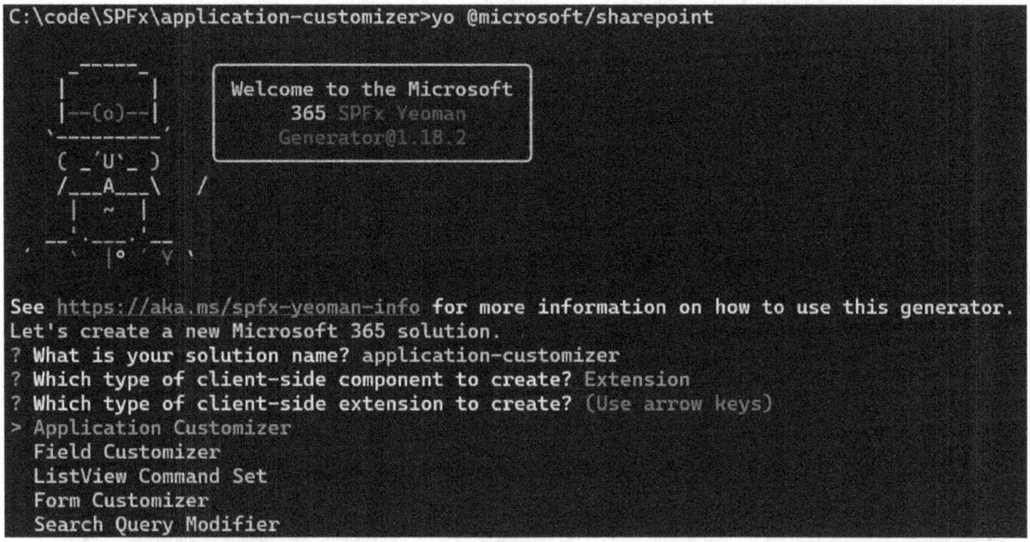

Figure 19.2 - Creating an application customizer

Once the project is created, the project includes the application customizer's main class and manifest for the extension.

```
∨ src                                                                        ●
    ∨ extensions \ teamArchivedApplicationExtensions                         ●
        ∨ loc
            JS en-us.js
            TS myStrings.d.ts
        {} TeamArchivedApplicationExtensionsApplicationCustomizer.manifest.json
        TS TeamArchivedApplicationExtensionsApplicationCustomizer.ts          6
    TS index.ts
```

Figure 19.3 - Extension project structure

Let's extend the default project to display a message bar in the top placeholder when the Teams team connected to the SharePoint site is set as archived. React and Office UI Fabric components are used in this example to render the message bar.

The first step is to add the React component for rendering the message bar. Let's create a folder called components underneath the src folder and add a file called SiteArchivedMessageBar. tsx. On the React component, the MessageBar and MessageBarType components from the Office UI Fabric need to be imported (*Figure 19.4*).

```
import {MessageBar, MessageBarType} from 'office-ui-fabric-react/lib/MessageBar';
```

Figure 19.4 - Import Office UI Fabric

Next, use the MessageBar compoment on the React components render method.

```
public render(): React.ReactElement<ISiteArchivedMessageBarProps>
{
    return(
        <MessageBar
        messageBarType={MessageBarType.severeWarning}
        >"This site is archived"
        </MessageBar>
    );
}
```

Figure 19.5 - React component's render method

The full source code of the `SiteArchivedMessageBar` React component can be found at https://github.com/PacktPublishing/Customizing-and-Extending-SharePoint-Online/blob/main/ch19/spfx-team-archived-extension/src/extensions/teamArchivedApplicationExtensions/components/SiteArchivedMessageBar.tsx.

The next step is to retrieve the Microsoft 365 Group ID of the site in the Application Customizer's main class. Group ID can be retrieved from the `pageContext` object.

```
// Get the group ID of the current site
this._groupId = this.context.pageContext.site.group.id;
if(this._groupId != null)
{
    this._renderPlaceHolders();
}
```

Figure 19.6 - Getting the group id and calling rendering

If the group Id is found, then the extension calls `_renderPlaceHolder` function.

The `_renderPlaceHolder` function first checks that the `topPlaceholder` element is available. If it is found, the Graph API's Teams resource is called using `MSGraphClientV3` client with Microsoft 365 Group Id as a parameter.

```
private _renderPlaceHolders(): void {

  if (!this._topPlaceHolder) {
    this._topPlaceHolder =
      this.context.placeholderProvider.tryCreateContent(
        PlaceholderName.Top,
        { onDispose: this._onDispose });
    if (this._topPlaceHolder && this._topPlaceHolder.domElement )
    {
      this.context.msGraphClientFactory
      .getClient('3')
      .then((client: MSGraphClientV3): void => {
        client.api('teams/'+this._groupId).get((error, team) => {
          if(team != null && team.isArchived)
          {
            const element: React.ReactElement<ISiteArchivedMessageBarProps> =
            React.createElement(SiteArchivedMessageBar, { context: this.context });
            ReactDOM.render(element, this._topPlaceHolder!.domElement);
          }
        });
      });
    }
  }
}
```

Figure 19.7 - Rendering the React component

If the Graph API call returns an object where isArchived property is true, the SiteArchivedMessageBar is rendered.

Testing the application customizer

To test this example, the linked SharePoint site's URL of a team (which is set as archived) is needed. It can be directly set to the pageUrl parameters on the serve.json configuration file, and the site is automatically opened when gulp serve is run. The required URL query string parameters are automatically added, and since parameters hold the Application Customizer's IDs in a specific format, running gulp serve is the easiest way to test it.

When the page is loaded for the first time, debugging scripts need to be allowed.

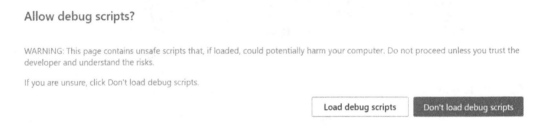

Figure 19.8 - Allowing debug scripts

And when the page is loaded on a SharePoint site linked to an archived team, the message bar is displayed on the top placeholder.

Figure 19.9 - Message bar visible on the top placeholder

Deploying the application customizer

To make the application customizer visible on all sites, the solution needs to be bundled and packaged using:

```
gulp bundle -ship
gulp package-solution -ship
```

After packaging, the solution's `.sppkg` file (found in the `sharepoint/solution` folder) is uploaded to the SharePoint App Catalog in the SharePoint Admin Center.

Deployment can also be targeted to specific site types, such as Microsoft 365 group-connected team sites. This is achieved by adding a `WebTemplateId` property to the `ClientSideInstance.xml` file found from the `sharepoint/assets` folder. The ID of the Microsoft 365 group-connected team site is GROUP#0.

```xml
<?xml version="1.0" encoding="utf-8"?>
<Elements xmlns="http://schemas.microsoft.com/sharepoint/">
    <ClientSideComponentInstance
        Title="TeamArchivedApplicationExtensions"
        Location="ClientSideExtension.ApplicationCustomizer"
        ComponentId="d001f520-afd7-4aae-ac0f-665a6fdb9ec5"
        Properties="{&quot;testMessage&quot;:&quot;Test message&quot;}"
        WebTemplateId="GROUP#0"
        >
    </ClientSideComponentInstance>
</Elements>
```

Figure 19.10 - ClientSideInstance.xml

The full source code of this example can be found at `https://github.com/PacktPublishing/Customizing-and-Extending-SharePoint-Online/tree/main/ch19/spfx-team-archived-extension`.

Customize Fields with SharePoint Framework

SharePoint Framework Field Customizer extension can be used to customize the behavior of a specified column on the list or library. The customization can be visual, such as an animated indicator of a missing value, a visual bar graph of progress, or functional (like a slider for changing the column value).

Creating a new Field Customizer starts again with `yo @microsoft/sharepoint` on the newly created project folder. The type of the client-side component is `Extension` and the type of the client-side extension is `Field Customizer`, and for the next example, React is chosen as the JavaScript framework.

The example is a simple toggle, which can be used to visualize and control *Yes/No* typed list columns. The example is utilizing Office UI Fabric for rendering the toggle. For accessing and updating the column values, PnPjs libraries are used to simplify the utilization of SharePoint REST APIs. PnPjs is a community-driven initiative, which develops and maintains a collection of libraries for accessing different Microsoft 365 REST APIs in a type-safe way.

Office UI Fabric and PnPjs are not automatically included in the project and need to be separately installed using Node Package Manager.

```
npm install office-ui-fabric-react –save
npm install @pnp/sp
```

After that, let's first open the `ToggleFieldExtension` React component, and import the Toggle Office UI Fabric Component:

```
import { Log } from '@microsoft/sp-core-library';
import * as React from 'react';
import styles from './ToggleFieldExtension.module.scss';
import {Toggle} from 'office-ui-fabric-react/lib/Toggle';
```

Figure 19.11 - Import Office UI Fabric and Toggle component

The next step is to add the Toggle to the React component's render method.

```
public render(): React.ReactElement<{}> {
  return (
    <div className={styles.toggleFieldExtension}>
      <Toggle
        defaultChecked={this.state.checked}
        onChange={this._onChanged.bind(this)}
        onText='Yes'
        offText='No'
      />
    </div>
  );
}
```

Figure 19.12 - Add Toggle component to render method

In *Figure 19.12*, the Toggle component's `onChange` event is wired to `onChanged` event handler, which also needs to be created.

```
private onChanged(checked: boolean): void {
  const sp = spfi().using(spSPFx(this.props.context));
  let _listTitle: string = "";
  let id = this.state.id;
  let checkedValue = checked ? true : false;
  if (this._context.pageContext && this._context.pageContext.list != undefined) {
    _listTitle = this._context.pageContext.list.title;
    sp.web.lists.getByTitle(_listTitle).items.getById(parseInt(id))().then(i => {
      let updateObject: any = {};
      updateObject["Complete"] = checkedValue;
      sp.web.lists.getByTitle(_listTitle).items.getById(parseInt(id)).update(updateObject).
      then((response: any) => {
        console.log("Item updated");
      });
    });
  }
}
```

Figure 19.13 - OnChange method

The `onChange` event handler uses PnPjs `pnp/sp` fluent API library to access SharePoint REST API and updates the `Complete?` field's value when the toggle is changed. Also, the PnPjs libraries need to be imported into the React component (*Figure 19.14*).

```
import { spfi, SPFx as spSPFx } from '@pnp/sp';
import "@pnp/sp/webs";
import "@pnp/sp/lists";
import "@pnp/sp/items";
```

Figure 19.14 - Importing PnPjs libraries

On the list view, the toggle is displayed like in *Figure 19.15*.

Figure 19.15 - Field Customizer visible on the list

As seen in this example, Field Customizer Extensions can be helpful for updating the field value without entering edit mode. On the same event, other updates related to the list item can be made.

Testing and debugging

As with all SharePoint Framework Extensions, the easiest way is to fill the list URL to serve.json file's pageUrl properties and change the name of the field to the fieldCustomizers section. The ID is added automatically during project creation. When running gulp serve, all needed properties are added to the list URL, and the Customizer is activated automatically.

Deploying the Field Customizer

Before deploying the Field Customer, the first thing is to check the elements.xml configuration file on the sharepoint/assets folder. The elements file should stand for the field to which the Customizer is linked to. In this case, it's the Completed field (*Figure 19.16*). ClientSideComponentId must also match the ID in the manifest.json file. The Field is added as a site column to sites during the deployment of the solution.

```xml
<?xml version="1.0" encoding="utf-8"?>
<Elements xmlns="http://schemas.microsoft.com/sharepoint/">
    <Field ID="{e7718687-fd24-476a-b262-c7471dc694ce}"
           Name="Completed"
           DisplayName="Completed?"
           Type="Boolean"
           Group="SPFx Columns"
           ClientSideComponentId="2cc69764-0431-4df6-a386-f46ddfc25355">
    </Field>
</Elements>
```

Figure 19.16 - Elements.xml configuration

After the configuration, the solution needs to be bundled and packaged using Gulp. And `.sppkg` file found from the `sharepoint/solution` folder was uploaded to the SharePoint App Catalog in the SharePoint Admin Center. After the field customizer is deployed to the site, the site column to which the customizer is linked can be added to lists and libraries.

The full source code of this example can be found at `https://github.com/PacktPublishing/Customizing-and-Extending-SharePoint-Online/tree/main/ch19/spfx-team-archived-extension`.

Extend SharePoint with Command Sets

The ListView Command Sets can be used to create new actions to SharePoint command surfaces. A Command Set can run client-side code to implement custom actions. A Command Set can be made available on the SharePoint list's or library's command bar (*Figure 19.17*), context menu, or both.

Figure 19.17 - Command bar

Creating a new ListView Command Set project starts with `yo @microsoft/sharepoint`. The Type of the client-side component is `Extension`, and the type of the client-side extension is `ListView Command Set`.

The example is an archive function, which moves a list item to a folder called `Archive`. The command is only available when a list item is selected and is visible on the command bar and the context menu.

Once the project is completely created, let's open the `manifest.json` file and change the items object to include just one command, like in *Figure 19.18*.

```
"items": {
    "ARCHIVE_COMMAND_1": {
        "title": { "default": "Archive item" },
        "iconImageUrl": "",
        "type": "command"
    }
}
```

Figure 19.18 - Command introduction in the manifest

If an icon is needed for the command, it can be added as base64 encoded to the `iconImageUrl` parameter, or reference publicly available icon.

The next step is to initialize the command on the main classes' `onInit` method.

```
public onInit(): Promise<void> {
  Log.info(LOG_SOURCE, 'Initialized ArchiveItemCommandSet');

  // initial state of the command's visibility
  const archiveCommand: Command = this.tryGetCommand('ARCHIVE_COMMAND_1');
  archiveCommand.visible = false;
  archiveCommand.title = `Archive item`;

  this.context.listView.listViewStateChangedEvent.add(this, this._onListViewStateChanged);

  return Promise.resolve();
}
```

Figure 19.19 - Initializing the command

At this point, the command is set as hidden since it should be available only when an item is selected. Also, event handlers for list view state changes, such as selections, are added.

On the `_onListViewStateChanged` event handler, the command is set as visible when a single item is selected, and the item type is not a folder.

```
private _onListViewStateChanged = (args: ListViewStateChangedEventArgs): void => {
  Log.info(LOG_SOURCE, 'List view state changed');

  const archiveCommand: Command = this.tryGetCommand('ARCHIVE_COMMAND_1');
  if (archiveCommand) {
    // This command should be hidden unless exactly one row is selected.
    archiveCommand.visible = this.context.listView.selectedRows?.length === 1 && this.context.listView.selectedRows[0].getValueByName('FSObjType') === '0';
    archiveCommand.title = `Archive item`;
  }
}
```

Figure 19.20 - List View State Changed event handler

Command execution is wired to the `_archiveItem` method in the `onExecute` method:

```
public onExecute(event: IListViewCommandSetExecuteEventParameters): void {
  switch (event.itemId) {
    case 'ARCHIVE_COMMAND_1':
      this._archiveItem(event.selectedRows[0].getValueByName('ID'));

      break;
    default:
      throw new Error('Unknown command');
  }
}
```

Figure 19.21 - Handling the execution

Finally, in the `_archiveItem` method, the selected list item is moved to the `Archive` folder using `spHttpClient` and SharePoint REST API.

```
const _listName = this.context.pageContext.list?.title;
console.log(_listName);
this.context.spHttpClient.get(`${this.context.pageContext.web.absoluteUrl}/_api/web/lists/getbytitle('${_listName}')/items(${itemId})?$select=*,FileLeafRef,FileRef`,
SPHttpClient.configurations.v1).then((response: SPHttpClientResponse) => {
  if(response.ok){
    response.json().then((item) => {
      console.log(item);
      const _fileRef = item.FileRef;
      const _fileLeafRef = item.FileLeafRef;
      console.log(_fileRef); //CORRECT ONE
      console.log(_fileLeafRef);
      this.context.spHttpClient.post(`${this.context.pageContext.web.absoluteUrl}/_api/web/getfilebyserverrelativeurl('${_fileRef}')/moveto(newurl='
${this.context.pageContext.list?.serverRelativeUrl}+
      "/Archive"/${_fileLeafRef}')`, SPHttpClient.configurations.v1, spOpts).then((response: SPHttpClientResponse) => {
        if (response.ok) {
          location.reload();
        }
      });
    });
  }
});
```

Figure 19.22 - Archive item using SharePoint REST API

Testing the Command Set

As with earlier examples, the easiest way is to add the URL of the list to the `serve.json` configuration file and run `gulp serve`. The required properties are automatically added to the list URL when the browser is opened:

Figure 19.23 - Archive item button on the command bar

The location of the Command Set is set with the location parameter on the `serve.json`. Possible values are:

- The `ClientSideExtension.ListViewCommandSet.CommandBar`
- command is displayed on the command bar.
- The `ClientSideExtension.ListViewCommandSet.ContextMenu`

- command is displayed on the context menu.
- The `ClientSideExtension.ListViewCommandSet`
- command is displayed on both.

Deploying the ListView Command Set

For deploying the solution to SharePoint, the location of the Command Set is configured with location parameters in the `elements.xml` or `ClientSideInstance.xml` files on the `sharepoint/assets` folder on the project depending on the method of deployment.

To deploy the solution to all lists and libraries on the tenant, bundle and package the solution:

```
Gulp bundle -ship
Gulp package-solution -ship
```

Then, upload the `.sppkg` file from the `sharepoint/solution` folder to the **Manage apps** list on the tenant's app catalog in the **SharePoint Admin Center**.

Figure 19.24 - Uploading the extension to the SharePoint App catalog

The full source code of this example can be found at `https://github.com/PacktPublishing/Customizing-and-Extending-SharePoint-Online/tree/main/ch19/spfx-team-archived-extension`.

Customize List and Library Forms with Form Customizers

Form Customizers enable overriding the default form on SharePoint lists and libraries, adding custom logic to display, editing and adding items, and customizing the layout of the form. Form Customizers have been introduced on the SharePoint Framework v1.15.

Let's create a simple example, this time using PnP Reusable React Controls created and supported by Microsoft 365 and Power Platform Community, which is an open-source developer community sharing and contributing on samples, reusable components, and knowledge. In this case, let's use the DynamicForm component for creating the custom form. And the first step after creating the project is to install these controls using:

```
npm install @pnp/spfx-controls-react
```

Using the DynamicForm is simple, just add it to the render() method of the React component.

```
public render(): React.ReactElement<{}> {
  return  <div className={styles.dynamicForm}>
  <h1>{"Custom Form"}</h1>
  <DynamicForm
      context={this.props.context as never}
      listId={this.props.context.list.guid.toString()}
      listItemId={this.props.context.itemId}
      onCancelled={this.props.onClose}
      onSubmitted={this.props.onSave}
      onSubmitError={(listItemData: unknown, error: Error) => { console.log(error.message); }}
      disabled={this.props.displayMode === FormDisplayMode.Display}
      //fieldOverrides={fieldOverrides}
  />
</div>;
  }
```

Figure 19.25 - DynamicForm on the Reach component

The DynamicForm will automatically render the item's fields, and allow modifying field controls if needed. In *Figure 19.25*, the **Title** and **Description** fields are set as disabled, and field values cannot be changed.

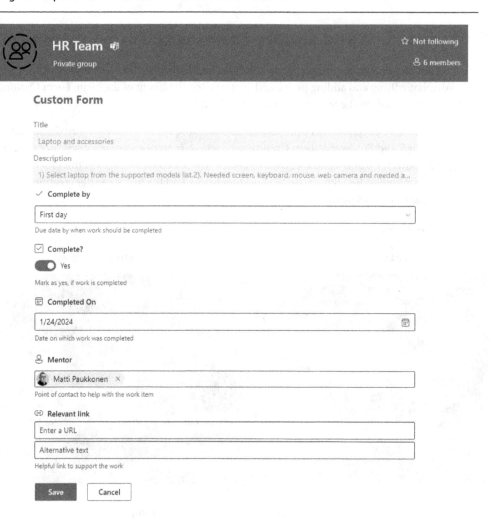

Figure 19.26 - Dynamic Form

Fields can be changed with the `fieldOverrides` object which is passed as a parameter to the DynamicForm components.

```
const fieldOverrides: { [columnInternalName: string]: (fieldProperties: IDynamicFieldProps) => React.ReactElement<IDynamicFieldProps> } = {
  'Title': (fieldProps: IDynamicFieldProps): React.ReactElement<IDynamicFieldProps> =>
    <TextField disabled={true}
    label={fieldProps.label}
    defaultValue={fieldProps.fieldDefaultValue}/>,
    'Description': (fieldProps: IDynamicFieldProps): React.ReactElement<IDynamicFieldProps> =>
    <TextField disabled={true}
    label={fieldProps.label}
    defaultValue={fieldProps.fieldDefaultValue}/>,
};
```

Figure 19.27 - Field overrides

In *Figure 19.26*, the `Title` and `Description` fields are set as disabled. It's also required to set `label` and `defaultValue` properties, otherwise, these fields would look empty. The `label` and `fieldDefaultValue` properties are stored in the `fieldProps` object.

Form Customizers are a handy method for building app-like experiences on top of lists and libraries. Form Customizers can implement custom logic in how list item fields are displayed, created, and updated. Sometimes it's useful to disable editing of specific fields after the list item has been created, and it's quite simple to achieve with Form Customizer.

The full source code of the example can be found at `https://github.com/PacktPublishing/Customizing-and-Extending-SharePoint-Online/tree/main/ch19/spfx-dynamic-form-customizer`.

Extending Viva Connections with Adaptive Card Extensions

Viva Connections experiences can be extended with Adaptive Card Extensions (ACE) using SharePoint Framework. Adaptive Card Extensions are used to bring custom experiences to the Viva Connections Dashboard, which is shown on the Viva Connections Home Experience and can be added to the SharePoint Home site using the Viva Dashboard web part. Viva Connections is introduced in *Chapter 10*.

Adaptive Cards Extensions have two layouts: medium and large.

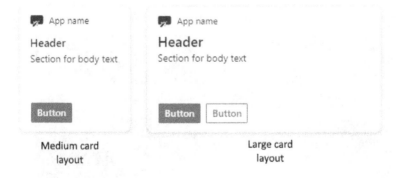

Figure 19.28 - Adaptive Card Extension layouts

Anatomy of the card contains:

- Icon, which can be a Fluent UI icon or custom icon. A custom icon needs to be 24x24 pixels in size, with a transparent background, and either in PNG or SVG format.

- App name beside the icon, which should describe the card, for example, Safety or Time off.

- Header section, which should include a descriptive header or action.

- Body section uses text to provide more detail about the card. The body section can also include a text input field or a search box. It can also be dynamically updated.

- The footer section, which can contain action buttons, a text input, or a search footer.

Available components with the current SharePoint Framework v1.18 are:

- Card Bar Component, for the icon and the name

- Text

- Text input

- Action button

- Search box

- Search footer

Create an Adaptive Card Extension

Let's create an Adaptive Card Extension example, which uses a SharePoint list on the back end for displaying days without accidents.

The first thing is to create a project for Adaptive Card Extension using Yeoman.

```
yo @microsoft/sharepoint
```

This time, the type of the client-side component is an Adaptive Card Extension for a Generic card template.

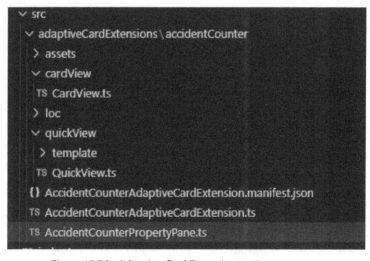

Figure 19.29 - Adaptive Card Extension project structure

The project consists of several files and folders like:

- `CardView.ts` is the class for rendering the Adaptive Card contents.
- `QuickView.ts` is the class for dynamically filling the Quick View contents.
- `QuickViewTemplate.json` is an Adaptive Cards template that is used to render the Quick View.
- `AccidentCounterAdaptiveCardExtension.ts` is a main class for the extension.
- `AccidentCounter PropertyPane.ts` is a class for controlling the property pane of the extension, for example, which properties card editors can manage.
- `manifest.json` describes the extension, and default settings.

The next step is to create a SharePoint list on the SharePoint Home Site for storing the required data. Let's call it Accidents. The list needs just the Title column and Accident Date column, which is typed as DateTime.

Let's again use PnPjs libraries to access the data on the list and install the needed package.

```
npm install @pnp/sp --save
```

And import libraries to the project similarly as in *Figure 19.14*.

Next, information that should be displayed on the card needs to be added to the Adaptive Card Extension's state. For this example, we want to show the number of days without accidents and the date of the most recent accident.

```
export interface IAccidentCounterAdaptiveCardExtensionState {
    daysWithoutAccident: number;
    lastAccidentDate?: Date;
}
```

Figure 19.30 - Update Adaptive Card Extension's state

Let's create a `getAccidentsCount` function to retrieve data using PnPjs from the list created earlier. We'll then calculate the number of days since the last accident and retrieve its date.

```
private getAccidentsCount(): void {
  const sp = spfi().using(spSPFx(this.context));
  sp.web.lists.getByTitle("Accidents").items().then((items) => {
    const today = new Date();
    const mostRecentItem = items.reduce((prev, current) =>
    { const prevDate = new Date(prev["AccidentDate"]); const currentDate = new Date(current["AccidentDate"]);
      return prevDate > currentDate ? prev : current;
    });
    const mostRecentDate = new Date(mostRecentItem["AccidentDate"]);
    const daysWithoutAccident = Math.floor((today.getTime() - mostRecentDate.getTime()) / (1000 * 60 * 60 * 24));
    this.setState({
      daysWithoutAccident,
      lastAccidentDate: mostRecentDate
    });
  });
});
```

Figure 19.31 - getAccidentCount method

The function first retrieves all list items from the Accidents list, then calculates the date of the most recent item and the number of days between the most recent item and the current date. Both pieces of information are stored in the extension's state. And finally, let's open the `CardView.ts` to display the state on the card. Since we want to include text to the body of the card, the returned card type on the get `cardViewParameter` function needs to be changed to `PrimaryTextCard`.

```
public get cardViewParameters(): ComponentsCardViewParameters {
  return PrimaryTextCardView({
    cardBar: {
      componentName: 'cardBar',
      title: this.properties.title
    },
    header: {
      componentName: 'text',
      text: this.state.daysWithoutAccident.toString()+
      ((this.state.daysWithoutAccident == 1) ? " day without an accident":" days without an accident")
    },body: {
      componentName: 'text',
      text: "Last accident happened on "+this.state.lastAccidentDate?.toLocaleDateString()
    },
    footer: {
      componentName: 'cardButton',
      title: strings.QuickViewButton,
      action: {
        type: 'QuickView',
        parameters: {
          view: QUICK_VIEW_REGISTRY_ID
        }
      }
    }
  });
}
```

Figure 19.32 - Modifying the CardView

The `daysWithoutAccident` is shown on the header section of the card, and `lastAccidentDate` is in the body of the card.

Now we can run `gulp serve` and test the extension on the Workbench, which can be accessed at `https://tenant.sharepoint.com/_layouts/workbench.aspx`.

Figure 19.33 - Adaptive Counter Extension on the workbench

Adding the Quick View

Let's extend the example by using Quick View to include the number of accidents from the current month, last month, and current year.

By default, Quick View is added to the project automatically and the Quick View button on the card opens the default Quick View.

First, let's extend the state of the extension with the following:

```
accidentsInThisMonth: number;
accidentsInLastMonth: number;
accidentsInThisYear: number;
```

Also, remember to initialize the variables above in the onInit function of the extension. The next step is to get the values for these and set them to the state in `getAccidentsCount` function (see the example code).

The layout of the Quick View is based on Adaptive Card, which is a structured JSON representation of the card contents. Microsoft has created a great tool called Adaptive Cards Designer for designing Adaptive Cards, which can be found at `https://adaptivecards.io/designer/`. Let's create a simple layout with three rows and two columns, and text boxes for each column. The left columns are for header text and the right columns include the number of accidents in this month, last month, and during the current year. These values need to be marked with a placeholder formatted like ${accidentsThisMonth}. Variables for these placeholders are then introduced in the IQuickViewData interface and filled with values within the code (*Figure 19.33*).

```
public get data(): IQuickViewData {
  console.log("IQuickViewData");

  return {
    accidentsThisMonth: this.state.accidentsInThisMonth.toString(),
    accidentsLastMonth: this.state.accidentsInLastMonth.toString(),
    accidentsInThisYear: this.state.accidentsInThisYear.toString(),
    thisMonthStyle: this.state.accidentsInThisMonth < this.state.accidentsInLastMonth ? 'good' : 'attention',
    lastMonthStyle: this.state.accidentsInLastMonth < 4 ? 'good' : 'attention',
    thisYearStyle: this.state.accidentsInThisYear < 10 ? 'good' : 'attention'
  };
}
```

Figure 19.34 - Setting adaptive card placeholder values

The example also includes setting some styles to columns to indicate the value in the expected range.

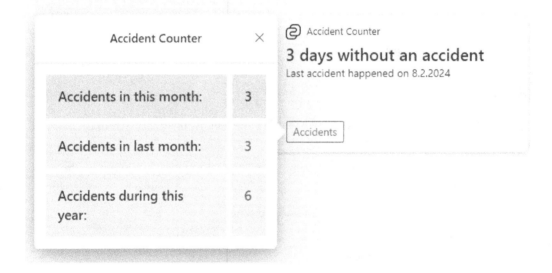

Figure 19.35 - Adaptive Card with QuickView

Full example code can be downloaded from https://github.com/PacktPublishing/ Customizing-and-Extending-SharePoint-Online/tree/main/ch19/ ace-accident-counter.

Deploying Adaptive Card Extensions to SharePoint

Adaptive Card Extensions are deployed similarly to other SharePoint Framework solutions.

First, bundle and package the solution using the following:

```
Gulp bundle -ship
Gulp package-solution -ship
```

Then upload the `sppkg` file found from `sharepoint/solution` folder to the SharePoint App Catalog in the SharePoint Admin Center.

Location in Adaptive Card Extensions

Viva Connections supports two location capabilities for fetching the user's current location, allowing the user to pick the location from the map or show a predefined location to the user. Location capabilities can become useful, for example when reporting on a place that needs maintenance or displaying an office location to users.

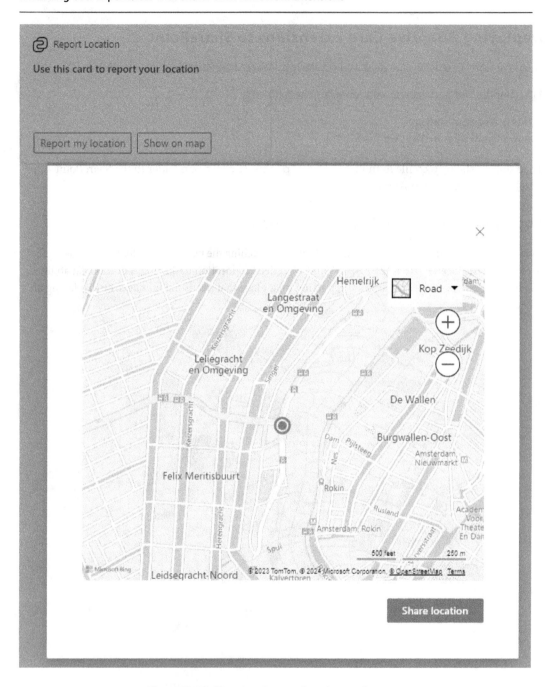

Figure 19.36 - Showing the user location on the map

To obtain the current location of the user or allow the user to select a location, you can utilize the VivaAction.GetLocation action type.

```
footer: [{
    componentName: 'cardButton',
        title: "Report my location",
        action: {
            type: 'VivaAction.GetLocation',
        parameters: {
        chooseLocationOnMap: false
        }
        }
    }
}
```

The example above adds a button to the card's footer and gets the location of the user when the button is pressed.

The `chooseLocationOnMap` parameter determines the behavior. When set to `false`, it retrieves the user's current location. If set to `true`, it opens a map interface for the user to select the desired location.

When the user has selected the location, the action can be caught with the `onAction` function.

```
public onAction(action: IGetLocationActionArguments): void {
    if (action.type === 'VivaAction.GetLocation') {
    console.log('action.location', action.location);
        this.setState({
            latitude: action.location?.latitude.toString(),
            longitude: action.location?.longitude.toString()
        });
    }
}
```

Retrieved coordinates are added to the state of the extension for later handling.

> **Note**
> Viva Connections location capabilities are currently available in Teams mobile and on SharePoint when used with a browser.

Media capabilities of Adaptive Card Extensions

Adaptive Card Extensions facilitate the uploading of images, audio files, and documents, with a current file size limitation of 1 MB per file. . The feature is implemented using `VivaAction.SelectMedia` action.

```
{ componentName: 'cardButton',title: "Upload photo",    action: {type:
"VivaAction.SelectMedia",parameters: {mediaType: MediaType.Image}}}
```

And again, values and file contents can be retrieved on the `onAction` function.

```
public onAction(action: ISelectMediaActionArguments): void {if
(action.type === 'VivaAction.SelectMedia') {              action.media.
map(attachment =>
{ //Handle attachment content });
}}
```

Currently, media handling capabilities are a bit limited because of the file size limitation but can be handy for simple use cases, like reporting a service ticket with an image to a central repository.

Summary

In this chapter, you were first introduced to Application Customizer, which can be used to bring custom elements to SharePoint page HTML and include custom JavaScript to pages.

Next, we learned about Field Customizers and how they can be used to customize the behavior of fields. Next, we delved into extending SharePoint command surfaces with custom commands, and how to use them to interact with items in a list or library.

Next, we learned how to customize SharePoint lists and library forms with Form Customizer Extension.

And finally, we covered extending the Viva Connections dashboard using Adaptive Card Extensions.

In the next chapter, we will be introduced to several SharePoint developer community solutions that can be used to extend and manage SharePoint.

20
Community Solutions for Extending SharePoint Online

The open source community, called the Microsoft 365 Platform Community or M365 PnP community, maintains and shares documentation, samples, reusable controls, and other open source resources for SharePoint development. The community is coordinated by the Microsoft 365 engineering team and it has members and participants across the globe.

The community has developed great quality tools and solutions, which can be used without any payment or license. Anyone can start contributing their solutions, fix issues, or maintain documentation. The community takes care of the quality of the provided code.

PnP provisioning templates offer a flexible way to create, duplicate, and configure different resources of the Microsoft 365 tenant. They can be used, for example, for creating an onboarding list to SharePoint or being a complete solution for provisioning a complete SharePoint site.

PnP PowerShell is a cross-platform PowerShell module for managing the Microsoft 365 environment and its services using a single set of PowerShell cmdlets. Modern Search web parts are a complete solution for building search-based solutions, such as search center with custom search results and filters, more comprehensive people search results, or the PnP Search Result web part as a search-based content roll-up with custom layout on SharePoint pages.

In this chapter, we're going to cover the following main topics:

- Using community solutions in SharePoint Online

- PnP PowerShell

- PnP provisioning templates

- PnP Modern Search

Using community solutions in SharePoint Online

The Microsoft 365 and Power Platform Community supply lots of samples and solutions, helpful articles, and tools to help developers and organizations gain more value from their environments. The community runs dozens of initiatives centered around different technologies. It's led by Microsoft Engineering but involves hundreds of professionals around the globe who are eager to share their knowledge and examples.

The community also hosts several community calls on different topics where everyone can join in. Calls can be joined easily using Microsoft Teams and are open to everyone.

All community examples, tools, and solutions can be used in your organization's SharePoint Online environment to extend the user experience, build automation, and maintain the environment.

I present three community initiatives—PnP PowerShell, PnP Site Templates, and PnP Modern Search—which I use as part of my daily work with different customers and environments.

I would also like to express my sincere gratitude to the community for the amazing job they do.

PnP PowerShell

PnP PowerShell should be found in every SharePoint Online administrator toolbox.

It's not just a SharePoint administrator tool; PnP PowerShell also supports configuring commands to manage a Microsoft 365 tenant, Microsoft Teams, Microsoft Planner, and more. The module includes close to 700 cmdlets and can be used on Windows, Linux, and MacOS platforms. Besides maintenance and configuration tasks, PnP PowerShell can be used for various kinds of automation that are run on Azure, a Docker container, or other platforms. Detailed documentation of the PnP PowerShell can be found at `https://pnp.github.io/powershell/index.html`.

Installing PnP PowerShell

For installing PnP PowerShell, PowerShell version 7.2 is needed. The legacy version of PnP PowerShell also works on Windows PowerShell, but it's not maintained actively anymore, so it's not recommended.

The easiest way to install PnP PowerShell is from the PowerShell Gallery:

```
Install-Module PnP.PowerShell -Scope CurrentUser
```

This installs the module to the current user's scope and does not require administrator permissions on the target machine.

It's also possible to install pre-release versions of the module:

```
Install-Module PnP.PowerShell -Scope CurrentUser -AllowPrerelease -
SkipPublisherCheck
```

When an updated version of the module is released, the module needs to be updated using the following command:

```
Update-Module PnP.PowerShell -Scope CurrentUser
```

Uninstalling the module can be done using the following command:

```
Uninstall-Module PnP.PowerShell -AllVersions
```

Authentication and connection to Microsoft 365 tenants

PnP PowerShell supports multiple authentication methods. The first thing to do is to set up access either using PnP PowerShell's multi-tenant application or creating an application registration for the tenant. This needs to be done once.

To use PnP PowerShell's multi-tenant application, use this command:

```
Register-PnPManagementShellAccess
```

Running the command will direct the user to authenticate and give permissions to the application:

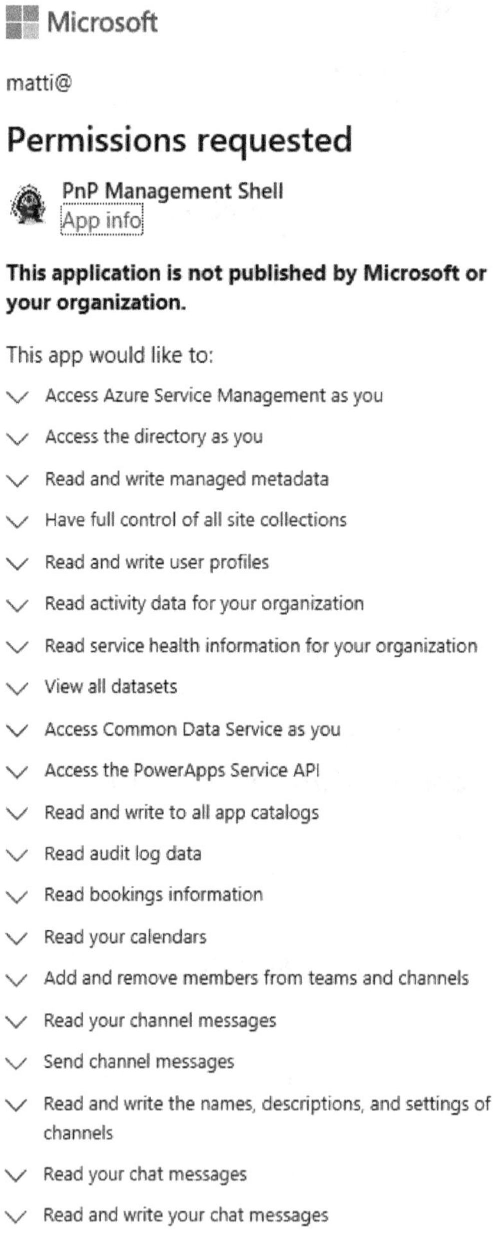

matti@

Permissions requested

PnP Management Shell
App info

This application is not published by Microsoft or your organization.

This app would like to:

∨   Access Azure Service Management as you

∨   Access the directory as you

∨   Read and write managed metadata

∨   Have full control of all site collections

∨   Read and write user profiles

∨   Read activity data for your organization

∨   Read service health information for your organization

∨   View all datasets

∨   Access Common Data Service as you

∨   Access the PowerApps Service API

∨   Read and write to all app catalogs

∨   Read audit log data

∨   Read bookings information

∨   Read your calendars

∨   Add and remove members from teams and channels

∨   Read your channel messages

∨   Send channel messages

∨   Read and write the names, descriptions, and settings of channels

∨   Read your chat messages

∨   Read and write your chat messages

Figure 20.1 - PnP PowerShell permissions

The application is added as an enterprise application to Entra ID, and if there is a need to revoke permission, the application can be removed.

For setting up access with an Azure application managed in your tenant, it's possible to use the following command:

```
Register-PnPAzureADApp -ApplicationName "Your name for the
application" -Tenant tenant.onmicrosoft.com -OutPath c:\temp\
certificate -DeviceLogin
```

This command will add an application registration to the provided Microsoft 365 tenant's Entra ID with a limited set of permissions. Permission can be expanded using Entra ID's application registration management or supplying permissions when running the command. More detailed information can be found in PnP PowerShell's documentation at https://pnp.github.io/powershell/articles/authentication.html.

PnP PowerShell can be connected using user credentials or using an Entra ID application's client ID with a certificate.

To connect using user credentials, it's recommended to use interactive login, which supports strong authentication:

```
Connect-PnPOnline -Url https://tenant.sharepoint.com -Interactive
```

One choice for connecting PnP PowerShell to Microsoft 365 using an application ID is to use the Connect-PnPOnline command with the client ID, tenant, and thumbprint parameters. Client ID refers to the application ID of the application registered Entra ID, and Thumbprint is the thumbprint of a certificate, which is used for authentication:

```
Connect-PnPOnline -Url https://tenant.sharepoint.com -ClientId <Client
ID> -Tenant tenant.onmicrosoft.com -Thumbprint $thumbprint
```

More choices for connecting can be found on the PnP PowerShell's documentation: https://pnp.github.io/powershell/articles/connecting.html

Example—copying a list with current items between sites

In this example, PnP PowerShell is used to copy a list and list items on that list to another site on the tenant.

1. The first step is to connect to the source site using the following command:

    ```
    Connect-PnPOnline -Url https://tenant.sharepoint.com
    -Interactive
    ```

2. The next step is to copy the list to another site using the following command:

    ```
    Copy-PnPList -Identity "Accidents" -DestinationWebUrl https://
    tenant.sharepoint.com/sites/another-site
    ```

3. Next, let's read all list items from the **Accidents** list to an object. We are interested only in the `Title` and `AccidentDate` fields:

```
$listItems = (Get-PnPListItem -List "Accidents" -Fields
"Title","AccidentDate").FieldValues
```

4. Now let's add list items to a list just copied to another site. First, disconnect a current connection using `Disconnect-PnPOnline`. Then, connect to another site, go through `$listItems` in a loop, and add list items.

```
Connect-PnPOnline -Url https://tenant.sharepoint.com/sites/
another-site -Interactive
foreach($item in $listItems){
     Add-PnPListItem -List "Accidents" -Values @
{"Title"=$item["Title"];"AccidentDate"=$item["AccidentDate"]}}
```

5. Finally, close the connection using `Disconnect-PnPOnline`.

PnP PowerShell is a community-built solution that can be used without additional costs or licensing. PnP PowerShell also includes commands that can be used to manage the same tenant settings as the SharePoint Online Management Shell, which was used in earlier examples of this book. It might be reasonable to focus on learning the more comprehensive PnP module thoroughly and use SPO Management Shell for some specific tasks that are not available in PnP.

PnP site templates

PnP site templates become handy when there is a need to provision different artifacts on SharePoint sites. PnP site templates are based on the Open XML file format and the schema of the template is open source and maintained by the community. PnP site templates offer a more comprehensive approach compared to SharePoint site design and site scripts, with a wide range of capabilities.

PnP site templates can be also used for smaller-scale provisioning or automation, such as creating content types and site columns, documenting libraries with specific settings and views, or provisioning assets between SharePoint sites.

It's also possible to create a new template for a specific SharePoint site and use it to create and configure new sites. In the next example, PnP PowerShell is combined with PnP site templates to get a site template from a site. Then, it is applied to another site:

```
Connect-PnPOnline -Url https://tenant.sharepoint.com/sites/
source-site -Interactive
Get-PnPSiteTemplate -Out c:\temp\template.xml
```

This command extracts these artifacts from the connected site:

- Site settings and regional settings

- Site memberships and security settings

- Navigation

- Content types and site columns

- Lists and libraries

- Activated features

- Modern pages and page templates with content

- Header and footer settings and theme settings

The template can be applied to another site with the following:

```
Connect-PnPOnline -Url https://tenant.sharepoint.com/sites/
targetsite -Interactive
Invoke-PnPSiteTemplate -Path c:\temp\template.xml
```

It's also possible to get and apply just specific artifacts of the template using the -Handlers parameter, which is used in the next example.

Example—copying page templates across a site with PnP provisioning

Sometimes it might be reasonable to distribute modern page templates across sites to keep uniform page structure and content, especially when having a hub site and associated sites. Currently, there is no out-of-the-box functionality for that purpose.

1. The first step is to connect to the source site that contains the templates you want to copy:

    ```
    Connect-PnPOnline -Url https://tenant.sharepoint.com
    -Interactive
    ```

2. Next, let's extract modern pages and templates using special parameters to retrieve all pages and branding files, such as images on pages, as an object:

    ```
    $template = Get-PnPSiteTemplate -Handlers Pages,PageContents -
    IncludeAllPages -PersistBrandingFiles -OutputInstance
    ```

3. Next, create a new site template object, which just includes templates. It takes the exported object from the previous phase and creates a new object that includes just page templates. A template page can be identified when the PromoteAsTemplate property is set to true.

```
$newTemplate = New-PnPSiteTemplate
$pageTemplates = $template.ClientSidePages | Where-Object {$_.
PromoteAsTemplate -eq $true}
foreach($pageTemplate in $pageTemplates)
{
    $newTemplate.ClientSidePages.Add($pageTemplate)
}
//To include all files to the new template
$newTemplate.Files.AddRange($template.Files)
```

4. After building a new template, it can be applied to a new site with the following command:

```
Connect-PnPOnline -Url https://tenant.sharepoint.com
-Interactive
Invoke-PnPSiteTemplate -InputInstance $newTemplate
```

PnP site templates can be used as part of automation or complete provisioning solutions developed using PowerShell or .NET. One possibility could be creating a Teams team provisioning solution using the Power Automate functionality and calling an Azure function at the end to provision some specific artifacts to SharePoint using PnP site templates.

PnP Modern Search

PnP Modern Search is an open source and community-maintained solution that includes a set of SharePoint web parts to build search-driven solutions.

The solution includes separate web parts for search results, search filtering, search verticals, and a search box. Web parts can be used on any modern SharePoint page. Web parts can be used and connected to build a comprehensive search solution. You can use just results and a search box to create a simple search center or you can use just the **Search Results** web part with predefined queries to create a customized roll-up for specific content with a customizable layout. The solution can use SharePoint's search engine and Microsoft search capabilities using Microsoft Graph API.

Since the solution is completely open source, the source code can be downloaded from the GitHub repository and the solution can be built and packaged using Gulp. It's also possible to start building a separate solution based on the source code.

The GitHub repository for PnP Modern Search can be found here: `https://github.com/microsoft-search/pnp-modern-search/`

Installing Modern Search web parts to Microsoft 365

The solution itself is installed similarly to any other SharePoint Online solution. The latest release of the solution, the `sppkg` package, can be downloaded from the GitHub repository (`https://github.com/microsoft-search/pnp-modern-search/releases`). Navigate to the SharePoint App Catalog in the SharePoint Admin Center and upload and deploy the package. The solution requires several Microsoft Graph API permissions. Utilizing SharePoint search capabilities doesn't require approving these permissions.

Creating a search center with PnP Modern Search

Once PnP Modern Search is installed and deployed, it can be used within the SharePoint site. For this example, let's build a search center with a search box, search results with a couple of filters, and a couple of search verticals for searching documents and people.

Let's first create a new site for the search center so that it's possible to use the site's home page without any page headers. A blank site template is the best choice since everything will be removed from the front page.

Let's create a layout for the page, with the top section in one column layout and the next section in the one-third left column layout.

Configure the search box

Let's add the **PnP – Search Box** web part to the top column by clicking the small plus icon at the top and searching for the web part as in *Figure 20.2*.

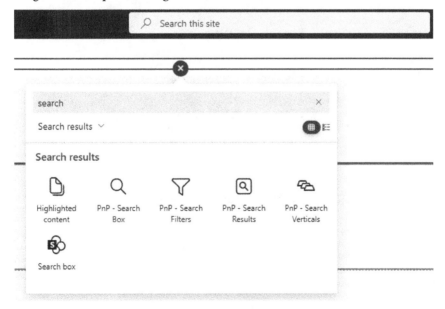

Figure 20.2 - Adding the search box

Configure Search Verticals

Next, add **PnP – Search Verticals** underneath the search box web part and open the **Property** pane for configuration. On the **Property** pane, open the **Configure vertical view**:

Configure search verticals

Add a new vertical to allow users to search in a predefined scope or data source. To use it, you must connect this Web Part to one or more 'Search Results' Web Parts as verticals control visibility over

	Tab name *	Fluent UI icon name	Tab value	Is hyperlink
1 ⌄	Documents	Document	1	☐
2 ⌄	People	People	2	☐
	ex: 'SharePoint'	ex: 'Document'		☐

Figure 20.3 - Adding Search Verticals

When using search verticals, each vertical needs a separate result and filter web parts to work correctly. It's also a clever idea to have separate sections for web parts connected to different vertical tabs so that it's easier to distinguish which web parts are connected to the same vertical. Let's duplicate the lower section.

Configuring search results

Let's add the first **Search Results** web part on the right side of the middle section and open the **Property** pane. The first configuration step is to choose which search is used, and here, SharePoint Search is the correct choice:

Figure 20.4 - Choosing the search data source

The choice opens all the settings of the **Search Results** web part, which can be used to customize the search result experience. Let's change a couple of settings to get PDF documents as results:

1. Add `isDocument:true` to **Query template**. This will limit the results only to files.

Figure 20.5 - Setting Query template

2. Add `FileType:equals("pdf")` to the refinement filters. This will limit the results to only include PDF files:

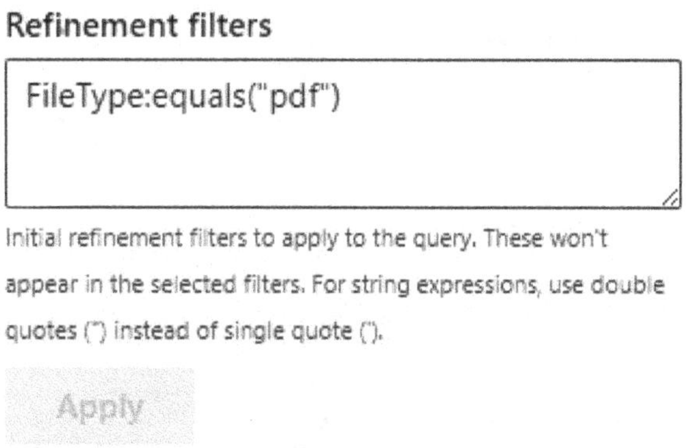

Refinement filters

FileType:equals("pdf")

Initial refinement filters to apply to the query. These won't
appear in the selected filters. For string expressions, use double
quotes (") instead of single quote (').

Apply

Figure 20.6 - Setting refinement filters

3. Navigate to the next page of the web part's settings and select **List** as the layout. You can change layouts and see the results on the web part. The custom option can be used to create customized layouts using *HandleBars*, which is a simple HTML templating language:

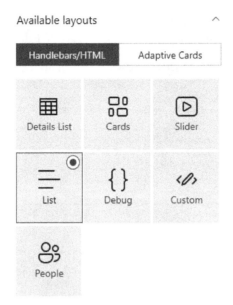

Figure 20.7 - Selecting the layout

4. Navigate to the third settings page of the web part and enable input query, select **Dynamic value**, and connect to the **PnP – Search Box** added to the page:

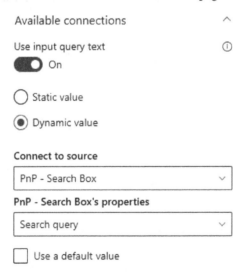

Figure 20.8 - Connecting the results web part to the search box

5. Enable the **Connect to vertical** settings, select **Search Vertical Web Part** added to the page as a component. For the **Display data only** setting, select **Documents**.

Figure 20.9 - Connecting verticals

With these settings, the **Search Results** web part will display PDF files in a list format. The web part is visible only when the **Documents** vertical is selected.

Configuring filters and connecting them to results

Add the PnP – Search Filter web part to the left side of the middle section and open the property pane. Take the following steps:

1. Connect the web part to the **Search Results** web part (*Figure 20.10*). Add the connect to verticals web part as we did with the results web part:

Figure 20.10 - Connecting to search result

2. Open **Customize filter view** and filter like in *Figure 20.11*:

Figure 20.11 - Add filters

3.   The final thing to do is to connect the filters on the **Search Results** web part setting's third page:

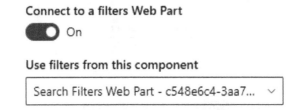

Figure 20.12 - Connecting filters on the Search Results web part's settings

The complete PDF document search looks like that in *Figure 20.13*:

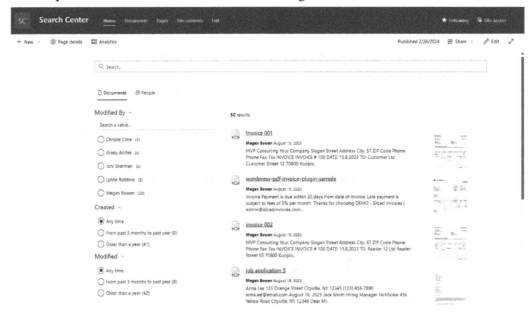

Figure 20.13 - Document search

The search box can be used to search for PDF documents using specific keywords and filters on the right side to narrow the returned results.

Adding filters and results to the People vertical

The next step is to add filters and search results web parts to the bottom section of the page with the same layout as with web parts added earlier. The easiest way is to duplicate the search results and filter web parts and drag them to the bottom section of the page:

1. First, let's open the settings of the **Search Results** web part we just duplicated. For **Query template**, add `{searchTerms}` *, change **Result Source Id** to **Local People Results**, and clear the **Refinement** filter.

2. On the second page of the settings, change **Layout** to **People**.

3. On the third page of the settings, change the **Display data only vertical** setting to **People** and connect the web part to another filters web part available.

    Open the settings of the filters web parts we just duplicated. For the **Use data from these Web Parts** setting, select the second **Search Results Web Part** (*Figure 20.14*), and for the **Display filters only when the following verticals are selected** setting, select **People**:

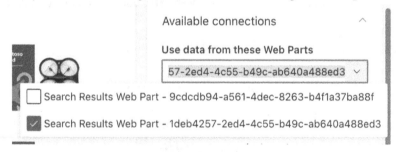

Figure 20.14 - Selecting the Search Result Web Part

4. Finally, let's change the search filter to something more suitable for filtering people:

Edit filters

Configure search filters by adding or removing rows. You can select fields from the data source results (if already selected) or use static values for filters.

	Display name	Filter field *	# of values	Template *	Filter type	Expand by default	Show count	Multi values
1 ⌄	Job title	JobTitle ⌄	5	Check box ⌄	→⌐	☑	☐	☐
	Department	Department ⌄	5	Check box ⌄	→⌐	☑	☐	☐

Figure 20.15 - People search filters

When connecting filters and **Search Results** web parts, it's important to make sure that the correct web parts are connected to each other; otherwise, the filtering is not working correctly. To help with this, each PnP Modern Search web part added to a page has its web part instance ID available on the last page of the web part's settings.

Figure 20.16 - Web part's instance ID

This ID is visible on the connection settings after the web part's title, as seen in *Figure 20.17*:

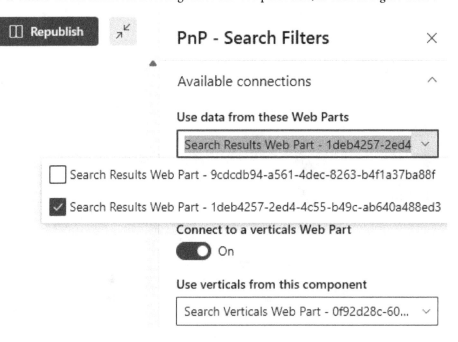

Figure 20.17 - Web part instance ID in the connection settings

Finally, the **People** search is ready to be published:

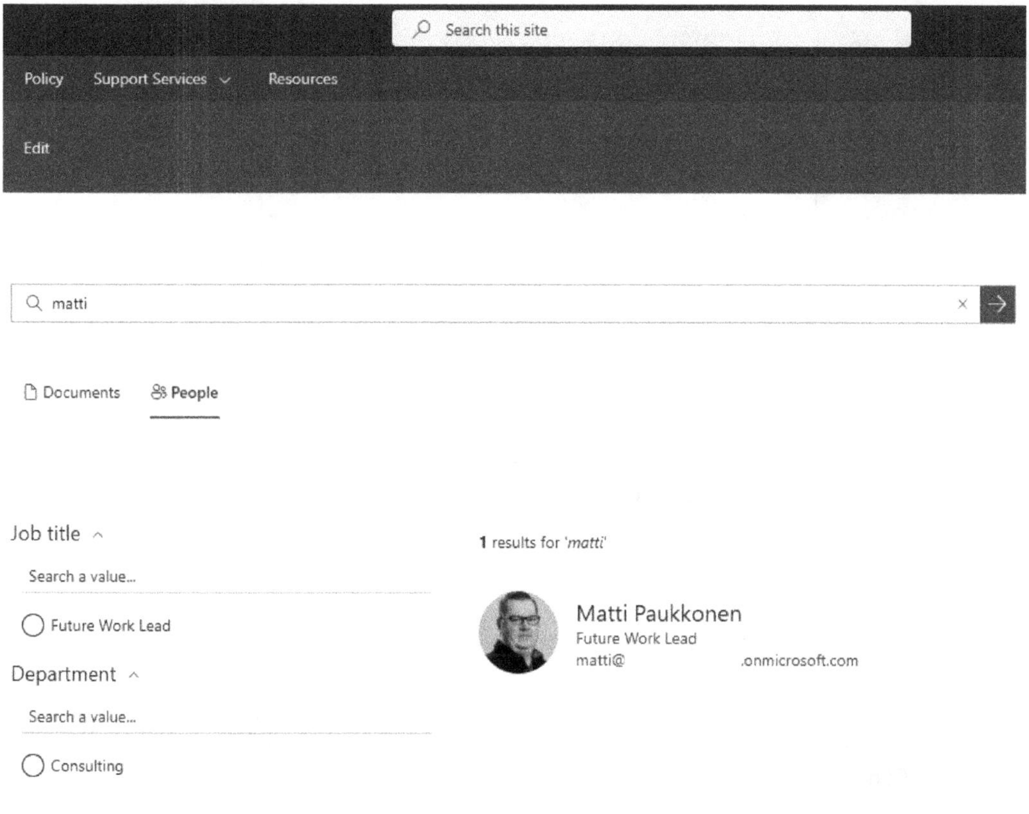

Figure 20.18 - People search results

Using the PnP Modern Search Results web part to roll up content

As mentioned earlier, the **Search Results** web part can be used as a dynamic content roll-up part. This can be achieved by formalizing a search query, which returns wanted results, and adding it as a query template to the web part settings. Let's create an example that displays people from the consulting department on a SharePoint page:

1. Add the PnP **Search Results** web part to the page and open the **Settings** pane.

2. Add `Department:Consulting` to **Query template** and select **LocalPeopleResults** for the **Result Source Id** setting:

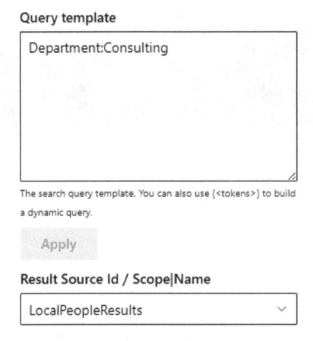

Figure 20.19 - Query template and result source settings

3.   On the second **Settings** page, select **People** as the layout. Now it's done.

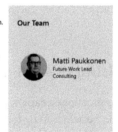

Figure 20.20 - The Search Results web part within the page

As seen in these examples, the PnP Modern Search solution offers a flexible way of building search-driven solutions. Since it's using SharePoint's search engine or Microsoft Search with underlying Microsoft Graph API, data is always retrieved using users' permissions. Permission checks cannot be bypassed using search queries or web part settings.

Summary

In this chapter, we were introduced to the Microsoft 365 and Power Platform Community and some solutions the community has developed to enhance user experience and simplify maintenance and automations.

First, we delved into PnP PowerShell and how to install and authenticate with it. We also saw a couple of small examples of how to use it to manage SharePoint content.

Next, we learned about PnP site templates, which are a mechanism to provision artifacts to SharePoint. We also investigated how to export templates from existing SharePoint sites and how to use them to distribute page templates.

Finally, we learned how to use PnP Modern Search web parts to create search-enabled solutions. We looked at how to build a search center and how to use web parts as part of SharePoint page content.

Congratulations! You have reached the end of this book, I hope you have got a good idea of how to use SharePoint's out-of-the-box features, Power Platform, and the SharePoint framework to extend the user experience of SharePoint.

Index

S

packtpub.com

Subscribe to our online digital library for full access to over 7,000 books and videos, as well as industry leading tools to help you plan your personal development and advance your career. For more information, please visit our website.

Why subscribe?

- Spend less time learning and more time coding with practical eBooks and Videos from over 4,000 industry professionals

- Improve your learning with Skill Plans built especially for you

- Get a free eBook or video every month

- Fully searchable for easy access to vital information

- Copy and paste, print, and bookmark content

Did you know that Packt offers eBook versions of every book published, with PDF and ePub files available? You can upgrade to the eBook version at packtpub.com and as a print book customer, you are entitled to a discount on the eBook copy. Get in touch with us at customercare@packtpub.com for more details.

At www.packtpub.com, you can also read a collection of free technical articles, sign up for a range of free newsletters, and receive exclusive discounts and offers on Packt books and eBooks.

Other Books You May Enjoy

If you enjoyed this book, you may be interested in these other books by Packt:

Microsoft 365 and SharePoint Online Cookbook, Second Edition

Gaurav Mahajan, Sudeep Ghatak, Nate Chamberlain, Scott Brewster

ISBN: 978-1-80324-317-7

- Manage content on SharePoint Online and create workflows with SPFx
- Build and deploy custom applications using Power Apps
- Automate repetitive business processes with Power Automate
- Learn with Microsoft Copilot for real-time intelligent assistance
- Prepare Microsoft Teams to be your organization's central hub of collaboration
- Gather feedback using polls and surveys created with Microsoft Forms
- Make content and tools easily accessible with Microsoft Search
- Read more with the bonus supplement covering Viva Engage, Delve, and more

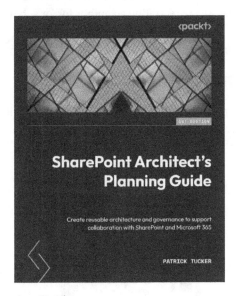

SharePoint Architect's Planning Guide

Patrick Tucker

ISBN: 978-1-80324-936-0

- Find out how to build or migrate to an effective modern intranet
- Explore how SharePoint works with other Microsoft 365 tools
- Discover best practices for extending SharePoint
- Understand the ways to implement effective metadata
- Plan for successful adoption and change management
- Explore best practices for site and data architecture

Packt is searching for authors like you

If you're interested in becoming an author for Packt, please visit authors.packtpub.com and apply today. We have worked with thousands of developers and tech professionals, just like you, to help them share their insight with the global tech community. You can make a general application, apply for a specific hot topic that we are recruiting an author for, or submit your own idea.

Share Your Thoughts

Now you've finished *Customizing and Extending SharePoint Online*, we'd love to hear your thoughts! Scan the QR code below to go straight to the Amazon review page for this book and share your feedback or leave a review on the site that you purchased it from.

https://packt.link/r/1-803-24489-5

Your review is important to us and the tech community and will help us make sure we're delivering excellent quality content.

Download a free PDF copy of this book

Thanks for purchasing this book!

Do you like to read on the go but are unable to carry your print books everywhere?

Is your eBook purchase not compatible with the device of your choice?

Don't worry, now with every Packt book you get a DRM-free PDF version of that book at no cost.

Read anywhere, any place, on any device. Search, copy, and paste code from your favorite technical books directly into your application.

The perks don't stop there, you can get exclusive access to discounts, newsletters, and great free content in your inbox daily

Follow these simple steps to get the benefits:

1. Scan the QR code or visit the link below

https://packt.link/free-ebook/978-1-80324-489-1

2. Submit your proof of purchase
3. That's it! We'll send your free PDF and other benefits to your email directly

www.ingramcontent.com/pod-product-compliance
Lightning Source LLC
Chambersburg PA
CBHW080607060326
40690CB00021B/4615